THE CULT OF KEAN

To the Kean I was....

The Cult of Kean

JEFFREY KAHAN
University of La Verne, USA

ASHGATE

Published by
Ashgate Publishing Limited
Gower House
Croft Road
Aldershot
Hampshire GU11 3HR
England

Ashgate Publishing Company
Suite 420
101 Cherry Street
Burlington, VT 05401-4405
USA

Ashgate website: http://www.ashgate.com

British Library Cataloguing in Publication Data
Kahan, Jeffrey, 1964-
   The Cult of Kean
   1.Kean, Edmund, 1787-1833 2.Kean, Edmund, 1787-1833 –
   Appreciation – History – 19th century 3.Actors – England –
   Biography 4.Fame – Case studies
   I.Title
   792'.028'092

Library of Congress Cataloging-in-Publication Data
Kahan, Jeffrey, 1964-
      The cult of Kean / by Jeffrey Kahan.
         p. cm.
      Includes bibliographical references.
      ISBN 0-7546-5650-0 (alk. paper)
   1. Kean, Edmund, 1787-1833. I. Title.

PN2598.K3K34 2006
792.02'8092 – dc22

QM LIBRARY
(MILE END)

2005032503

ISBN-10: 0-7546-5650-0
ISBN-13: 978-0-7546-5650-0

Contents

List of Illustrations

Acknowledgements

I would like to thank Deborah Smith, HRC, Leah Marcus, Stanley Stewart, Haley Stokes, Heidi Oberdank, Christine Lewis, Jim Shaw, Shakespeare Institute, The Theatre Museum in Covent Garden, the University of La Verne, and the Ashgate Editorial team, including the splendid efforts of Anthea Lockley, Peter Coles, Anne Keirby, and Erika Gaffney.

Introduction

GENTLEMEN—If you think the following particulars worth the space they will occupy in your excellent journal, perhaps you will not object to their insertion. I was in one of the boxes of Covent-Garden theatre, on Monday, the twenty-fifth of March, 1833; the last night that great actor, Edmund Kean, appeared on the stage. His health, for months, had been so rapidly declining, and his physical energies become so visibly impaired by those long-indulged irregularities, which had broken down a naturally vigorous but abused constitution, that his acting was rendered generally feeble, unsatisfactory, and often painful, and even his inability to appear at all when announced, was by no means a rare occurrence…. There was nothing distinguishable in Kean's performance of the first and second acts, from his usual personification of Othello, except a more than ordinary feebleness in his voice, action and gait; which, as he had not many weeks previous broken down in the midst of the part, was imputed to a designed reservation, or perhaps the fear of too early exhausting what physical strength he might otherwise be enabled to call up in order to sustain the third and latter acts: when, however, he came to that memorable apostrophe—'Now, forever, farewell!' etc., the whole of it was breathed forth with all that melodious melancholy, so noted in his brighter days, and so happily described by the critic, Hazlitt, as 'striking upon the heart and imagination like some divine music,' only mingled with a far greater degree of feeling than I had ever before observed; in fact, so deeply affecting were his tones, that, as he half sobbed out the last line, 'Farewell!—Othello's—occupation's—gone!' I remarked to a friend near me, "Poor fellow! I fear that a consciousness of Othello's despairing moans being applicable to himself personally, has touched his own feelings.' I seldom remember Kean's failing, in this particular point, to elicit less than three hearty rounds on ordinary occasions; but on *this*, they were increased in number and duration. He remained abstracted and motionless, his chin resting on his breast, and his eyes fixed on the ground for many seconds after every murmur of applause had subsided then raising his head from his chest, as from a forgetful slumber, he seemed partially aroused into a sense of his situation with the audience and the necessity of proceeding; but, instead of that sudden and infuriate alternation—that towering passion which used to threaten the destroyer of his peace with irresistible and immediate annihilation; he turned slowly and feebly, tottered a few steps towards Iago, (who seeing his sinking state, approached him,) and, leaning on his arm for support, and unable to seize him by the throat, he uttered in disjointed accents, only audible to those quite near him—'Villain—be—sure—you—prove'—then throwing himself upon his son's neck, in a faint and faltering voice, added, *'Oh God! I am dying! speak to them, Charles!'* The house, though somewhat prepared for a result of the kind, did not anticipate such a decided prostration of his faculties, and kept up their applause for nearly a minute. … I have the honour to be, gentlemen, very respectfully your friend and obedient servant,

JAMES H. HACKETT.[1]

---

1   James Henry Hackett, "Kean's Last Appearance on the Stage," *New York Mirror*, 22 February 1834, p. 270, in Press Clippings, Personal Collection.

If the audience's applause for Kean's death throes seems out of place, we might recall that this same audience had been seeing Kean die on stage for years. Often, his death was the highlight of the evening. Indeed, it's likely that, as Kean lay dying, many assumed that he was merely acting. One audience member wrote in his journal that the climax of any Kean performance was his realistic rendering up of the ghost: the actor "did not spare the spectator the groans, the convulsions, the death-rattle, in such a way that the dramatic interest of the character's death is already submerged in the kind of anguish one feels oneself when one has occasion to be present at the last moments of a dying man."[2]

Even Kean's declaration to his son that he had only moments to live seemed both genuine and theatrical. Even as he was being carried off the stage, the dying actor, still archly aware of his audience, stopped his attendants and, "in token of his sense of their [the audience's] kind indulgence," feebly attempted a bow.[3] Six weeks later, on 15 May 1833, the performance was almost over. Kean, now bedridden, turned to his tearful son and recited Lear's tender lines, "pray do not mock me."[4] Later that day, he died. He was, if we can trust the actor, 43 years old.

Kean's end is appropriate, if only because of the perverse mixture of stage *éclat* in his personal life. One of Kean's most celebrated stage moments had been his performance opposite his son Charles in John Howard Payne's *Brutus*, but the spectacle had little to do with the play. Kean's life was a public show. After a notorious sex scandal and messy divorce, Kean and his son, as audiences were well aware, had been estranged for years. With Kean's health failing, the two decided to mend their relationship. To publicly confirm their reconcilement, Kean agreed to act with his son. On Kean asking his son, as the play demanded, to "embrace thy wretched father," a tearful audience watched Charles fall into his father's arms. Overcome by the fusion of staged and private sentiment, the spectators erupted into heartfelt applause.[5] As the crowd thundered, Kean hugged his son in artful emotion and then whispered opportunely, "We are doing the trick, Charley."[6]

---

2   Etienne-Jean Delécluze, *Journal de Delécluze, 1824-1828*, 492; translation my own. Audiences might have also been confused because at one performance, on receiving his death wound, an exhausted Kean fell unconscious to the floor and had to be carried from the stage. See James Winston, 26 February 1827, *Drury Lane Journal*, 143. Playwright Bruce G. Bradley retells a story—"story" being the operative word—concerning Edmund Kean, who was asked on his deathbed by his son: "Is dying hard, father?" Kean replied, "Dying is easy. Comedy is hard." See Doug Moe, "Mixing mysteries and fine cuisine."

3   James Henry Hackett, *Notes and Comments*, 131.

4   James Henry Hackett, "Kean's Last Appearance on the Stage," *New York Mirror*, 22 February 1834, p. 245, in Press Clippings, Personal Collection.

5   John Howard Payne, *Brutus, or the Folly of Tarquin*, V.iii.57. Signaling that this may have been play-acting on Charles' part as well, John William Cole writes that this reconciliation was "temporary" (*The Life and Theatrical Times of Charles Kean*, I:163).

6   F.W. Hawkins, *The Life of Edmund Kean*, II:329. Kean also made up to Charles' wife, Ellen Tree. She played Portia to his Shylock on 21 March 1833 at Covent Garden (Gordon Craig, *The Life and Theatrical Career of Edmund Kean*, 21). Some libraries catalogue Craig's

What are we to make of Kean quoting Shakespeare on his deathbed or of his turning so artfully to his son during a performance of *Brutus*? Pierce Egan suggests that Kean often pretended to be injured, even dying, just to deliver a Shakespearean phrase. On a drunken dare, for example, the actor once jumped out a second story window. After lying unconscious for some hours, he crawled to the hut of a fisherman and addressed the old man therein with the following sepulchral speech:

Angels and ministers of grace
Be thou a spirit of health,
Or Goblin—

When the old man interrupted, "I am no *speerit*, but poor old Sandy Pike, the fisherman, at your bidding!" Kean countered in a "theatrical sort of rage" with virtually the same line he would use years later on his deathbed: "Do not mock me, sir." When the fisherman remained unmoved, Kean dropped the act and asked, "You did not know me?" The fisherman replied that he did not. Whereupon, Kean rose up majestically and declared, "Know then, good old man, that my name is Kean, the actor." He then gave the old man five pounds and "darted like lightning into the post-chaise, and very soon afterwards was in bed at his own lodgings."[7]

Egan might simply have been recording a tall tale, but the actor's first biographer, Bryan Waller Procter, *née* Barry Cornwall, recognizes that, when writing about Kean, fact and fiction are inextricably bound by the actor's own puckish personality—"in regard to the accounts given by Kean himself, (to say nothing of their differing *from each other*,) [*sic*] he was at once so fond of mystification … that no reliance whatever can be placed upon them."[8] In his own day, Kean was the subject of rumors, fantasies, and falsifications.[9] An actor who reshaped London theater, Kean played a number of characters on stage and just as many off: he was an impish impresario who staged a variety of *impromptu* street festivals, a demagogue who toyed with the careers of playwrights and actors, a popular working-class hero, a Don Juan who made Byron's fictional hero look positively demure. He slept with actresses, prostitutes, and wives of the wealthy; he drank a great deal and spent a fortune on frivolous expenses, including seasonal boat races on the Thames; he staged carnivalesque boxing matches at Drury Lane; he fed fresh meat to his prize pet lion, which roamed

---

book as by Ifan Kyrle Fletcher, with Craig the author of the foreword. However, Fletcher's name is not on any copy I have consulted.

7   Pierce Egan, *The Pilgrims of the Thames. In Search of the National*, 355.

8   See his *The Life of Edmund Kean*, I:3-4. For the rest of this study, Barry Cornwall will be referred to by his pen-name, Bryan Waller Procter.

9   Lord Essex, a member of the Drury Lane Committee, wrote to Kean's wife that she'd do well to ignore the "many idle stories about my friend Kean." The letter is undated and was only printed in the 30 April 1836 issue of the *Athenæum*. The letter is reprinted in Harold Newcomb Hillebrand, *Edmund Kean*, 165.

freely through his house.[10] Kean was alternately and simultaneously perceived as a Whig and a Tory, a radical and a conservative, a disciplined genius and an intuitive actor, a Hamlet, a Lear, a Macbeth, all inextricably fantastical and/or real.

In general, there seems to be at least two versions of nearly every Keanian event. In consequence, Procter advises his readers to disregard the standard foundations of biography, those letters and conversations traced to the subject himself: "One [version] is derived from Kean, and the other rests on very respectable authority."[11] Yet, in the case of Kean, even the most "respectable authority" cannot be trusted. One of the earliest biographies of the actor, the anonymous *A Memoir of Edmund Kean* (1825), is filled with fantasy and contradiction. We learn, for example, that Kean spent his childhood in leg irons but was sought after for his skillful dancing. Perhaps most amazingly, Kean was in two places at the same time. As a child, he appeared with Kemble at Drury Lane *and* served as a cabin boy aboard a ship bound for Madeira.[12] Likewise, as a teenager, he rubbed shoulders with duke's sons at Eton *and* toured the provinces with farmboys. Robert Elliston, who hired Kean at Drury Lane, recalled that the actor sometimes fancied himself the bastard son of the Duke of Norfolk, at other times he claimed to be the offspring of a West-Indian merchant by the name of Duncan. On yet other occasions, he asserted that he was son of Edward Kean, who was in the employ of Mr. Wilmot, a builder. "Thus, under the names of *Howard, Duncan, Kean,* and sometimes *Clarke* (which latter he assumed from one of his early patronesses), he variously amused his own imagination, and completely mystified the fact to others."[13]

Journalists of the era only muddled matters still further. Some said that his mother was an actress, others said she was a prostitute, still others that she sold perfume. As for his father, some writers believed that he really was the son of the Duke of Norfolk; other journalists were so convinced by Kean's performances of Shylock that they mistook him for a Jew. One even affirmed that Kean's real name was Cohen.[14] After his success as Iago, he was described as having Italian "swarthiness, his eyes very large and dark."[15] As for the rumor that Kean went to Eton, the famed showman,

---

10 On Kean's tame African lion, see Otis Skinner, "Three Madmen of the Theatre II," 631.

11 Bryan Waller Procter, *The Life of Edmund Kean*, I: 58. Procter adds that "no such information exists as his biographers can use with *entire* confidence. One statement is perpetually opposed to another, and date after date is encountered by denials, and sometimes utterly refuted by subsequent well established facts. Without impeaching the veracity of his historians, we may fairly doubt the fidelity of their memories" (I:3). At another point, he writes, "We cannot vouch for the correctness of the next extract, but it has been given in print, and may be true. The reader will judge for himself" (I:212).

12 *A Memoir of Edmund Kean*, 2-3.

13 George Raymond, *The Life and Enterprises of Robert William Elliston, Comedian,* 225.

14 A journalist for the *New Monthly Magazine* recalled that the actor looked more like a Jew than a Christian child. See Harold Newcomb Hillebrand, *Edmund Kean,* 6.

15 Henry Sedley, "The Booths—Father and Son: Some Personal Reminiscences," 1083.

John Richardson, who employed Kean at Smithfield for the Bartholomew's fair and at the Theatre Royal in Rochester, averred that "there were a number of Lies circulated about *Mr. Kean* as well as by himself[;] it was stated that *Mr Kean* was educated at Eton School; that was all a lie for he was never at Eton in his life...."[16] But *The Champion*, looking into the report, countered: "It is certainly true, that this gentleman has had the benefit of instruction at Eaton School; he continued there, we understand, for more than three years."[17]

Later writers and enthusiasts habitually selected one yarn over another, modified or combined them. Harry Houdini, a collector of Kean memorabilia, preferred to see Kean making his debut at Drury Lane but not with the aforementioned Kemble.[18] Henry Barton Baker's Kean was a dancer at age three, but at age seven was put in corrective leg irons.[19] Otis Skinner's Kean was not crippled but did wear leg irons while he served aboard a ship heading for Madeira. Skinner rationalized his selection by arguing that the boyish Kean, not taking to hard work, had faked being a cripple—a handy rehearsal for *Richard III*. Thus, Skinner proposed with

---

16 See Richardson manuscript in "Story of Mr. Kean," Manuscript, HRC-TA.

17 See the clipping for *The Champion* in Press Clippings, Kean, Edmund C. Newspaper Articles Messmore Kendall Collection, HRC. *The Champion* may be referring to John Roach's *Authentic Memoirs of the Green-Room* (1814), which also mentions his three-year stint at Eton (247). In all likelihood, Kean never attended school of any kind, although his wife, a former governess, did attempt to teach him smatterings of Greek and Latin. Bryan Waller Procter, always one to ridicule Kean, writes: "He was rewarded in the end with the Latin dictionary, with which he busied himself for a long time afterwards, culling words and phrases from it, and using and misusing them upon every occasion. He was as proud of his little incursions into the classical country, as an Oxford or Cambridge professor"(*The Life of Edmund Kean*, I:174).

18 Houdini wrote his surmise on a playbill for 2 November 1796 performance of *Douglas*. Neither Kean nor Kemble is listed on the playbill. See Kean, Edmund E. –1m.-1. Programs, 1796.

19 Henry Barton Baker states that at the age of three Kean danced the part of Cupid in "Cymon," at the Opera House. See *Our Old Actors*, II.i.166-7. Leg irons are mentioned on the following page. John Roach agrees that Kean first appeared on stage at age three, but in the role of a sleeping cupid, which, obviously, would not entail dancing. Roach then has Kean acting the part of Falstaff's page. Kemble is not mentioned. See his *Memoirs of the Green-Room*, 247. Shakespeare's Falstaff has no page, but he does in William Kenrick's *Falstaff's Wedding* (1766). The play only staged once in 1766 and was revived infrequently. Gordon Craig records the earliest of Edmund Kean's theatrical appearances as 8 June 1796, when he appeared as "Robin" in *The Merry Wives of Windsor*, performed at Drury Lane, but with Palmer, not Kemble. The theater manager and dramatist Charles Dibdin recalls that he hired Kean, then calling himself "Master Carey", in June of 1801, to perform short poems (*Professional & Literary Memoirs of Charles Dibdin the Younger*, 5). One advertisement, dated to 1801, has Kean performing for his widowed mother (Gordon Craig, *The Life and Theatrical Career of Edmund Kean*, 5-6).

Wordsworthian insinuation, "early did the boy become father to the man."[20] But how early? According to Harold Newcomb Hillebrand, Kean's date of birth is either 4 November 1787 or 17 March 1789, but even here "there is no reason to suppose that either is correct...."[21]

It is not difficult to accept that Kean enhanced details of his life, or that collectors and enthusiasts have embraced these stories, some probably of Kean's own making, others born of rumor and fantasy. What seems harder to accept is that even his biographers happily embrace these contradictions.[22] Julius Berstl (1946), for example, claims that Kean's life creates, in effect, the ultimate Shakespearean play, mixing, as the Bard does, aspects of both comedy and tragedy:

> There is to be found in the changing phases of Kean's destiny everything that the fantasy of a writer could invent. Tension and climax; crime and punishment; the happiness, the sadness of a human being who reaches out for the fire of the gods, but who—alas! a prey to his earthbound impulses—is hurled into the dark and swampy places of the underworld.
>
> Are there not all the essentials of a novel, of a powerful drama?[23]

Likewise, Gerald Weales (1989) declares that even the "verifiable events" of Kean's life "seem to have been designed for melodrama."[24]

---

20 Otis Skinner, "Three Madmen of the Theatre II,"622-3. John Doran also inferred that Kean's later dramatic flair for wearing his Indian costume could be traced to his childhood: "A young Huron ... could not have lived a more savage, but certainly enjoyed a more comfortable and better tended boyhood." See John Doran, *"Their Majesties' Servants." Annals of the English*, II: 413. On Kean's adolescence, Doran added: "He journeyed on foot, and when he came to a river, swam it ... as readily as an Indian would have" (II: 381).

21 Harold Newcomb Hillebrand, *Edmund Kean*, 3. On the subject of Kean's age, *The Morning Chronicle* of April 6, 1789 states that:

> This evening, Mr. Kean, will give a SENATORIAL, THEATRICAL, and various other IMITATIONS, in which he will be assisted by his brother.
>   Mr. E. KEAN.

This would mean that Edmund Kean either lied about his age, since, in April 1789, Kean was only three weeks old, or that we have the wrong Kean. Presumably, if a child actor were involved in the above-cited theatrical, it would have been mentioned advantageously in the advertisement. It's possible that one of these two theatrical Keans fathered the boy.

22 William R. Siebenschuh sees little problem with the concept *per se*. He writes that "factual works" can borrow techniques from fiction "without compromising generic credibility." He adds, however, that "there are dangers involved" (*Fictional Techniques and Factual Works*, 132-3).

23 Julius Berstl, *The Sun's Bright Child*, 8.

24 Gerald Weales, "Edmund Kean Onstage Onstage," 151. After hearing of Kean's sudden rise to fame and fortune, his sister-in-law Mary Chambers wrote that the tale was "more enchanting than reality." See transcription of letter dated 29 March 1814 in Jonathan Reynolds, *Dramatis Personæ*, 20 (1991):17.

Indeed, Kean's biographers are often far more interested in the fictional than the demonstrable. Sometimes their imaginative interludes actually attempt to suppress the historical record. For example, Bryan Waller Procter's narrative, *The Life of Edmund Kean* (1835), stridently avoids any impropriety. On the subject of Kean's many affairs, the biographer states primly: "It is not a part of our purpose to enter into any detail of the tragedian's love affairs. It is better that they should rest in obscurity."[25] On his drunken orgies with "The Wolves' Club," he writes, "whether he was a member or not of that community, are questions which may be passed over, without injury either to our hero's reputation, or to the sincerity or completeness of this present narrative."[26] To fill the space, Procter gives us a variety of comic intermissions, many of which he knows are clearly calumniating. Nonetheless, he justifies their inclusion: "It is enough if he [Procter's constructed Kean] be witty himself; or the cause of amusement to others." Usually, Procter's comedy concerns Kean's drunkenness. At one point in Procter's biography, Kean is arrested for intoxication and thrown in jail, then escapes with keystone cops giving chase:

> It would be difficult to describe this night-hunt; but one may imagine the mischievous player, running off at a pace of ten knots an hour, and the hounds of justice loud behind him (loud, but not swift, for we know them.... One may imagine the tumult of the pursuit, the stamping of feet, the clattering of lanterns, the flourishing of shillelahs... and finally the yells and cries and denunciations (to which no English translation could do justice) of the rogues whose dexterity had been outwitted by a stranger, and whose hearts no 'tinpinny' had softened.[27]

At another point, Kean comes home one night (or rather morning) "tipsy as usual," and announces that he had bought a yacht, which he intends to sail to the theater each night. Since Drury Lane is not built next to or near to a dock, it's difficult to follow Kean's reasoning here. Procter's punch line seems to come straight from a Tobias Smollett novel:

> the servant glided into the breakfast-room, and intimated that 'a person' had called about 'the yacht!' This stunning announcement put a period to the pleasures of breakfast. The cold fowl appeared to have a fishy flavour: the eggs tasted as though they had come from an aquatic nest: the chairs seemed to undulate,—the table to rock, beneath the unexpected intelligence.[28]

Procter goes on to describe how, when the actor sobered up, he reneged on the deal.

Such comic additions serve a serious purpose. Noting that most biographies attempt to "supply a system for the improvement of mankind," Procter's Kean is a clown, and his narrative fights any attempts to see Kean as anything other than a coarse, though sexually staid, entertainment for his readers: "We ourselves cannot

---

25 Bryan Waller Procter, *The Life of Edmund Kean*, II: 215.
26 Ibid., II:179.
27 Ibid., II: 101.
28 Ibid., II: 119.

at present enter upon the subject. We are, indeed, well inclined to be philosophical, but we must refrain, seeing that some of our contemporaries occasionally muddy the stream of their narrative by profound paradoxes, and impenetrable observations on men and things."[29]

Others took this reproach as a challenge. F.W. Hawkins' *The Life of Edmund Kean* (1868) repeatedly asserts its Victorian values by arguing that Kean's theatrical successes were offset by his personal dissipation. Kean's life is nothing to be celebrated; it is, asserts Hawkins, a tragedy of Shakespearean dimensions. J. Fitzgerald Molloy's *The Life and Adventures of Edmund Kean* (1869) responds to Hawkins' biography by replacing Kean's social excesses with tear-jerking accounts in which the actor provides food or finance to old, worn-out actors and, just as importantly, censures an economy that refuses to care for the aged and indigent. Thus, Molloy notes that when Kean became famous, he embarked on a variety of provincial tours, revisiting the theaters that had once treated him with contempt. Now demanding and getting more for one performance than he had formerly received for an entire season, Kean enjoyed belittling the managers who had once mistreated him. In one scenario, a provincial manager comes to Kean bearing bags of gold, but the actor treats him with disdain. Yet, when Kean hears that this same manager is on the brink of financial collapse, the actor instantly offers his services for a benefit. As Molloy continues the story, Kean saves the day, his fans flock to see him, and the receipts rescue the theater from ruin. That night, as Kean treats the actors of the company to a round of drinks, the thankful manager joins them. We can defer to Molloy's rendering of the scene:

> In the midst of loud acclamations which followed Kean stood up, and the light in his eyes and pallor of his face caused sudden silence. Turning to the [manager], he said in cold and measured tones, 'Don't let us misunderstand one another. I am bound to you by no ties from my former acquaintance. I don't play for you because you were once my manager, or a manager, for if ever a man deserved his fate it is you; if ever there was a family of tyrants it is yours. I don't play for you from former friendship, but I play because you are a fallen man.'[30]

Kean is not interested in rewarding the just; if he were, he would have refused to aid his ex-manager.[31] The actor is only interested in alleviating poverty.

---

29 Ibid., I:109.

30 J. Fitzgerald Molloy, *The Life and Adventures of Edmund Kean*, I:271-2.

31 Henry Barton Baker has an obsequious manager thanking Kean, who replies:

Look you, sir, now I'm drawing money to your treasury, you find out I am a fine actor. You told me when I rehearsed Shylock it would be a failure. Then I was a poor man, without a friend, and you did your best to keep me down. Now you smother me with compliments; 'tis right I should make some return; there, sir, to the devil with your fine speeches, take that[!]

Kean then dumps a bucket of punch on his head. See *Our Old Actors*, II.ii.198.

These sorts of philanthropic accounts may have been inspired by Alexandre Dumas' play *Kean* (1836), in which the actor is always ready to give the shirt off his back to help and to hearten the poor and just as ready to remove his pants to seduce and to humiliate the rich. But Dumas' play is just too good to pass up for some of Kean's later biographers. Thus, in the last chapter of Maurice Willson Disher's biography *Mad Genius: A Biography of Edmund Kean* (1950), one of Kean's mistresses, Charlotte Cox, attends a performance of Dumas' play. After the performance, a friend stops her:

> 'Charlotte, my dear. Forgive the intrusive nature of my question, but was it really like that?'
>
> Dabbing her eyes daintily with a square of scented lace, [Charlotte] suppressed a sob and thought again how brilliantly the French actor's piercing black eyes resembled her Edmund's.
>
> 'Oh, exactly—*exactly.*'[32]

Disher told friends that his new "facts" had been culled from James Winston's then-unpublished Drury Lane diaries. In 1959, Disher died and the diaries were sold at auction. In 1974, they were published. While they contain many interesting (and often smutty) details concerning the actor, the above-mentioned vignette is entirely the biographer's invention.[33] Even Kean's latest biographer, Raymund FitzSimons is unable to fully separate Kean from fiction. After completing *Edmund Kean: Fire From Heaven* (1976), the biographer turned his materials into a work of "Faustian proportions": the play *Kean* (1981).[34] Starring Ben Kingsley, *Kean* toured for a number of years and was televised on BBC TV in 1983.[35] Although the play is based on a biography of the actor, it uses Kean's Shakespearean performances to explain his life and his genius. For example, when describing his youthful, poverty-stricken years as an itinerant actor, Kingsley's Kean falls into Lear's lines, "Art cold fool? I'm cold myself."

Our first chapter begins by looking at farfetched stories of Kean sparring with professional fighters both in his house and on the stage boards of Drury Lane— materials, which, if this were an orthodox biography of the actor, we might be forced by a lack of historical verification to disregard. But yarns have their own value. The historical Kean may or may not have brawled with boxers at Drury Lane, but he certainly used the aesthetics of boxing to change the way his audience saw him as an actor.

---

32 Maurice Willson Disher, *Mad Genius: A Biography of Edmund Kean*, 193.

33 See George Speaight's conversation with Disher in his Preface to James Winston, *Drury Lane Journal*, VII.

34 *Kean*, starring Ben Kingsley, opened at the Harrogate Theatre, Yorkshire, in July 1981. In taking the role, the actor reportedly gave up a million dollars to star in a John Schlesinger movie.

35 A copy is available at the Shakespeare Institute, University of Birmingham.

If the first chapter suggests that a golden grain of historical truth can be panned from the fool's gold of fiction, the second chapter, concerning Kean and the playwrights, argues the opposite. Kean's acting, described as physical, natural, unthinking, Romantic, was so finely wrought that it has continued to blind his biographers to his innumerable and oftentimes brilliant ploys to control Drury Lane. Sifting for value in both fact and fantasy, Chapters Three and Four examine the Keanian creations of two major canonical figures, Alexandre Dumas and Mark Twain. For Dumas, Kean offered a character capable of exposing aristocratic pretensions. For Twain, Kean's America tours suggested that his audiences were more interested in titillation than tragedy, more interested in bare bottoms than bare bodkins. Chapter Five explores Charles Kean's attempt to reformulate his father's acting legacy into a tidy, conservative philosophy. Chapter Six turns to Sartre's Kean, an existential Everyman who acts both on and off stage because he sees no escape from the false consciousness of a theatrical life. The final chapter suggests that we are still living very much in a Keanian world of illusion.

Rather than suggest that the uninitiated situate themselves in relation to the numerous and widely differing studies of Kean, not to mention the various plays and films the actor inspired, each chapter starts with some aspect of the actor's lively mythography. What follows, however, is not straightforward theater history. Much of this book uses storytelling to explore the changing dynamics of appropriation, representation, and recollection.[36] The result is a narrative that is (hopefully) fraught with elements of rhetorical expectation. At the same time, this book encourages the reader to halt, or at least slow, at decisive rhetorical twists and turns.[37]

A word or two on the stylistic choices of this book is also necessary. A man who made his career acting on the public stage, whose sex life was known and discussed in Britain, America, and France, Kean's life leaped artfully between high and so-called low culture, and the language of the former cannot always address the intrinsic perceptions of the latter. This study attempts to accommodate audiences interested in both. In the coarsest sense, to say that the writer need be vulgar to discuss Kean is absurd, but appropriations of Kean—and studies of those appropriations—do not mushroom *ex nihilo*.[38] Kean's shameless and often vulgar behavior was the epitome of bad taste, but it was his spectacular audacity that was often of political and social consequence, a direct critique of, and response to, the *status quo*. Given the peculiar subject at hand, an actor who is often, though not always, better suited to the campus

---

36 Hayden White has argued that even a stolid history adopts "a manner of speaking about events, whether real or imaginary…" (*The Content of the Form*, 2).

37 More recent literary theorists, including the maverick Bryan Reynolds (2003), have asked scholars and readers not only to be aware of (self or re)constructed patterns of intelligibility but also to look at these forms of intelligibility as options, not answers. See his *Performing Transversally: Reimagining Shakespeare and the Critical Future*, 4.

38 See Arthur Danto who writes: "the instrument of representation imparts and impresses something of it own character in the act of representing it…. The structure of style is like the structure of a personality" (*The Transfiguration of the Commonplace*, 197, 207).

bar than the classroom, it seems best to avoid a model of popular culture that imagines potential readers to be homogeneously academic or unreflectively popular.[39]

This book appears at a time when Kean's reputation in the theater is again on the ascendancy. Some of our greatest actors, including Derek Jacobi and Anthony Hopkins, have played the actor on stage and screen; Kean's ghost flits through Peter O'Toole's memoirs; one of London's more successful West End transfers in recent years was a musical based on Edmund Kean, and, as of this writing, acclaimed director Georij Paro is preparing a new Kean play for Croatia's National Theatre and a tour of Eastern Europe's capitals. Kean, at least as a fictional figure, remains an ongoing source of enjoyment and apparently retains a continual potential for transformation and impersonation, an ever-evolving cultural dynamic, shaped by the emotions, desires, and processes of an actor who never forgot he was always playing to the crowd.

---

39 Park Honan, writing on why style counts in a biography, argues that: "Biographers as a rule are not concerned with theory, but anxious to avoid mistakes. ... Yet in avoiding every gaucherie, they may dehydrate their product" (*Authors' Lives: On Literary Biography and the Arts of Language*, 4).

Chapter 1

Bare-Knuckle Kean

In Julius Berstl's *The Sun's Bright Child: The Imaginary Memoirs of Edward Kean*, our unreal actor tells us that he likes to frequent prizefights. Moreover, he fancies himself a capable combatant. The actor has a boxer's sense of "perseverance" and to prove it, Kean invites two fighters, Mendoza and Richmond the Black, back to his house. They clear the dining room and have a free-for-all:

> Bang—bang! Beautiful straight lefts and right swings, a good lot of solid slogging, right and left, right and left, round after round, until Mendoza sinks to his knees, absolutely groggy, and Richmond the Black, like a tiger, in a most amazing fashion becomes the winner on points. Very clever, indeed![1]

What with the all the swings and upper cuts, we're unsure until the close of the passage that it is Richmond and not Kean himself who is fighting (and beating!) Mendoza, who was champion from 1784 to 1820. The narrative confusion is multiplied in Tomaso Smith's screenplay, *Kean, gli amori di un artista* [*Kean: The Loves of An Artist*] (1940), which opens with Kean engaging in a boxing match at the local pub. After the punch up, Kean rushes to Drury Lane to perform his unusually aggressive *Hamlet*. Conflating both stories, Peter O'Toole suggests that Kean essentially boxed while he was performing Shakespeare at Drury Lane because "In the older days, the 1800s, theatre was on a par with present-day boxing. It had as much excitement, as much fancy."[2] From O'Toole's perspective, Kean was doing more than learning the art of the jab. He was using aspects of boxing to improve his ability to stage excitement and to awaken fancy, in effect to score theatrical points. Very clever indeed!

The above-cited renderings should not be discounted either in sum or in part as fictional or fanciful. Giles Playfair recorded that Kean did learn the art of boxing from Mendoza.[3] And the idea of learning something of acting from these fighters is not as mad as it initially sounds. Pierce Egan argued that the ring was a kind of theatrical stage, and that the boxers of his era were merely second-rate performers: "the *milling stage* cannot boast so often of the advantages of *criticism* as the boards of the more classic theatres, nor the qualities of the performers so *generally* the theme as the

---

1   Julius Berstl, *The Sun's Bright Child*, 80.
2   "Reckless, courageous and a little bit crazy." *The Guardian* 19 March 2003.
3   Giles Playfair, *Edmund Kean*, 144.

extraordinary flights of genius elicited by a KEMBLE or a KEAN....">[4] Further, even if Kean had little to learn from Mendoza about performing Shakespeare, he might still have seen Mendoza as a respected rival of sorts. In Bury St. Edmunds, for example, a troop of actors entreated the boxer to join the company. He did, and met with great success.[5] Thereafter, Mendoza was a regular in pantos, which were often designed with a specialty spot in which he could give a boxing exhibition.[6]

Likewise, Tomaso Smith's story of Kean brawling in bars, whether historically accurate or not, still sheds some light on the actor's relationship with his core audience. John Cowell writes of Kean as if the actor were Prince Hal: "His chosen associates were selected from the lowest dregs of society—prize-fighters, thief-catchers and knaves and fools of low degree."[7] The descriptive "low degree" is worth bearing in mind. John Rule discusses how working-class Londoners were noticeably shorter than the aristocracy. Kean—as opposed to the tall and stately John Philip Kemble—was not just a man of the people; he was a man of their stature.[8] Further, while Kean did not look like a star Shakespearean, he did look like many of the era's greatest boxing champions: Jack Scroggins was 5' 4"; Dutch Sam (or Sam Elias) was 5' 6", Daniel Mendoza was 5' 7".[9]

What these stories really stress, however, is that the historical Kean was a fighter, a working-class actor who banged on doors, if not heads, until they opened. Although testaments of his life vary greatly, if we can trust the most consistently told stories

---

4   Pierce Egan, *Boxiana*, II: 15. He also suggested that the loser of a boxing match was "not altogether unlike JULIUS CÆSAR, in receiving the unkind stab from his beloved BRUTUS" (Pierce Egan, *Boxiana*, I:148). In addition, William Hazlitt, Kean's greatest supporter, would go on to write a still-celebrated essay on boxing, "The Fight" (1822).

5   Mendoza joined the company in 1791. Mendoza gives no account as to what roles he played. See Daniel Mendoza, *The Memoirs of the Life of Daniel Mendoza*, 77. Written in 1807, well before Kean's rise, the memoir is of no use on the topic of his sparring with Kean. In 1809, Mendoza worked, albeit briefly, for Kemble. See chapter three. He retired as Champion of the boxing ring in 1820, at age 55.

6   Gerald Frow, *"Oh Yes It Is"*, 160. Frow does not list any Mendoza performances in London.

7   *Actors and Actresses of Great Britain and the United States: Kean and Booth*, 33. We might further note that boxing matches were not just the sport of the ill-educated. Byron loved the sport, as did the Prince of Wales, who considered Pierce Egan's *Boxiana* among his favorite reads. If boxing did, as Bob Mee writes, help "create a false image of 'one nation' with a common interest" (*Bare Fists*, 38), Kean may have used aspects of the sport to broaden his appeal—not among "the lower orders" but among the aristocracy.

8   See John Rule, *The Labouring Classes in Early Industrial England 1750-1850*, 379. According to John Howard Payne, Kemble, already tall, also used "additional elevation" in his shoes to tower over his cast. See *Actors and Actresses of Great Britain: The Kembles*, 86.

9   There were yet other fighters who were taller: Tom Cribb was 5' 10"; John Jackson and John Gully were 6'. These taller fighters were often associated with the upper classes. Jackson, whom Byron labeled the "Emperor of Pugilism," was hired as a bodyguard for George IV's coronation. See Bob Mee, *Bare Fists*, 42.

as "facts," it's clear that Kean had fought long and hard to become an imp of fame, a lad of life, the sun's bright child:

The bastard son of a second-rate actress turned prostitute, Edmund was raised by Charlotte Tidswell, a minor actress at Drury Lane, who specialized in playing whores and other "parts the most obnoxious to human nature."[10] "Aunt Tid," as the youngster called Charlotte, brought Edmund to Drury Lane where she performed. The child was taken under the wings of many actors and actresses, who, in turn, taught him the craft of acting. He made his stage debut as an imp in John Philip Kemble's 1794 production of *Macbeth* and, by 1801, became known as "The Celebrated Theatrical Child," performing at Covent Garden and Drury Lane with his "aunt."[11]

His height (full grown, he stood 5' 4") did not keep pace with his talent or his ambition and lead roles were difficult to come by. Nonetheless, Kean remained convinced that he was England's finest actor. The problem was that no one paid much attention to him. Kean often doubled and tripled parts for a mere fifteen shillings a week. But far from being seen as valuable or even talented, Kean was rarely given the leading roles, unless it was as a trade-off, an exchange for the much-acclaimed physical theater of his Harlequin.

Kean married, and his wife, Mary, soon became pregnant. Edmund, desperate for proof of his genius, began to drink heavily before and after performances. The family's situation became dire. He was hired in Birmingham for thirty shillings a week. Kean continued to drink after these shows. He then tried his luck in Swansea for twenty-five shillings a week. Unfortunately, he was so badly in debt, having owed the Birmingham company £15, that he and Mary and their son Howard had to travel the one hundred and fifty mile distance by foot.

Kean promised that Swansea would be the turning point for them. It wasn't. The crowds didn't react any better to Kean than they had in Birmingham. They considered him a second-rate actor and a loud-mouth. As late as 28 July 1813, Kean's Richard III was met with "shouts of derisive laughter" in Guernsey.[12] Mary gave birth to their second son, and Edmund found himself sliding deeper and deeper into debt. Mary wanted him to leave the theater, but Kean was convinced of his own preeminence.

After years of toiling in the unappreciative provinces, the family returned to London where Kean begged for work, and Howard, despite an advancing illness, did dramatic recitals at parties. After agreeing to play at the Olympic Theatre in London, Kean was eventually signed by Drury Lane, which had just spent the enormous sum of £150,000 on renovations but had no famous actors to fill its 3,611 seats. Kean was hired for £6 a week on a conditional trial run of six shows. When the actor arrived at Drury Lane, one actress asked "where the little wretch had been picked up"; John Cowen wrote that when Kean first came on stage, he was "astonished. I was prepared to see a small man; but … [by] mental comparison with Kemble's princely person,

---

10 *The Secret History of the Green-Room,* I:288.

11 Raymund FitzSimons, *Edmund Kean: Fire From Heaven,* 2, 6.

12 Gordon Craig, *The Life and Theatrical Career of Edmund Kean,* 7.

he appeared a perfect pygmy...."[13] Taller actors complained, "God renounce me! 'tis only necessary nowadays to be under four feet high, have bandy legs and a hoarseness, and mince my liver! but you'll be thought a great tragedian."[14] Nevertheless, on the night of 26 January 1814, this little man trudged through a miserable winter night to conquer Drury Lane and the theatrical world.

When he first came on stage, the reaction from the half-empty house was unfavorable. They wished he were half-a-head taller, but by the middle of his first speech, the audience began to cheer. They were drawn to Kean's energy and seeming simplicity. By the third act, the audience was on its feet and the din was so loud that stagehands, startled by the noise, appeared in the wings. The age of Kean had begun.

Kean and the Aesthetics of Boxing

That a new star had arrived on the London stage was not in-and-of itself surprising. The era's principle star, the aforementioned John Philip Kemble, was aging. It was inevitable that audiences would find someone new. What must have been surprising to audiences was that, even after conquering London, Kean continued to portray himself as a brawler who had fought his way up through the provincial ranks, and, confident of his powers, now welcomed all challengers.

The rationale for that portrayal was almost surely related to the actor's 1817 mandate that Drury Lane, home to Shakespearean performance, begin to stage prizefights each Monday evening. Kean may have even appeared *in* boxing matches *after* his Shakespearean performances. The impresario John Richardson saw Kean fight and recalled that the star was certainly skilled "*with the gloves*," but he does not say how often Kean fought or with whom.[15] Reticence seems to have been shared by all, including *The Fancy*, a publication of the era dedicated to reporting on the pugilistic sport, which noted only that matches were often staged at Drury Lane on "*the sly.*"[16] What a lovely and telling phrase. These bouts were not advertised, even though having London's newest star actor boxing professional fighters was, obviously, a sensational novelty. Instead, Kean had these scraps staged as if they were clandestine affairs.[17] In so doing, the actor maintained his role as an antiestablishment

---

13 J. Fitzgerald Molloy, *The Life and Adventures of Edmund Kean,* I:125 and I:185. A lack of height had impeded his early career as well. Kean complained:

> Mr. Long kept me in the background as much as possible and frequently gave those characters which undoubtedly were mine to fellows who certainly would have adorned the handles of a plough but were never intended for the stage; but these met with Mr. Long's approbation because they were taller than me. (Raymund FitzSimons, *Edmund Kean: Fire From Heaven*, 12)

14 Eleanor Ruggles, *Prince of Players*, 9.
15 See John Richardson, "Story of Mr. Kean," in HRC.
16 *The Fancy*, 162.
17 Monday night playbills do not advertise Kean boxing before or after any play.

figure; someone who was taking perilous risks, going against the stated wishes of his employers, willing to break the rules for his loyal fans.[18] Yet, if these matches did meet on "*the sly,*" what can we say about them? A lack of facts, we have already noted, didn't stop Kean's aforesaid biographers, playwrights, and actors from having their fun. But there is no need to leave it at that. What we can say with some certainty is that Kean used the aesthetics of the boxing match to change the way his audiences judged his acting.

Kean ushered in a sportive and competitive atmosphere, a new kind of theater with not merely a show and a star, but a spirited contest with a winner and a loser. His audience soon learned to keep the mental equivalent of scorecards and counted who won the theatrical rounds of each scene.[19] In sum, Kean, with his supposedly spontaneous physical bursts, punctuated by his signature "flashes of lightning," flouted widely understood cultural and physical boundaries, and his career would be measured as no Shakespearean before him: not for his skill in reciting Shakespeare, but for his ability to knockout his theatrical rivals.

Kean's First Great Combat

Meanwhile, Covent Garden, the rival playhouse, scrambled to find their own short and energetic actor, and it found one in a young upstart, Junius Brutus Booth, who had been making a name for himself in the provinces. When he showed up at Covent Garden, the cast was amazed. Booth looked so much like Kean that he could have passed for a twin. William C. Macready stated that at first glance Booth, "might have been thought Kean himself."[20] J. Fitzgerald Molloy wrote that "the audience was struck with astonishment at the strong resemblance he bore in complexion, stature, figure, and face to the Drury Lane actor."[21] It wasn't just height and hair color.[22] On 16 February 1817, Hazlitt observed that "almost the whole of his [Booth's]

18 These matches continued even while Kean was in America. Thus, the following dispatch for June 1821: "there was some excellent Sparring at Drury-lane Theatre, on Monday night. Ben Burn and Shelton made a very scientific display, *and drew forth much applause.*" Drury Lane manager Robert Elliston seems to have recorded the event for *The Fancy.* See p. 139.

19 On theatrical scorecards, see Alan S. Downer, ed. in James Henry Hackett, *Oxberry's 1822 Edition of King Richard III,* XVII-XVIII; C. Douglas Abel, "Venom in His Blood: Edmund Kean's Othello Contests," 71-2. Julian Charles Young noted that when Kean acted with Young, his father's "happiest hits were the result of natural sensibility"—that is, in adopting Kean's style (*A Memoir of Charles Mayne Young,* 55). "Hits" seem to be related to the older system of "points," discussed in Lisa A. Freeman, *Character's Theater,* 31-4. The scoring of "points" is also mentioned in George Henry Lewes, *On Actors and the Art of Acting,* 5 and in Raymund FitzSimons, *Edmund Kean: Fire From Heaven,* 50.

20 William C. Macready, *Macready's Reminiscences,* 105.

21 J. Fitzgerald Molloy, *The Life and Adventures of Edmund Kean,* II: 3.

22 Stephen M. Archer states that Booth was "about five three" (*Junius Brutus Booth: Theatrical Prometheus,* 3). Raymund FitzSimons writes that Booth "was a romantic-looking

performance was an exact copy or parody of Mr. Kean's manner of doing the same part. It was a complete, but at the same time a successful, piece of plagiarism." Nonetheless, he counseled, "[w]e do not think this kind of second-hand reputation can last upon the London boards for more than a character or two."[23]

Kean wasn't taking any chances and demanded that Drury Lane hire Booth immediately and that the two appear together in *Othello*. Drury Lane's rationale for acquiescing has never been questioned. Was the theater simply caving in to the demands of its principal actor, or was it actively trying to humble, if not undermine him? Undoubtedly, hiring Booth had its advantages. The move made good financial sense. Kean might have demanded more money than other actors, but he had single-handedly saved the theater from ruin.[24] Two Keans might mean double the profit. The two actors would not, after all, be appearing together all the time. And Booth might be used as a kind of insurance. If Kean grew sick, he might be replaced by Booth and/or vice versa. Further, Covent Garden would have no answer to this stable of Kean actors. Lastly, having Booth might be just the trick in further dealings with Kean. If, in later contract negotiations, Kean snubbed Drury Lane, Booth might still be retained. Perhaps Booth might be used to weaken Kean's position?

In short, Kean's fans certainly had much to be upset about. Admittedly, the notion that Drury Lane wanted to humble Kean, and hired Booth to do just that, is speculative. What is not is that the press, sensitive to Kean's recalibration of the theater into a violent, sportive event, judged everything concerning the performance in terms of tactical advantages. In selecting the part of the Moor, Kean, the papers noted approvingly, had already outmaneuvered Booth. The *New Monthly Magazine* wrote:

> In the Cast of Othello, Mr. Kean has immensely the advantage, for while the Moor is one of the most noble and diversified characters on the stage, no one can make Iago prominent, except by rendering him absurd—by making his villainy so plain, gross, and palpable to the eyes of the audience, as to deprive Othello of all shadow of excuse for listening to his slanders.[25]

---

youth, with … lustrous back hair and, like Kean, he was below average height" (*Edmund Kean: Fire From Heaven*, 105-6).

23 William Hazlitt, *Complete Works*, V:354. The compiler of Booth's memoirs defends the actor: "No, *there is not the smallest foundation for the assertion that Mr. Booth is an imitator*" (*Memoirs of Junius Brutus Booth*, 60).

24 We get a sense of Kean's impact from a hand-colored caricature from 1816, which reads "A Kean Manouver to Pay Old Debts-or-Drury is itself again!!!" and shows Kean's goblet filled with coins, which spill down to awaiting creditors. See Jonathan Reynolds, *Dramatis Personæ*, 88 (2005):11.

25 *New Monthly Magazine* 9 (1 January 1823): 7 in Press Clippings, in Kean, Edmund C. Newspaper Articles Messmore Kendall Collection, HRC. The point is made in reference to Kean's battle with Young but is equally relevant to Kean's match with Booth. See Press Clippings, Huntington Manuscript Collection, Huntington Library 182799.

Booth could either play Iago as a straight man or clownish foil; either way, advantage Kean. As the performance of *Othello* began, "Mr. BOOTH was welcomed by thunders of applause"[26] but was unprepared for Kean's power:

> The fury and whirlwind of the passions seemed to have endowed him [Kean] with supernatural strength. His eye was glittering and blood-shot, his veins were swollen, and his whole figure restless and violent. It seemed dangerous to cross his path, and death to assault him.[27]

The language suggests Kean's power to galvanize crowds and to waken in them a kind of theatrical blood lust. Booth walked around the stage half-stunned and hid in the greenroom at the first intermission, but the actor soon "overcame his fear, and went through the part of Iago manfully."[28] Procter described Kean's knockout blow: "Kean ... seemed to *expand* ... and to assume the vigour and dimensions of a giant. He glared down upon the now diminutive Iago; he seized and tossed him aside, with frightful and irresistible vehemence."[29] The *Morning Post* recorded that in "the subsequent scenes he [Booth] was sometimes feeble, frequently very good, but never transcendent. With another actor in that character, the *Iago* of the evening might have been thought great, but by the side of KEAN we could discover in him nothing strikingly original."

After his debacle with Kean, audience interest in Booth, and his confidence in his own powers, waned. Years later, Booth recalled that Kean's Othello "smothered Desdemona and my Iago too."[30] The fast-rising actor William C. Macready had not been able to attend the theatrical duel, but his brother, who had attended, informed him, "Booth was not only obscured, but hidden; no one seemed to give a thought to him. The question of comparison was completely set at rest."[31]

Kean vs. Young

If Kean's interest in boxing was part of a campaign to ally himself with the people's affections, to suggest that, having scuffled and scraped to the summit of London's theatrical world, he was more than man enough to take on all rivals, in reality, Kean was less than ready to enter into any and all matches with his acting contemporaries. Indeed, private letters and backstage practices suggest that Kean used his position to delay theatrical contests and entered into them only as a last resort. Naturally, Kean could not forever maintain the illusion of being willing to face all comers, although he tried. On stage, and, as we will see, in the press, Kean continued to promote himself

---

26 *Morning Post*, 21 February 1817, in Press Clippings, Huntington Manuscript Collection, Huntington Library, 182799.

27 Bryan Waller Procter, *The Life of Edmund Kean*, II:167.

28 Ibid., II:166.

29 Ibid., II:166-7.

30 Charles Wingate, *Shakespeare's Heroes On The Stage*, I:36.

31 William C. Macready, *Macready's Reminiscences*, 105.

as a man of the people. But, backstage, he aspired to the company of aristocrats and wanted to be recognized as the monarch of his profession. Thus, while Hazlitt was promoting the actor as a *"radical* performer," Kean was also secretly and actively attempting to suppress the very revolutionary impulses that had made him a star.[32]

In 1822, Drury Lane hired away Charles Mayne Young from Covent Garden. Stiff and artificial, it was said that Young plunged a dagger into his breast with the same elegance and lack of emotion as he handed a chair to a lady. Kean knew the actor and his limitations well. Indeed, they had acted together before.[33] On 26 May 1814, Henry Crabb Robinson noted that Young had been hired by Drury Lane as "Kean's inferior."[34] But by 1822, Young was a star in his own right, though not of the magnitude of Kean. Nonetheless, the hiring outraged Kean. Drury Lane tried to pacify him, reminding him that he was still its principal star. Still, Kean objected to performing with Young. In a letter to Elliston, Kean wrote:

> ... is Mr. Young to act Iago with me ....[;] did Mr. Young's Hamlet ever bring to the treasury the same Money that mine has[;] is there any Country manager [that] will give Mr. Young *10£* for his acting Hamlet[?]... I am prepared for *war*—, you make some references in your letter.
>   I am tired of Pimps and Sycophants.
>   Yours Edmund Kean
>   Veritas vincit[.][35]

Kean did not want a staged competition, but, being forced into one, he did not run. He did, however, get drunk for a week.

Sensing an upset, Procter recalled that it seemed to him that Kean was avoiding a "fight to the finish." Procter was right. Kean had tried to shun this fight or even any direct comparisons between the two actors. When booking one of his lucrative tours, Kean found that, due to scheduling, Charles Mayne Young would play one of his roles the night after the great actor finished his run. Kean was having none of it: "if he [Young] plays after me the same part I have just played, I will throw up my engagement, and you may seek your redress in a court of law."[36] The theater, anxious

---

32 Wrote Hazlitt: "Mr. Kean's acting is not of the patrician order; he is one of the people, and what might be termed a *radical* performer.... aristocratical pretensions .... did not seem *legitimate* in him, but upstart, turbulent, and vulgar" (William Hazlitt, *Complete Works*, XVIII:290).

33 According to one outlandish report, Charles Mayne Young and Edmund Kean had met, albeit briefly, under embarrassing circumstances. When Kean was a child, he accompanied his prostitute-mother Nance (or Nancy or Ann) Carey on her visits to various gentlemen. While she did her business with Mr. Young, his son, Charles, then ten years of age, sat patiently in the hallway with Edmund. See Henry Barton Baker, *Our Old Actors*, II.i.169. Donald Wolfit prefers to have Kean raised in a carnival atmosphere. As a child, Kean "sold medicines at fairs" (Speech, [p1]).

34 Henry Crabb Robinson, *The London Theatre 1811-1866*, 58.

35 Harold Newcomb Hillebrand, *Edmund Kean*, 231.

36 Julian Mayne Young, *A Memoir of Charles Mayne Young*, 54.

not to offend so great a star, agreed to Kean's terms. But now that there were no more tricks, no more managers to threaten or to deride in merciless contempt, Kean was going to have to act with Young.

To Drury Lane's manager Elliston, Kean dropped the bravado: "I am not ashamed to say I am afraid of the contest. ....I am told he is wonderfully great.... If so, I am beaten." That being said, Kean was not going down without a fight: "As the Covent Garden hero comes upon my ground the challenger, I have doubtless my choice of weapons; he *must* play Iago...."[37] Elliston agreed. Young and Kean would appear together in *Othello*, a night of "mighty expectation," as it was called in the *Morning Post*. According to Charles Mayne Young's son, Julian, playbills "were posted all over London, advertising the early appearance on the same boards of the two men who had long been regarded as the rival representations of two opposite schools of art."[38]

As with the Booth match, the reviews stress the physical nature of their encounter: "In figure, stature, and deportment, Young had the advantage over Kean.... [who] in his gait shuffled. Young trod the boards with freedom." Kean, weak of body, conserved "his powers for a point, or for an outburst of impassioned feeling."[39] But, in the end, Young was no match for Kean, who was "fierce, ungovernable, dangerous. You knew not what he would do next, in the madness of his spirit:—he knew not himself what he should do!"[40] It is Kean's "ungovernable" actions that stand out. According to the above-cited reviewer, the working-class vulgarian overthrows Young, the tall, stately aristocrat. Moreover, it seems the brutality Kean unleashes against his opponent is part of a larger class struggle of payback. Kean strikes back at Young's social advantages, not unlike the ungovernable fury of the peasants of revolutionary France.

Not everyone rated Kean the victor. Hazlitt, usually one to praise Kean, argued that, in surviving the encounter, Young had established his position as Kean's greatest rival and likeliest successor.[41] For his part, Young was delighted with the outcome

---

37 J. Fitzgerald Molloy, *The Life and Adventures of Edmund Kean*, II:99.

38 Julian Charles Young, *A Memoir of Charles Mayne Young, Tragedian*, 53.

39 Ibid., 55.

40 *The London Magazine*, 7.37 (January 1823): 99-100, in Press Clippings, in Kean, Edmund C. Newspaper Articles Messmore Kendall Collection, HRC. Hillebrand, continuing the trope of physical combat, writes:

> If the audience looked for another slaughter, they were disappointed; their hero was no longer capable of exerting himself so mightily, he was tiring already under the strain of constant expenditure, the sinews of his will had lost their tautness. Yet though Kean did not play Young off his feet, as he had played Booth, he played better than he had done for a long time. He may have given a *finer* performance than on that other historic occasion, but not so electric; the time for demonic energy had passed, the time for finesse had come, for those rarifications of art which seek to replace the vigor of prime. (*Edmund Kean*, 232)

41 Imagining the prospect of Kean's death, Hazlitt lamented: "A Kemble school we can understand; a Kean school is, we suspect, a contradiction in terms" (William Hazlitt, *Complete Works*, V:355). Thus, a Kemble successor was inevitable.

and looked on all further bouts as irritating superfluities. One night, on learning he had again been matched with Kean, the upstart complained that he had "to play again with that bloody, thundering bugger."[42] Soon after, Young left, and Drury Lane hired William C. Macready to fill the gap. Macready had been making £20 a week at Covent Garden. Drury Lane offered him £20 a night. Kean was raised to £30 a night.

Kean's Fading Skills

If Kean comes across as someone who brilliantly stage-managed his own image, he could also unbutton—indeed, unravel—suddenly and alarmingly. Increasingly, Drury Lane posted notices that Kean was unable to perform due to "illness." Illness here might mean a variety of things. Kean might have been too drunk or might have simply been too lazy to perform. His power over the theater was such that he often knew ahead of time when he would be too debauched to appear. For example, he wrote to the Drury Lane Committee on 23 November 1817 that he would be ill on the following night. Another actor, Maywood, took his part. On 6 December 1817, Kean was supposed to play in *Richard, Duke of York*. Again, he canceled due to "continued and severe indisposition." It was not until 15 December, an interval of six weeks, that Drury Lane announced that "Mr. Kean will have the honour of resuming his professional duties this evening, when he will perform the character of Richard the Third."[43]

After a few years of riotous excess, however, Kean's body seemed to give out. Keats, hearing of Kean's exhaustion, publicly urged the actor to "Have a carefulness of thy health ... in these cold and enfeebled times."[44] On 18 December 1818, Kean's Luke was "very fine indeed" but he "had a very bad voice throughout"; on 13 December 1819, Kean looked "old and haggard" in *Hamlet*; on 10 June 1823, Kean

---

On the other hand, Jeremy Diddler suggested that copying Kean was very much in vogue:

> He is indeed, the glass, wherein
> The day's tragedians now do dress themselves;
> They have no skill that practice not his gait....

Concluding, he noted that copyists of Kean could not hope to match the actor's genius:

> In standing, action, or in speech,
> He is the mark and glass, copy and book
> That fashions others; his defects combined
> They mimic,—all things, save creative mind. (Jeremy Diddler, "Kean and his Imitators," p.31)

Esther Cloudman Dunn records that as early as 1817, many American actors were imitating Kean (*Shakespeare in America*, 159).

42 Raymund FitzSimons, *Edmund Kean: Fire From Heaven*, 171.
43 Maurice B. Foreman, in John Keats, *Poetical Works,* 5:cf.228.
44 John Keats, *Poetical Works,* 3:232.

had grown stout "and his face has lost some of its fine expression. He gave little pleasure."[45] By age 33, Kean, was already seen as an old man, yet another sign that he had turned acting into an athletic—thus, young man's—sport. This gradual physical deterioration was mirrored in his fading popularity. But rather than Kean embarking on a regime of sound and healthy living, he, as will be detailed in Chapters Three and Four, continued to live hard, as if expecting to die young. Whether he was aware of his sadomasochistic diligence, the actor was at least perceptive enough to understand that his power over Drury Lane was no longer complete. To stave off further combats that might prove physically costly, Kean found new ways to encumber his theatrical competition.

Attempts to Contain and Marginalize Macready

In the eighteenth and nineteenth centuries, each major Shakespearean actor had his set of effects and carefully selected roles to highlight them. Kemble was masterful at playing aristocrats. His main roles were Hamlet, Brutus, King John, and Coriolanus. Kean was a far earthier actor and preferred Shylock, Othello, Iago, and Richard III. This difference in parts and approach was not entirely by accident. Kean in part rose by differentiating himself from Kemble. Thus, when Kean first made his mark in London, he studiously avoided all of Kemble's principle roles, and he expected other actors to avoid his.[46]

All that changed with the rise of Kean's greatest rival, William C. Macready. Hazlitt stated that, even as early as 1816, Mr. Macready was "by far the best tragic actor that has come out of our remembrance, with the exception of Mr. Kean."[47] The actor had first come to Covent Garden's notice after he received rave reviews as Luke in *Riches; or, The Wife and Brother*, an adaptation of Massinger's *The City Madam* (at Bath, 18 February 1815). Like Kemble and Young, Macready was stately and aristocratic, a "better orator than an actor."[48]

Initially, Macready was hired by Covent Garden as a transitional replacement for the aging Kemble, who had last put in a full season in 1811-12. In 1813, Kemble

---

45 Henry Crabb Robinson, *The London Theatre 1811-1866*, 80, 90, 102.

46 According to Procter, Kean felt that his parts were his and his alone, even when he was a player in the provinces. When playing in Birmingham, Kean demanded that no one play Hamlet, Richard, or Othello. "If John Kemble came down," said he, "he should not have them. *They are mine!*" (Bryan Waller Procter, *Life of Edmund Kean*, I:97) This account is mitigated somewhat by yet another report that while acting Laertes in the provinces opposite Master Betty, Kean swore that he'd "play seconds to no man, save John Kemble" (Henry Barton Baker, *Our Old Actors*, II.i.177). In any case, this behavior was not new. Some fifteen years before the rise of Kean, Kemble had been criticized for trying to wrestle the part of Richard III from the hands of George Frederick Cooke. An anonymous writer defended Kemble: "Competition constitutes the very essence of human actions" (*Kemble & Cooke*, 9).

47 William Hazlitt, *Complete Works*, V:334.

48 Ibid., V:340.

remained inactive but returned 15 January 1814 for a performance of *Coriolanus*, which he reprised on 22 and 25 January. In that same season he also played other favorites: *Cato* (20 January), *Macbeth* (18 and 25 January), and *Hamlet* (27, 29 and 31 January). Kemble's final performance would not be until 23 June 1817—a last performance of his Coriolanus. However, in these final three years (1814-17), Kemble performed only a handful of times.

As decorum dictated, Macready showed respect for the elder star. True, Macready did play Coriolanus, but this was not attempted until two years after Kemble's official retirement; the role of Coriolanus was Kemble's and everyone knew it. But Macready did not extend the same respect to Kean.[49] On 10 October 1816, Macready, in his first London season as a headliner, appeared as Othello; on 15 October 1816 he appeared as Iago.[50] This was an outrage! Kean had made a point of exploiting *Othello* as a showcase for his virtuosity. One night he would play the Moor, and then the very next night Kean would reverse roles, playing Iago. Now Macready was doing the same thing, making Kean's formerly distinctive talent seem ordinary. Kemble had all but retired from the stage and, since Kean wasn't playing Kemble's roles, Macready was, of course, entitled to them, but Othello and Iago were another matter.[51]

Kean decided to fight fire with fire. If Macready could play Kean's parts, Kean could play Macready's. He began with the part that had first brought Macready to Covent Garden's attention: Luke in *Riches; or, The Wife and Brother*. Kean had strong reasons to attempt the part: (I) the play was originally by Massinger. One of Kean's principal roles was Sir Giles Overreach in Massinger's *A New Way to Pay Old Debts*. If Macready established *Riches* as his own, might his growing audience want him—indeed, expect him—to play in other Massinger plays? Kean had to stop

---

49 Despite the facts, William Archer argues that "Kean's parts were barred" from Macready (*William Charles Macready*, 33).

50 William Archer, *William Macready*, 37. Hazlitt thought Macready's Othello was inferior to Kean's: "We have been rather spoiled for seeing any one else in the character, by Mr. Kean's performance of it" (*Complete Works*, V:338). But by 2 January 1821, Crabb Robinson judged Macready to be Kean's equal (*The London Theatre 1811-1866*, 94). Thus, Kean, even by 1817, was correct in seeing Macready as a real threat.

51 It should be pointed out that on 3 January 1816 Macready did star in *Hamlet*, a part claimed by both Kemble and Kean. This exception to the proprietary nature of Shakespearean parts seems simply that: an exception. Even Kean understood that every major actor was entitled to try Hamlet. That being said, Macready continued to show at least some deference. Yes, he played Hamlet, but in Bath, not in London. The same pattern is seen in Macready's reaction to Kean's title role in *Alexander the Great*. Kean played the Greek hero on 8 June 1818, and again on 27 June 1818, as his season's close at Drury Lane. The next fall, on 18 October 1819, Macready appeared in the play, but only as Clytus, not as Alexander. Macready would not touch the part until 24 May 1823, when Kean's skills were in steep decline. Even then, Macready knew better than to raise Kean's ire. Yes, he'd play Alexander, but, again, only in Bath, not in London. That same month, also in Bath, Macready played Shylock for the first time.

Macready now, while Sir Giles was still firmly Kean's; (II) Kean had played Luke once before, at Bath, on 25 May 1814. Macready, we remember, played the same part in Bath on 18 February 1815. Mulling his strategy in 1817, Kean decided that it was time to revive the role. Not that the part would become a mainstay. The performance dates of Kean's minor roles indicate that he simply abandoned characters as soon as he had secured them as his own or returned to them when some new upstart threatened his hold. In the case of Luke, Kean only played the role four times in total: 25 May 1814, 18 December 1817, 22 December 1817 and 31 January 1818, but the performances, few as they were, did the trick. Macready never played the role again. Kean may have also played Paris in Massinger's *The Roman Actor* on 22 June 1822 to keep Macready away from it.

On 4 July 1815, Kean appeared as Octavian in *The Mountaineers.* The role had been a standard of Kemble's and, with that actor in semi-retirement, Kean may have wanted to secure the part. Despite the occasion of Kean performing a new role, the house was not crowded.[52] Yet Kean still found reason to revive the role: on 18 and 19 June 1818, again on 5 September 1819 and yet again years later, on 22 June 1822. These repetitions took place even though the theater historian John Genest assures us that "his Octavian was not capital."[53] *Town and Country*, "a miserable play," was revived on 27 February 1815 only to let Kean play the part of Reuben Glenroy, a man who, in the course of being abandoned by his mistress, expresses both passionate outrage and despair.[54] On 16 and 17 June 1818, 29 and 30 August 1820, and on 11 June 1823, Kean revived this seemingly minor part. On 14 May 1817, Kean played Eustace de St. Pierre in *The Surrender of Calais*. The play ran for only two performances. Yet Kean revived it five years later on 5 June 1823. Kean not only kept his minor roles from becoming Macready's, he also tried any new Shakespearean role his rival appeared in. For example, on 29 November 1819, Macready played *Coriolanus* at Covent Garden for the first time. Kean followed suit a month later, playing the same at Drury Lane on 24 December 1819.[55] Macready, of course, was trying a similar tactic. For example, when John Dillon's play *Retribution* premièred on 1 January 1818, Macready noted that its run of just nine initial performances was enough to "establish me more firmly in public opinion as the undisputed representative of the disagreeable [character]."[56]

Let Macready have that minor part, so long as he stayed away from Richard III and Shylock. But for the London 1819 season, Macready, launched a counterattack, playing Richard III on 25 October. (The actor had previously avoided the role for fear

---

52 John Genest, *Some Account of the English Stage*, VIII:462.

53 Ibid., IX:178.

54 Henry Crabb Robinson, *The London Theatre 1811-1866*, 61.

55 On 25 January 1820, Kean mounted a production of *Coriolanus*, in part to answer Macready's performance in the role (Raymund FitzSimons, *Edmund Kean: Fire From Heaven*, 135). See also David George, who argues that Macready raced to perform Coriolanus before Kean secured the part as his own ("Restoring Shakespeare's *Coriolanus*: Kean Versus Macready," esp. 103).

56 William C. Macready, *Macready's Reminiscences,* 120.

that Kean would see it as an "affront."[57]) Genest saw both Macready's and Kean's respective Richards and noted that Macready "was inferior to Kean, till the Ghosts appeared—he was then superiour."[58] Now emboldened, Macready soon appeared in another of Kean's principal roles: Zanga in *The Revenge*, a part nineteenth-century audiences had come to accept as our actor's.[59] Given Macready's growing powers and prominence, it looked as though Kean would have no choice but to fight Macready head on.

Macready vs. Kean: A Fight Neither Actor Wanted

William Macready had been just a boy when Kean began performing Shakespeare. He even remembered Kean when the King of Drury Lane had only been a bit player in the provinces:

> It was on my return home from one of my Christmas holidays that in passing through Birmingham I found the theatre there... had sent tickets for a box.... a little mean-looking man, in shabby green satin dress (I remember him well), appeared as the hero, 'Alonzo the Brave.' . ... How little did I know, or could guess, that under that shabby green satin dress was hidden one of the most extraordinary theatrical geniuses that have ever illustrated the dramatic poetry of England! ... an actor of the name of Kean.[60]

If Macready was reluctant to clash directly with his boyhood hero, Kean, for his part, was none too anxious to combat with Macready. When his rival was in London, Kean discreetly retired to his country home—his recently purchased Bute Castle in Scotland—or toured the provinces. He even spread the rumor he was in France for his health, but really he was in a bar and brothel in Brighton. Elliston tracked him down and brought him back to London. Kean alternately thought of retirement and accepting the challenge, stating, "Yet, a breath—a breath, I say, of Kean shall confound a generation of Youngs and Macreadys."[61]

Macready was far from confident about the match. His diary entries speak for themselves:

---

57 William Archer, *William Macready*, 50.

58 John Genest, *Some Account of the English Stage*, IX: 223.

59 On the part of Zanga: Hillebrand records that many critics were outraged that Kean was trying one of Kemble's roles (*Edmund Kean*, 148). Kemble tried and failed in the role on 19 January 1798. Kean first performed the part on 24 May 1815. Macready played the part on 30 September 1820.

60 William C. Macready, *Macready's Reminiscences,* 18-19. On the other hand, as years passed, Macready came to despise Kean's lifestyle and only went to his funeral because it was expected of him. He felt that he was "under such a *surveillance*" (*Macready's Reminiscences*, 283).

61 Raymund FitzSimons, *Edmund Kean: Fire From Heaven*, 179.

November 22nd.—Rehearsed Iago. Very nervous, in extremely low spirits. Came home. Thought over Iago, a very unhappy state of mind....

November 26th.—Read Iago in bed. Rehearsed Iago. Met Kean. Lay down on bed. Acted, not satisfactorily, nervous.

Even years later, Macready wrote that he could not appear as Othello without "blushing through his black" at his inferiority to Kean.[62]

Critics, however, did not share Macready's apprehension. Most expected an easy victory. Again, the language was suggestive of physical combat. Hazlitt wrote that "there is no vacant pause in [Kean's] action," but *The Morning Post* for 2 October 1818 dismissed Kean's now only occasional bursts of restless energy as "sometimes approximated to vulgarity."[63] Macready, on the other hand, was described as an immovable and formidable object: "tall enough" with "no sweeping outlines, no massy movements in his action."[64] In boxing terms, it was a classic case of differing styles: Macready, the young contender, was an imposing, immovable object; Kean, the aging champion, was short, energetic and, while not in his prime, dangerous.[65] One cannot help but feel that if Hazlitt were a betting man, his wager would have been placed upon Macready.

How stunned the audience must have been by that evening's performance, in which Kean, the aged actor, demolished Macready. George Henry Lewes was a boy when he saw the match but recalled: "how puny he [Kean] appeared beside Macready, until the third act when, roused by Iago's taunts and insinuations, he moved towards him with a gouty hobble, seized him by the throat, and, in a well-

---

62 William, Archer, *Eminent Actors: Macready, Betterton, Macklin*, 51.

63 *Morning Chronicle*, 27 January 1814, in Press Clippings, in Kean, Edmund C. Newspaper Articles Messmore Kendall Collection, HRC. According to C. Douglas Abel, Kean's defects were also his assets. It was his very lack of height that forced the actor to be more active: "Because he had no grandeur in repose, and because his acting was so powerful when it was energized, Kean needed to be animated...." See his essay, " 'Alexander the Little': The Question of Stature in Edmund Kean's Othello," 102. A caricature published 29 March 1819 refers to Kean as "Caesar the Little," a joke which not only suggests his height deficiency, but which may also recall the similar diminutive stature of Napoleon. See Gordon Craig, *The Life and Theatrical Career of Edmund Kean*, 16.

64 William Hazlitt, *Complete Works*, V:339. Macready's height (5' 7") is listed in *Oxberry's Dramatic Biography*, V:51.

65 The general outline of this scene, in which one large man is tormented by a shorter, faster man, may be an allusion to Thomas Fuller's famous, though apocryphal, story of Jonson and Shakespeare trading jests: "Master Jonson ... was built far higher in Learning; *Solid*, but *Slow* in his performances. *Shake-spear*, with the *English-man of War*, lesser in *bulk*, but lighter in *sailing*, could turn ... by all the quickness of his Wit and Invention." (Thomas Fuller, "Excerpt from *Worthies, Warwickshire* (1662)," 41). Kean's combats may have also affected nineteenth-century Shakespeare scholarship. Ian Donaldson argues that eighteenth- and nineteenth-century biographers often imagined Shakespeare as pitted in a variety of theatrical contests with his playwrighting rivals, most significantly with Ben Jonson. See *Jonson's Magic Houses: Essays in Interpretation*, 11-25.

known explosion, 'Villain! be sure thou prove,' etc., seemed to swell into a stature which made Macready appear small."[66] Macready later reiterated some of these details: Kean was "quite strong on his legs and in his voice."[67]

The mere necessity of noting both the unexpected strength of his leg and voice indicates how comparatively frail Kean had become. It's true that even in his greener days Kean's acting had been so exhausting that, while playing Othello, he was obliged to "rest on a sofa" during his dialogue with Desdemona, so as to gather strength before murdering her.[68] But some who had seen Kean in his heyday were shocked by the decline. Dr. Doran, commenting on his Richard, wrote: "The sight was pitiable. Genius was not traceable in that bloated face; intellect was all but quenched in those once matchless eyes and the power seemed gone, despite the will that would recall it. … [H]e moved only with difficulty, using his sword as a stick." And when playing Richard III, after a short fight, the actor playing Richmond was now compelled to help Kean by the hand, and "let him gently down, lest he should be injured by the fall."[69]

As great, surprising, and even suspicious, as this victory was, it came at a physical cost. James Henry Hackett noted that after defeating Macready, something seemed to go out of Kean: "the rival talents of Macready, in *Iago*, gave a stimulus to his [Kean's] powers of body and mind," though never again "did his genius display itself more triumphantly."[70] Backstage, a frequent visitor "found him, as was usual after the performance of any of his principal parts, stretched upon a sofa, retching violently, and throwing up blood."[71]

Fixing the Theatrical Scorecard

To what can we attribute such a sweeping, though physically costly, victory? Saying that Kean, hobbled by gout, weakened by his own social excesses, won on sheer force of will may not be sufficient. For all the talk of doing away with the old order, Kean did not win his matches on merit alone. Indeed, the actor had collaborated with factions of his audience in effect to "fix" the outcome of many of his theatrical matches.

---

66 George Henry Lewes, *On Actors and the Art of Acting*, 4.

67 William C. Macready, *Macready's Reminiscences,* 263. Kean's legs had been bothering him for years. A notice posted by Drury Lane on 13 June 1820 stated that he had "ruptured a considerable portion of the muscular flesh appertaining to the calf of his leg." (Gordon Craig, *The Life and Theatrical Career of Edmund Kean*, 8). In the latter part of his career, there was even talk of amputation. See James Winston, 12 February 1827, *Drury Lane Journal*, 142.

68 John Forster, *Dramatic Essays*, 16.

69 John Doran, *"Their Majesties' Servants." Annals of the English Stage*, II: 411-2. The story is repeated with slight variation in Charles E.L. Wingate, *Shakespeare's Heroes On the Stage*, II:317-8.

70 James Henry Hackett, "Kean's Last Appearance on the Stage," *New York Mirror*, 22 February 1834, p. 270, in Press Clippings, Personal Collection.

71 Harold Newcomb Hillebrand, *Edmund Kean*, 172.

Kean had a legion of fans and an official fan club, The Wolves, dedicated to hissing and booing anyone that the star actor disliked.[72] In time, the duties and functions of this club would alter—at least officially. Nonetheless, for the first half dozen years of its existence, the above-cited Wolves were Kean's ravenous pets. If Kean's genius could not defeat an up-and-coming performer, his Wolves might be released as audience enforcers.

Kean even published the proceedings of The Wolves' meetings, in which Kean discussed ways to block other actors from achieving fame. In the first of their meetings, Kean ordered his fans to "run down [all] pretenders"; given their marching orders, the club members agreed to a list of actors who were to be blacklisted: "Messrs. Meggott, Edwards, and Cobham, on their respective assumptions of *Richard the Third*."[73] True, none of these actors were household names, perhaps that is because Kean saw to it that they never succeeded. Genest, for one, thinks that it was clear that The Wolves formed some combination to prevent any new performer from succeeding in *Richard III*: "Meggett was most cruelly used by the bigoted admirers of Kean."[74]

The baying of Wolves also broke out at performances of plays Kean had considered and discarded. For example, Kean mulled acting in John Thelwall's play *The Castle of Glendower* but rejected it. Hearing that some other actor was to appear in a play that Kean had considered, The Wolves had the play booed off stage. When Kean rejected Charles Bucke's *The Italians* and the author had the gall to stage it anyway, Kean's legions shouted down the actors.[75] The next night, Bucke's supporters came to one of Kean's play and tried to interrupt his performance. Kean stopped the play to announce that he "had no apology to make"; The Wolves soon shouted down his opponents and demanded that Kean continue, which he did.

The Wolves did more than howl in derision. We get a taste of their more forceful tactics in the following article, which appeared in the *New York American*. On 1 February 1825, some audience members had the audacity to hiss Kean's performance. As soon as they began to express their opinion, the writer:

> observed several individuals borne down by numbers, thrust from their places and atrociously kicked and beaten into the bargain for daring to express an independent opinion. ... Several personal conflicts took place in the pit, and a few individuals were ejected with much violence; in every instance, we believe they [those ejected] were the opponents of Mr. Kean.[76]

---

72 F.W. Hawkins writes that a "club called the 'Wolf Club,' of which Mr. Kean was president, had pledged themselves by oath to damn every effort to rival him..." (*Life of Edmund Kean*, I:418).

73 *Oxberry's Dramatic Mirror*, 148.

74 John Genest, *Some Account of the English Stage*, VIII: 486.

75 On Kean's rejection of *The Italians*, Bucke writes that "I made one important alteration, (against my own judgment), in order to harmonize with the wishes of Mr. Kean" (Preface, *The Italians*, VIII). On Kean's management, he writes: "though Mr. KEAN is saving the establishment with his right hand, he is ruining it with his left..." (Ibid., XVIII).

76 *New York American*, 12 March 1825 in Press Clippings, Personal Collection.

CARTOON OF THE BOOTH-KEAN CONTROVERSY IN LONDON IN 1817.

Plate 1:   A Cartoon of the Kean-Booth Contest. Kean, on stilts, is propped up by his fans. Reprinted by kind permission of the Harry Ransom Humanities Research Center; The University of Texas at Austin.

   True, the organization of audiences to ruin theatrical careers predated the Age of Kean. On 22 February 1748, Lord Hubbard organized a party to ruin the premiere of *The Foundling*. The reason he gave was that it was too long.[77] How he knew it was too long is a matter of speculation, since he damned the play before it even ran. The anonymous author of the 1751 *Guide to the Stage* disapproves of the "ambitious youths, who thus love to signalize themselves." The old plays are to be respected. However, this same critic adds that he "shall leave a new play to their mercy."[78] Some new authors decided to fight fire with fire. For the premiere of Addison's *Cato*, Richard Steele secured an "Audience ... [so] it should be impossible for the Vulgar to put its Success or due Applause to any Hazard."[79] Similarly, Nicholas Rowe hired part of an audience for the premiere of his play *Lady Jane Grey*.[80] What is unusual, however, is that The Wolves fanclub was controlled by an actor and, more astonishingly, was directed against his own company and even segments of his ticket-buying public.

---

77 See *The London Stage, 1660-1800*, Part 4.1:CLXXXIV.

78 Ibid., 4.1:CLXXXIX.

79 Allardyce Nicoll, *A History of English Drama*, 2:17.

80 Ibid., 2:18.

Backstage Brawls: Destroying Up-and-Coming Rivals

Fair enough, Kean wanted to remain champion of the stage and used his influence to retain his title. After all, what was he to do? Kean had turned theater into combat, but he had met the chief rivals of his era. His bouts against Booth, Young, and Macready were fought amongst able contestants. If the better man (Kean) won, that was hardly his fault. And as for The Wolves, every actor had his fans. What of it?

Not everyone—Booth's aforementioned supporters, for example—saw it that way. Some complained that Kean did far more than avoid other star actors; he destroyed an entire generation of potential rivals. In a pamphlet called *The New Way to Act Old Plays: A Familiar Epistle to the Management of Drury Lane Theatre on the Present State of the Stage* (1818), an anonymous author complained that since Kean had come to power:

> The … failure of this house, of late, seems to arise from the circumstance of keeping the fore-ground isolated instead of the collective talent of the company. When we go to see a fine historical picture, it is not to see one figure in it— … it is the whole—the *tout*[e] *ensemble* that we hope to be pleased with.[81]

The charge is repeated a year later, when Elizabeth Macauley attacked Kean along similar lines. She knew what she was talking about: she had played opposite Kean three times. The first time she acted so poorly that Kean accused her of having a drinking problem. But an actress with a drinking problem evidently pleased him because he soon after found reason to employ her again, this time as Lady Randolph in *Douglas*. She performed well and, given Kean's temperament, he was probably irritated by that. Still, he rehired her as Constance to his King John; she again performed well. So Kean refused to act with her again. Macauley retorted in a pamphlet, *Theatrical Revolution, or Plain Truth Addressed to Common Sense* (1819), in which she accused Kean of ruining London theater with his bread and circus:

> Mr. Kean stands in general estimation, as the enemy of his profession, and … [the] hopes of Actors, and Authors, unless they made themselves subservient to him; as one who repayed the generosity of the public, by keeping from them all prospects of amusement but what centred in himself.[82]

Both pamphlets argue that Kean, in direct contradiction to the spirited and celebrated matches that sustained him as a star, was actively hostile to the idea of competition. Kean did not care for negative press, but the damage Macauley caused was negligible.[83] His most ardent fans were working class and probably did not read

---

81 *The New Way to Act Old Plays: A Familiar Epistle*, ix.

82 Elizabeth Macauley, *Theatrical Revolution*, 21. For Kean's attack on Macauley, see F.W. Hawkins, *Life of Edmund Kean*, II: 46-50.

83 Mrs. Garrick, on seeing an unhappy Kean, asked Mrs. Kean why he was upset. "Oh," replied Mrs. Kean, "you mustn't mind him; he has just read a spiteful notice of his *Othello* in one of the newspapers, which has terribly vexed him." "But why should he mind that?" said

pamphlets. Besides, people like Macauley missed the point entirely. The people wanted more, not less, of him.

But can we dismiss so cavalierly the charge that Kean was destroying all sense of competition within his own company? Here, we might begin by comparing Kean's practice to his predecessors. In the eighteenth century, David Garrick had wielded "inestimable professional power and had the ability either to promote or devastate the careers of playwrights and aspiring actors, actresses, musicians, and dancers."[84] Yet, Garrick, who, like Kean, was given a share of the theater, almost always used his power for the good of Drury Lane. When he became manager, he made a promise to Drury Lane's treasurer, William Pritchard, that he would "secure my property and my friends to the best of my judgment. I shall engage the best company in England if I can, and think it the interest of the best actors to be together...."[85] Garrick's successor, John Philip Kemble, also recruited the best actors available. Kemble's usual supporting cast featured his sister, Sarah Siddons, the preeminent female actress of her day, as well as Mrs. Jordan, "as dazzling a star in her way as Mrs. Siddons,"[86] "singly capable of supporting the interests of the theatre,"[87] Miss Farren, described as "beautiful and accomplished,"[88] and, for minor parts, John Palmer, whose acting was "serviceable to the theatre," Mr. Whitfield, a "tolerable" comedian and tragedian, and Mr. Trueman, "a useful and respectable actor."[89]

Whereas Garrick and Kemble saw cast members as important theatrical allies, Kean merely saw them as rivals who might one day become combatants. To further highlight his skills and to stave off all competition, Kean magnified the effect of his genius by making sure that no competent actor appeared near him. On 22 November 1815, Henry Crabb Robinson jotted down that in Kean's production of *Tamerlane*, the star:

> performed the character throughout under the idea of his being a two-legged wild beast. ... His tartan whiskers improved the natural excellence of his face—his projecting underlip and admirably expressive eye gave to his countenance all desirable vigour. And his exhibition of rage and hatred were very excellent.... But that was all I enjoyed. Mrs. Bartlett as Arpasia was offensive.[90]

This was not a "one off." Kean always made sure that the actress playing opposite him was incapable. For example, Kean selected Mrs. Glover for both *The Distrest*

Mrs. Garrick; "he is above papers, and can afford abuse." "Yes," observed Mrs. Kean; "but he says the article is so well written: but for that, he wouldn't care for the abuse" (John William Cole, *The Life and Theatrical Times of Charles Kean*, I:49).

84 Phyllis T. Dircks, *David Garrick*, 1.

85 Kalman A. Burnim, *David Garrick: Director*, 22.

86 Linda Kelly, *The Kemble Era*, 54.

87 William Henry Ireland, *Confidential Friend*, 56.

88 Linda Kelly, *The Kemble Era*, 118.

89 See entries in *The Thespian Dictionary*, vol. II. Regarding John Palmer, the actor in Kemble's company is not to be confused with his father, an actor of the same name.

90 Henry Crabb Robinson, *The London Theatre 1811-1866*, 66.

Mother and *Richard, Duke of York.* A fine comedian, Mrs. Glover's skills in tragedy were considered to be "worse than death."[91]

Kean was equally careful in selecting actors for minor roles. Kean's criterion was simple: the actor had to be terrible. Hazlitt, the age's most observant critic, noted, after a performance of Kean's *Othello*, that, aside from the star, "the play was by no means judiciously cast; indeed, almost every individual appeared to be out of his proper place."[92] In his review of Kean's *Richard II*, Hazlitt commented, "Of the other characters [read: actors] of the play, it is needless to say much. Mr. Pope was respectable ... Mr. Holland was lamentable ... and Mr. Elliston indifferent."[93] Keats, in his review of *Richard, Duke of York*, remarked that aside from Kean, every actor was appalling:

> There is little to be said of the rest. Pope as *Cardinal* (how aptly chosen) balances a red hat. Holland wears insipid white hair, and is even more insipid than the hair which he carries. Rae plays the adulterous Suffolk, and proves how likely he is to act amiss. Wallack as *Young Clifford*, 'towers above his sex.' *Mr. Maywood* is more miserable in *Henry the Sixth* than winter, or wet nights, or Death on a pale horse, or want of money, or deceitful friends, or any other crying evil. The comic parts are sadly mangled, owing to illness of Munden and Oxberry. *Jack Cade* dies of a locked jaw;—and *Dick* the butcher is become a graveman. Mrs. Glover chews the blank verse past all endurance....[94]

On 28 September 1816, Kean played Mortimer, the principal lead in Colman's *The Iron Chest*. Robinson saw the play on 2 December 1816 and averred that Kean was "very fine indeed." However, Wallack's Wilford "was without thought or conception of any kind—No other actor was worth notice."[95] With no competition, Kean allowed the play to run for another 15 performances, a palpable hit.[96] For Kean, cast support paradoxically called for ineptitude. No one was to rival his genius; even mediocrity was apparently frowned upon.

Not all his audience was willing to put up with such middling fare. In October 1814, Shelley walked out of a performance of Kean as Hamlet because of "the bad filling up of the inferior parts."[97] Earlier in that same season, on 14 May 1814, Henry

91 John Keats, *Poetical Works*, 5:245.

92 William Hazlitt, *Complete Works*, V:189.

93 Ibid., V:224. Hazlitt, while not directly commenting on Kean, suggested that it was natural for actors to be constantly looking over their shoulder and plotting ways to stymie their competition: "Suppose an actor ... *does* get at the top of his profession, he can no longer bear a rival near the throne; to be second or only equal, is to be nothing: he starts at the prospect of a successor, and retains the mimic scepter with a convulsive grasp..." (Ibid., VIII:94). The quotation is from the essay "On Living to One's-Self," which was published in 1821, at the height of Kean's power. Further, the passage alludes to *Macbeth*, one of Kean's favorite plays.

94 John Keats, *Poetical Works*, 5:244-5.

95 Henry Crabb Robinson, *The London Theatre 1811-1866*, 74.

96 John Genest tells us that in Kean's day, nine performances qualified the play as a success (VIII:687).

97 Jonathan Bate, *Shakespeare and the English Romantic Imagination*, 265-6. n14.

Crabb Robinson attended a performance of Kean's Iago in *Othello*. He opined that the "other characters were not well played."[98] Both, however, continued to praise Kean's acting, and, more crucially, no one blamed Kean for his casting selections.

Looking back on Kean's entire career, however, it becomes obvious that Kean's ability to select actors of such poor quality paradoxically indicated that he had an eye for real talent. In part, Kean's decisions in terms of casting might have been based on his early struggles, when he worked hard to differentiate himself from his acting company. In 1809, Andrew Cherry hired Kean to act Hamlet for a tour of Wales. But rather than simply approving of Kean, the local press, *The Cambrian*, focused on the minor actors in the cast: "All the prominent persons of the drama were most ably supported; Polonius, Grave Digger, Ghost, Ostrick, Laertes, Queen, Phelian were portrayed with great theatrical effect by Messrs, Cherry, Woulds, Bickerton, Mrs and Miss Cherry."[99] The many Cherrys in the cast comprised Andrew Cherry's own family. Clearly, the press was playing favorites. The pattern was repeated on 10 December 1810. *The Cambrian* again reviewed one of Kean's performances and again dwelled on a minor actor in Kean's supporting cast: "In those scenes where the child's character (Master H. Cherry) was prominent, we never witnessed more effect and the applause was general and unqualified."[100] After such reviews, Kean might have felt that unless he controlled casting absolutely, he had little chance of success.

If Kean alone succeeded, he deemed the production a success; if Kean succeeded and every one else failed, it was an even greater success; if other actors drew good reviews, Kean's own success was diminished. That would never do, even if it meant foregoing a hit, and the income needed to replenish Drury Lane's dwindling resources. On 18 May 1815, Kean played Penruddock in *The Wheel of Fortune*.[101] The play highlighted Kean's "several bursts of passion." Nevertheless, the piece was canceled. Robinson noted that Dowton, who played the part of Governor Tempest, "was good. Indeed he is an excellent comedian."[102] Any attention on Dowton was a detraction from Kean. This might also explain Kean's orders to pull prematurely Beaumont and Fletcher's *Beggar's Bush*. The old play was revived on 14 December 1815. Critics noted that, "One of the last scenes, in which *Clause* brings in the money-bags to the creditors, and Kean [playing Goswin] bends forward pointing to them, Munden [playing Vandunke] after him, repeating the same attitude, but caricaturing it, was a perfect *coup-de-théatre*."[103] Robinson noted that Munden, who had clearly upstaged Kean in the main piece, was equally amusing in the farce that followed.[104]

98   Henry Crabb Robinson, *The London Theatre 1811-1866*, 57.

99   *The Cambrian*, 23 June 1809 and 16 June 1809, in Press Clippings, Huntington Manuscript Collection, Huntington Manuscript Library,182799.

100   *The Cambrian* (1810), exact date not specified, in Press Clippings, Huntington Manuscript Collection, Huntington Manuscript Library,182799.

101   Again, this play had been part of Kemble's repertoire. With that actor in semi-retirement, Kean may have been trying to keep the part out of Macready's hands.

102   Henry Crabb Robinson, *The London Theatre 1811-1866*, 63.

103   William Hazlitt, *Complete Works*, V:265.

104   Henry Crabb Robinson, *The London Theatre 1811-1866*, 67.

The play appeared again on 19 December 1815 and then disappeared.[105] On 9 March 1816 at Drury Lane and, that summer, on 5 July 1816 at Bath, Kean appeared as the Duke in an adaptation of Massinger's *The Duke of Milan*. The highlight of the play is the final scene, wherein Francisco tells the Duke he has made love to the Duchess. The Duke stabs his unfaithful wife and then, in a sudden conversion, loves his dead wife all the more. Genest was pleased with both the play and performance: "we are much obliged to the person [Kean] that made [read: revived] it, for bringing so fine a Tragedy once more before the public."[106] This play is a tragicomedy and was well suited for Kean's histrionics, but its does call for a strong female lead. Kean acted the part of the Duke seven times in London and then never again. On 5 February 1817, Kean played a fine Oroonoko but the play was withdrawn. Robinson noted that Alexander Rae, a minor actor in the company, "got credit by playing Aboan," the slave who convinces Oroonoko to revolt.[107] On 8 March 1817, Kean played the title lead in R.C. Maturin's *Manuel*. The play builds on an *Othello* base. De Zelos, an Iago figure, convinces Manuel to kill the Desdemona-like Victoria. The piece was doing well with the box office and might have become a hit; but, if John Genest's comments are of any consequence, Kean had good reason to shelve the play; Alexander Rae's Iago-like De Zelos was getting too much attention.[108]

On the rare occasion when Kean found himself on stage with a decent actor, he had a variety of tricks to draw the audience's focus back to him, even when he wasn't speaking. When still a minor actor in the provinces, Kean, bored with the actor playing Hamlet opposite his Polonius and upset that he was not the star, did a double somersault on stage. He thereby stole the show.[109] By the time he became the most famous actor of his age, Kean relied on a more subtle ploy. For example, on 9 April 1816, Kean starred in Maturin's *Bertram*. Miss Somerville, who played the female lead, Imogene, complained that Kean kept himself "a little behind her, and did not give her fair play." Genest, who relates the story, sourced Somerville's complaint to the following explanation: "it is a method with an old stager [an experienced actor], who knows the advantageous points of his art, to stand back out of the level with the actor who is on with him, and thus he displays his own full figure and face to the audience" and, in so doing, diverts attention from the less experienced actor or, in this case, actress.[110] Somerville understood Kean's power and quickly learned to stay out of his way, but Kean fired her anyway, not for getting in his way, but because she was too tall, and was thus a visual distraction.[111]

---

105   John Genest saw the 14 December performance but does not mention Kean's acting (*Some Account of the English Stage,* VIII:521-4).

106   Ibid., VIII:531.

107   Henry Crabb Robinson, *The London Theatre 1811-1866*, 75.

108   *Oxberry's Dramatic Biography*, IV:189. See also Kean's torpedoing of *The Bride of Abydos*, discussed in the next chapter.

109   Otis Skinner, "Three Madmen of the Theatre II," 624.

110   John Genest, *Some Account of the English Stage*, VIII: 533-4.

111   William Archer, *William Charles Macready*, 46.

Running Actors Out of Town

On those nights Kean did not perform, Drury Lane tried out other actors. A star like Booth was now out of the question, but the theatre hoped one of its minor stand-ins might eventually replace—or lessen the power of—Kean. The first to be hired was David Fisher. A handwritten note on one of the playbills announcing Fisher states that the "Committee had imported [Fisher] to keep Kean down."[112] The choice must have rankled Kean. Fisher's father was a carpenter-turned-acting manager who "ran the Norfolk and Suffolk Company of Comedians and built up a circuit of twelve theatres in which he and his family performed."[113] In short, Fisher came from the kind of provincial and nepotistic companies that Kean felt had so unfairly ignored him. Worse yet, Fisher was actually a gifted actor, musician, and scene painter. Fortunately, audiences did not much like him, and Fisher stayed with the company only two years. Kean also took care that Fisher appeared in plays unsuited to his tragic skills. He even blocked the actor from appearing in *Hamlet* on his own benefit night.[114] Frustrated with his inability to garner good roles, Fisher asked Kean for advice. Kean suggested that he try his luck in other theaters—in America.[115]

Reassessing Kean

The record suggests that Kean stage-managed his own persona. Even after rising to the top of his profession, he presented himself as "the little guy," always willing to prove to his audience that he was the best actor of his age. In truth, he was reluctant to enter into all but the first of his matches, but, having entered, used every trick he could muster to "fix" the outcome.

Looking back on those few years of glory, as Kean reveled in his triumphs and squandered his wealth, it's sometimes difficult to remember the actor's acumen. The record shows that Kean was a wonderfully physical specimen and manipulated his audience and the press to see him in those terms. Kean had dealt with the actors, but there were still other enemies to consider....

---

112   John Keats, *Poetical Works*, 5:cf.228.
113   "An Exhibition About the Fisher Family," 3.
114   *Oxberry's Dramatic Biography*, IV:189.
115   Kean even wrote him a letter of introduction. See *The Times* 12 September 1818, [2], in Press Clippings, Personal Collection. The paper incorrectly cites the actor as Mr. Palmer Fisher.

Chapter 2

'The Throne is Mine and I Will Maintain It at Any Cost'

Kean's Power Over the Regency Stage

In 1827, Thomas Colley Grattan came to Kean's house and found it sumptuously redecorated like an eastern palace. He was ushered through the house by a black boy who led him to the consummate actor. Kean sat Buddha-like in a dark room, flanked closely by veiled sisters, described as "lovely creatures—the daughters of a clergyman."[1] These formerly-devout Christian sisters now formed part of Kean's seraglio, his personal and willing sex slaves, who demonstrated in their looks and gestures that they were fixedly and "desperately in love with him," and eager to offer themselves to the actor's pagan desires "with the most unlimited offers."[2]

These stagings were common events in the Kean household. Visitors sometimes found the actor in American Indian dress, a gift from the Huron Nation; at other times, he dressed as Lear, wandering the house with a vacant stare.[3] But much of Kean's magic was lost on Grattan, who never confused this garden of sensual delights with reality. Kean, he plainly noted, spoke in a "stage whisper" and his boy stood "with suitable mystery." Kean, sensing, perhaps, that this playlet was not fully producing its intended effect, quickly dropped the charade and explained that the tableau was merely part of his personal rehearsal process for Grattan's own play, *Ben Nazir*, which concerned a Byronian sociopath of Moorish origins.

Kean told Grattan that he was delighted with the play's long, blustering speeches. His first appearance on stage, for example, called for the actor to enter in a passion, exulting in his capricious plans to marry the chaste Emerance and to kill her father, Eudes:

Down sinks the sun, on other worlds to shine
And rob these realms of brightness and of joy,
All, all, but me—he rifles not my bliss.
Here is my warmth and light—it glows within,
To regions of high happiness I soar,

---

1   Thomas Colley Grattan, *Beaten Paths*, II:211.
2   Ibid., II:211.
3   Kean was made honorary Chief of the Huron Nation of Indians in Quebec, on 7 October 1826, and given the name "Alanienoudet, Son of the Forest."

Look down on Nature's gloom, and think it glory.
Emerance, divinest creature of this earth,
Thou art mine for ever! Holy Alla, view
My boundless transport! From thy starry throne
Smile down on thy poor worshipper! Yes, now
I triumph in my turn. Vile Christian, Eudes—
Late my fame's plunderer, now my baffled dupe—
Soon on thy low-bowed neck, with my spurning foot—
Who's there?[4]

From the opening speech, we get the idea. Ben Nazir is part Richard III, part Iago, part Shylock, dressed as Othello. In sum, Grattan had created a character from all of Kean's most successful Shakespearean parts.

Nonetheless, Kean still insisted upon one key change: he wanted yet more focus on himself, particularly in the last act. Grattan was unhappy with the request, noting that it was exactly this kind of heavy-handed demand that had "made him [Kean] so many enemies, and did him such mischief with the public."[5] Nonetheless, Grattan complied, adding a new fifth act which further puffed Kean's ego by referring to the actor's place in history:

Why search futurity? Why look
For further life? Enough, whene'er I die,
I live for ever! History shall bear
The weight of my renown; and worlds to come
Know that I dived in fame's unfathomed depths,
And rode in triumph on her glorious waters.[6]

Grattan was willing to swallow his pride. What success could the play have without Kean's support? And Kean was happy, or so he said, with the rewrites. Grattan attended the rehearsals and noted that the actor, though not yet off book, was splendid in the part, acting with "great energy and effect." The fact that Kean spent long hours alone studying the manuscript was a good sign. One actor recorded that, as with the rehearsal of all his parts, "He [Kean] used to mope about for hours, walking miles and miles alone with his hands in his pockets, thinking intensely on his characters. No one could get a word from him; he studied and slaved beyond any actor I ever knew. ..."[7]

Kean did more than simply polish the script. He personally oversaw Grattan's contract details, stipulating that the play be performed a minimum of twenty times. Kean boasted that this was just a formality. He fully expected that *Ben Nazir* might run 100 times in the upcoming season and saw to it that management splurged (50 guineas above and beyond the theater's own lavish production budget) on his costume.

---

4   Thomas Colley Grattan, *Ben Nazir*, I.ii.p.11.
5   Thomas Colley Grattan, *Beaten Paths*, II: 215.
6   Thomas Colley Grattan, *Ben Nazir*, V.iii.p.90.
7   Recorded in Henry Barton Baker, *Our Old Actors*, II.ii.208.

Further, in the weeks leading up to the première, the actor was frequently sighted declaiming his lines as he lolled up and down the Thames on his new pleasure-craft, which he christened the "Ben Nazir," a spectacle suggestive of Cleopatra sailing on a barge of burnished gold, dazzling equally the "watermen and the Naiads." At Kensington Gardens, Kean appeared dressed as an eastern sultan; amid groves of Arcadian splendor, he hallooed his lines to the four winds.[8]

For his part, Kean had his own reasons for promoting the play. As he explained to Grattan, *Ben Nazir* was a weapon Kean would use to maintain his stranglehold on London theater:

> He [Kean] knew that a crisis had arrived in his professional fate; the whole tide of public feeling was with him. … To confirm him there, beyond competition or cavil, there was only wanting one vigorous display of power in a new part, and that part was now ready written to his hand. Nothing, in short, could exceed the ardour with which he undertook the study of 'Ben Nazir.'[9]

After such conversations, Grattan came to see Kean as a Machiavellian showman, a careful and scrutinizing theatrical general, raising public awareness, leaving nothing to chance. "Do not think that [Napoleon] the greatest conqueror of his day is degraded by … [this comparison with the] greatest actor of England. And after all, which was most a stage-player…?"[10]

Grattan had no doubt that the play would be an immense success, as did the management of Drury Lane: "It was everything I could wish; no one had a shadow of a doubt as to the impression it would produce on an audience. Congratulations were poured on me on all sides, with premature profusion."[11] The playwright, we may be assured, slept well the night before the premiere. Yet on opening night, 21 May 1827, he woke to a nightmare. Kean's first entry had called for him "to rush rapidly upon the stage, giving utterance to a burst of joyous soliloquy."[12] Instead, Grattan watched as the curtain rose on an unmoving Kean, a seeming statue holding center stage:

> … a cold shower of perspiration poured from my forehead, and I endured a revulsion of feeling which I cannot describe, and which I would not for worlds one eye witnessed.

> I had all along felt, that this scene would be the touchstone of the play. Kean went through it like a man in the last stage of exhaustion and decay.

Worse yet, Grattan had written the opening scene with the specific stage direction that the lines be delivered in the star's signature "flashes of lightning," hurried, a rush of words. Instead, Kean delivered a stolid jumble of murmurs. The fifth act, which Kean had demanded be reworked to further highlight his genius, was all but

---

8   Thomas Colley Grattan, *Beaten Paths*, II:214.
9   Ibid., II:211.
10 Ibid., II:195.
11 Ibid., II:214.
12 Ibid., II:217.

EDMUND KEAN ESQ^r

Plate 2:   Kean in his Indian costume; he enjoyed wearing it around the house. Reprinted by kind permission of the Harry Ransom Humanities Research Center; The University of Texas at Austin.

abandoned: "He wholly omitted the soliloquies at the conclusion; and in many of the scenes, but more particularly in the last Act (the most important of all), he made scarcely an effort to speak a line of the text." Grattan tells us that as the final act closed, "a dead silence followed the last curtain; and I felt, though I could not hear, the voiceless verdict of 'damnation.'"[13] After Kean stumbled and fumbled through his part, Mr. Wallack came forward to apologize for the star's weak performance.

Understandably, Grattan was infuriated. He went immediately to Kean's dressing room and confronted the actor, who, shame-faced, admitted that his bravado during rehearsals had all been a great piece of acting meticulously designed to conceal the fact that he, Kean, the greatest actor of England, was so impaired by drink that he could no longer memorize new parts. Grattan's anger immediately dissipated: "I said

---

13 Ibid., II:218. James Winston agrees that Kean "cut every scene to atoms," but suggests a reason why he did not rush onto stage—the actor's gout had flared up (21 May 1827, *Drury Lane Journal*, 148).

something in return as cheering and consolatory as I could. I may say that all sense of my own disappointment was forgotten in the compassion I felt for him."[14]

And yet Grattan remained haunted by the suspicion that Kean had cheated him of fame and that, in accepting Kean's *mea culpa*, he had been hoodwinked yet again. When Wallack proposed that Kean write a public letter of apology, the actor steadfastly refused, "preferring to let the fault lie wholly on the author's shoulders." At last, it seems, Grattan realized that Kean had merely faked his loss of memory: "It was then I resolved to publish my preface to the play, in which, as everyone who read it thought, I dealt too lightly with *the culprit*."[15]

Had Kean confessed the truth, or had Grattan been seduced by yet more of Kean's acting? The question has been all but buried in favor of the tragic story. Grattan throws himself onto the sharp sword of critical opinion, sacrifices his playwrighting career, hushes up the entire episode so that Kean's career can continue, unrivaled and unscathed.

The Failing Genius

The story of the deteriorating actor does make for compelling, if maudlin, drama, at least as presented in Peter Yates' play, *The Burning Mask* (1948). At the climax of the play, Grattan meets Kean, who begs his forgiveness: "I have ruined a fine play and myself; I cannot look you in the face." The mortified actor admits that his memory has failed him, a result of years of continuous dissipation:

KEAN. I couldn't face you. I was too ... ashamed. Forgive me, Tom.
GRATTAN. There is nothing to forgive. I wrote the play for you. But for you, Ned, I should never have turned to authorship.
KEAN. I know ... and what hopes you had. *Ben Nazir!* How we discussed it, scene by scene *(There is a long pause.)* Why have you come?
GRATTAN. To say good-bye, Ned. I'm going abroad.
KEAN. Abroad? Are you leaving England, because ...
GRATTAN. Let us not speak of that. What's done is done. *(A pause.) Ben Nazir* ... it was a dream born of a friendship. The dream is over.
KEAN. The dreamer wakes ... finds the dream was a nightmare. *(A pause.)* Did you stay till ... the end, the very end?
GRATTAN. Yes.
KEAN. But—you have read ... the newspapers?
GRATTAN. They were unkind to us, I'm afraid. Forget them.

---

14 Thomas Colley Grattan, *Beaten Paths*, II:219.

15 Ibid., II:220, my own emphasis. In the "Preface" to *Ben Nazir*, Grattan states that "an apology was made from the stage" and thanks Kean for his "candour in acknowledging this [his fault]" (VII). No theatrical review has Kean doing so. It seems Grattan was referring to Wallack's apology; his reference to Kean implies that Wallack acted on Kean's behalf and with his sanction—both suggestions run counter to Kean's normal policy and Grattan's later, fuller account.

KEAN. For months ... flayed *by my* pride ... I've struggled on.
Clung to a crumbling edge, a precipice ...
And heard the abyss roar under me.
GRATTAN. I bear no malice, Ned. For me the stage was a pastime. No more.

It's not just dramatists who have embraced the story. Biographers, anxious to turn Kean's life into a cautionary tale of genius ruined by success, happily agreed with the actor's pitiable, if, perhaps, staged confession. In fact, the convenient excuse of drink was revived for many of Kean's failures. On the actor's disappointment as Henry V, for example, F.W. Hawkins writes:

> If the unsuccessful attempt to embody the character of Henry V. demonstrated beyond all doubt that the powers of Edmund Kean were on the decline.... It was this extraordinary energy, this ever active impulse, that hurried him on to his grave, for he endeavoured to rise equal to himself when violated nature had been deprived of her former resources, and then flew to brandy to alleviate the exhaustion consequent upon such forced, compulsive efforts.[16]

Molloy repeats Hawkins' story and produces a letter written (possibly forged) to a theater critic that indeed suggests Kean's powers were failing:

> DEAR HALPIN,
> Fight for me, I have no resources in myself; mind is gone, and body is hopeless. God knows my heart. I would do, but cannot. Memory, the first of goddesses, has forsaken me, and I am left without a hope but from those old resources that the public and myself are tired of. Damn, God damn ambition. The soul leaps, the body falls.
>
> 'EDMUND KEAN.'[17]

Molloy notes that because of this letter, Halpin gave Kean a pass on Henry V, when he might otherwise have blasted him with a bad review.

Another Possibility

Perhaps Kean's memory really did fade when he performed Henry V. But Kean played Henry V in 1830. This letter cannot be marshaled as evidence that Kean had already lost his memory as early as 1827, the year *Ben Nazir* was staged. Further,

---

16 F.W. Hawkins, *Life of Edmund Kean*, II: 341. According to W.J. MacQueen-Pope, before Kean even began the part, the audience began to hiss. Kean asked for silence and reminded them that acting was hard work. His audience heckled, "You have been well paid for it [Shakespearean performance]" and "Why do you drink so hard?" (*Theatre Royal Drury Lane*, 262) If the story is true, Kean may have simply destroyed *Henry V* out of pique.

17 J. Fitzgerald Molloy, *The Life and Adventures of Edmund Kean*, II:230. Molloy never documented his sources and, so far as I know, no one has ever seen the letter. If the letter is in fact genuine, it is by no means conclusive evidence that Kean was sincere.

Kean suffered no such impediments in 1828 or 1829, nor was his memory an issue after 1830. Is it possible that Kean lost, then regained his ability to memorize parts, lost the ability, and then regained it yet again for the remaining years of his career?

We might also ask ourselves whether memory alone accounts for Kean's lackluster performance in the opening act of Grattan's play? Surely, he would have known he was supposed to run onto stage in a passion, not stand like a stone. This begins to sound as if Kean purposefully ruined *Ben Nazir*. The idea is odd. Why would Kean purposefully court bad publicity? If the purpose of *Ben Nazir* were to solidify his hold over his audience, how would trashing a play accomplish the desired end? What of the other thread in Grattan's narrative—not of the failing actor, but of the ruthless, Napoleonic tactician?

Although constructions of Kean's excessive nature will be the subject of future chapters, at the moment, we might do better to concentrate on Kean's confessed aim—to increase his control over Drury Lane. As we saw in the last chapter, Kean carefully realigned Drury Lane along populist lines. While this realignment was not necessarily political, many Whiggish supporters, nonetheless, embraced the actor, who, seeing that Covent Garden's John Philip Kemble had in large measure alienated that demographic, played upon their sympathies.[18] The actor and the audience both made the Cult of Kean. But did the Kean of the stage, the Kean who performed the characters of playwrights, correspond to the Kean who managed Drury Lane? To understand Kean's motives and ambitions, we have to go beyond theatrical reportage; we have to glimpse an undisclosed backstage drama played out in a world of props, makeup jars, and sticky filth.

Kean Seizes Power

According to *The Theatrical Inquisitor* (August 1818), it was sometime in the 1816-17 season that Kean commanded "that every new piece in which he was to perform, was to be got up under his management."[19] And yet, under Kean's direction, play after play was withdrawn. Astonishingly, he even did away with a number of plays that were doing quite well. Was Kean simply a bad manager, or was this by design?

Let's deal with the possibility that Kean really was a poor director and a poor judge of drama. How else, for example, can we explain Kean's interest in such "gems" as George Soane's *The Dwarf of Naples* (1819)—the title tells us much of what we need to know about the play's plainly crass quality—in which Kean played the title role? Kean had been raised by actors and knew his trade. He had grown into manhood standing in the wings of Drury Lane, watching Kemble, hearing the audience applaud or hiss. He had toured for years and had come to know the tastes of provincial and London audiences.

---

18 This is in contradiction to W.J. MacQueen-Pope, who states that Kemble was "packing" Covent Garden (*Kean*, 33).

19 *Theatrical Inquisitor* (1818): 116. *The Theatrical Inquisitor* for September 1817 noted that Kean "supported an active part in every department of the drama" (163).

And we would do well to avoid putting all the bad theater of the era on Edmund Kean's capable shoulders. Some even suggested that Kean's fault lay in working too assiduously for his employers. On his playing Sir Pertinax Macsycophant in Macklin's *Man of the World*, one anonymous writer suggests that "What KEAN'S private opinion of this new species of announcement may be, we know not, but it is a duty of his friends, who have any care either for his reputation, or for his interest of the establishment, to inform him, that like all quakery, it is a short-sighted policy; exposing to the chance of a great future evil, for an insufficient, momentary good."[20] Facts, however, don't support that opinion. As we shall see, Kean was extremely particular in picking plays and, in most cases, went out of his way to discourage additions to his repertoire.

Kean might not have gone to an upper-crust prep school, or any school, but he knew his business; he had not stumbled into being an actor. He knew his strengths and his limitations. He knew, for example, that he was a great villain, a superb Shylock, Richard III, Othello, and Sir Giles Overreach. Equally, Kean knew that he had neither the temperament nor the talent for comedy. Elizabeth Macauley, a former actress turned critic, observed that:

> Some of the best plays of the inimitable SHAKESPEARE, are consigned to oblivion; he [Kean] *cannot* play them nor will allow others to try their skill: his talent is restricted; it is of that peculiar sort, which was never meant for common use. The plays of Mr. Kean's choice, are for the most part, those where his character is of the malignant cast; those that are written or altered for him, the principal object is (not to prepare a good play, from which a fair moral may be drawn) but to collect a number of scenes, where the vilest passions of human nature are held out, to shew the force of his powers....[21]

Returning to *The Dwarf of Naples* is instructive on this point. Written "to suit the peculiarities of Kean's acting ...[and] dedicated to Kean in a strain of fulsome flattery,"[22] the play, despite its unpromising title, featured a number of dramatic situations—Macauley preferred to call them an "assemblage of horrible passions"[23]— that highlighted Kean's talents. In five acts, this dwarf frames his best friend for treason, wins a duel, makes love to two women (Amanda and Imma), succeeds in a homicide (of Imma, who loves him), and attempts a regicide. Kean, it seems clear, was not simply picking plays willy-nilly.[24]

---

20 Anonymous, found in Press Clippings, in Kean, Edmund C. Newspaper Articles Messmore Kendall Collection, HRC.

21 Elizabeth Macauley, *Theatrical Revolution*, 24.

22 John Genest, *Some Account of the English Stage,* VIII: 686

23 Elizabeth Macauley, *Theatrical Revolution*, 27.

24 Soane was also a talented groveler. The dedication to his play reads: in "admiration for that brilliant genius which has placed you on the throne above flattery, as it is above detraction.... I indulge in the vain idea of ever being able to write a Drama adequate to your genius: ... there was but one Shakespeare; there is but one Kean; time cannot fashion a second to the dead; time cannot fashion an equal to the living."

Kean's demand for *Ben Nazir*, particularly his insistence for yet more focus on him—was nothing new or exceptional. As we saw in the last chapter, Kean dismissed any actor who drew audience attention away from him. Nor was he secretive about his requirements. When John Thelwall submitted to Drury Lane *The Castle of Glendower*, Kean wrote to him:

> Sir
> I shall read your manuscript with the strictest attention, when I receive it from Mr. Lamb, but you must excuse my candor when I say: unless the character allotted to me, is the chief object of the play, it will not be consistent with my reputation or the interests of Drury Lane Theatre to accept it.[25]

When Kean first read Charles Bucke's *The Italians* he complained that the secondary character of Manfredi was "too much in his line," that the character of the Blind Man was "too good," and "that no one should write a Tragedy for that House, without making the entire center in the character HE should perform."[26] Bucke fired back, through a friend, that playwrights had collectively "become a Martyr to Mr. Kean's ambition and caprice...."[27]

Kean's theatrical trademarks were soon stamped upon every play in his repertoire, including *Richard, Duke of York*.[28] The play had been performed more or less regularly since its debut on 17 March 1712 at Drury Lane.[29] Despite its long stage history, Kean had no qualms about changing the plot to suit his needs. Genest dismissed the rewrite as ludicrous because Kean, Bottom-like, assigned nearly all good speeches—no matter their logic in the story—to his own character, York:

> ... act 3d begins with the low characters in rebellion—then follows the 2d scene in Shakespeare's 3d Act—York speaks what belongs to Warwick, and 6 lines from Webster, badly brought in—Warwick speaks what belongs to Salisbury made for the sake of giving more importance to Kean's part....

---

25 The letter is stored in London's Theatre Museum archive.

26 Charles Bucke, Preface, *The Italians*, IX. Kean rejected the play. The anonymous author of *A Defence of Edmund Kean* countered that Bucke was lying. The play was rejected because it did "not present a single situation worthy the genius of Kean!" (14)

27 *The Assailant Assailed. Being A Vindication of Mr. Kean*, cf.21.

28 According to Foreman, Kean himself made the revisions to *Richard, Duke of York*, with possibly another hand helping him. Foreman suggests it was S. Penley, an actor in the company, who had adapted Marlowe's *Jew of Malta* for Kean. The playbill for *Richard, Duke of York* did state that it "will be produced under the Direction of Mr. Kean" (Foreman, in Keats, *Poetical Works*, 5:cf.242). That being said, it is unlikely and unnecessary that Kean did the adaptation himself. Kean was enough of an egotist to advertise that he was also a literary talent. The fact that he did not do so only confirms that he did nothing more than command Penley or some other hack to make him look good.

29 John Genest, *Some Account of the English Stage*, IX: 565.

Plate 3: Drury Lane carried on Kean's shoulders. Reprinted by kind permission of the Harry Ransom Humanities Research Center; The University of Texas at Austin.

Kean also demanded that the fifth act be reworked. In the original, York's death signals the rise of Richard, a principal role of Kean's. But to allow that scene would mean that audiences would see some other actor playing Richard. If successful, this might lead to a rival interpretation of *Richard III*; again, an unwanted possibility. The adapter came up with the only solution that would satisfy Kean. In the last scene, York/Kean comes on wounded and bleeding, declaims a soliloquy and dies. The curtain falls. Likewise, Kean demanded that *The Distrest Mother*, in which Kean played Orestes, end immediately after his character's death, even though *The Distrest Mother* is the story of Andromache, not Orestes.

On 24 April 1818, Kean premièred his Barabas, in an adaptation of Marlowe's *The Jew of Malta*. Kean had the poisoning of the nuns cut, so that Abigail's death became a meaningless bit of stage business. Kean added a song to the 4th act, which was encored, although one critic complained that he could not "help think it [Kean's singing] a perversion of talent."[30] Lastly, our actor had, according to Genest, "the manner of Barabas's death ... altered"—though it's difficult to see what could be more spectacular than being boiled in oil![31] Shakespeare's plays were correspondingly revamped. The ending of Kean's *Richard II*, which premièred 9 March 1815, was augmented with a few lines from *King Lear* to highlight his death.[32] Similarly, Kean's death in *Macbeth*, rather than simply being reported, was turned into something that was "very grand—He after receiving his mortal wound staggers and gives a feeble blow—After he crawls on the floor to reach again his sword and dies as he touches it."[33]

Dropping the curtain after Kean's stage-death didn't always bend the Bard to Kean's awe. On 10 February 1823, Kean restored Shakespeare's ending to the then-prevalent Nahum Tate adaptation of *King Lear*. Rather than Lear repossessing his crown, Kean had the king die and, with a few choice words from Kent, had the curtain drop.[34] Kean also modified *Richard III*, though, as with *King Lear*, this was, perhaps, not so great a sin. Like other actors of the period, Kean acted in the Cibber adaptation of Shakespeare's original. But the actor went so far as to deny the mandated action of the play. The first time he acted the part at Drury Lane, he

---

30 *The Times Review*, April 25, 1818; personal collection.

31 Ibid., VIII:647.

32 John Genest, *Some Account of the English Stage*, VIII:455.

33 Henry Crabb Robinson, *The London Theatre 1811-1866*, 59.

34 On Kean's *King Lear*, see George C.D. Odell, *Shakespeare From Betterton to Irving*, II:154-6. Kean may have purposefully destroyed the play. According to Austin and Ralph, Mrs. West played Cordelia. Kean was scarcely strong enough to carry her, causing the play to end with unwanted laughter from the pit, boxes, and gallery (Austin and Ralph, *The Lives of the Poets-Laureate*, 205). In 1820, Kean performed the traditional Tate-version, but Drury Lane added a wind-machine to the heath scene which drown the actor out. According to W.J. MacQueen-Pope, the wind-machine and other stage effects were added on the expressed orders of then-manager Robert Elliston, who hoped to "dwarf" Kean with these new and novel effects (*Pillars of Drury Lane*, 99). Nonetheless, I have a copy of a playbill for 13 May 1820 that refers to this same production as a "triumphant Success!!!"

allowed himself to be killed by Alexander Rae, the actor playing Richmond, but not before chasing Rae "round and round the stage."[35] One spectator, who saw Kean's *Richard III* at Bath on 18 July 1815, noted: "Kean... overdid his death—he came up close to Richmond, after he had lost his sword, as if he would have attacked him with his fists—Richmond, to please Kean, was obliged to stand like a fool, with a drawn sword in his hand without daring to use it." On another occasion, one actor playing Richmond, deferentially asked Kean, "Where shall I hit you, sir?" Kean replied scornfully, "Where you can, sir."[36]

Aside from *Macbeth*, *Lear*, and *Richard III*, none of these aforementioned plays figured prominently in Kean's repertoire, but these and other cast-offs were far from failures.[37] Keats thought the play *Brutus* "very bad" but a worthy theatrical endeavor since "Kean was excellent."[38] Macauley described Kean's performance in Marlowe's *The Jew of Malta* as "undoubtedly very great"; Genest called *Ina* "very dull" but had nothing bad to say about Kean's performance.[39] Hazlitt thought Kean's staging of Colman's *The Iron Chest* "unrivalled":

> The last scene of all—his coming to life again after his swooning at the fatal discovery of his guilt, and then falling back after a ghastly struggle, like a man waked from the tomb, into despair and death in the arms of his mistress, was one of those consummations of art, which those who have seen and have not felt them in this actor, may be assured that they have never seen or felt any thing in the course of their lives, and never will to the end of them.[40]

Before discussing why, given these successes, Kean did not repeat many of these roles throughout his career, it is important to note that Kean's virtual disregard for plot-logic was readily accepted by his audience: "the central character was so absorbing that an audience was willing to go along with anything he ... did."[41] While modern audiences might find a lack of a coherent plot troubling, most Romantic audiences were unperturbed. Instead, they concentrated on the emotional magnetism of the lines as set pieces and applauded Kean for his vocal and physical skills. Thus, when Henry Crabb Robinson saw *Richard II* at Drury Lane on 25 May 1815, he,

---

35 J. Fitzgerald Molloy, *The Life and Adventures of Edmund Kean*, I:150.

36 Otis Skinner, "Three Madmen of the Theatre II," 630.

37 In fact, only one commissioned play, *Brutus*, found a permanent home in Kean's repertoire. Why that play survived is discussed in the next chapter.

38 John Keats, Letter to George and Georgiana Keats, 16 December 1818, *The Letters of John Keats*, 248.

39 John Keats, *Poetical Works*, 5:228; Elizabeth Macauley, *Theatrical Revolution*, 25; John Genest, *Some Account of the English Stage*, VIII:457. Byron thought Kean "acted badly" in *Ina*, though he did not suggest purposeful incompetence (*The Selected Letters of Lord Byron*, 81). On the other hand, Fanny Brawne saw Kean's *Lear* and felt that the performance was not to the actor's "best advantage." She further added that "the play itself is spoiled" (*Letters of Fanny Brawne*, 31).

40 William Hazlitt, *Complete Works*, V:344-5.

41 John Russell Taylor, *The Rise and Fall of the Well-Made Play*, 12.

unsurprisingly, concentrated on Kean: the "admirable artifices of the actor gave great satisfaction ... the blending of opposite emotions is so curious as to resemble insanity."[42] Even Charles Lamb, who questioned whether any Shakespeare play could be properly staged, conceded that he found Kean's Macbeth to be "true and impressive."[43] As for plays such as *The Jew of Malta*, which had been rendered nonsensical by the actor's modifications, the *Times* critics noted that "We have seldom known a more indulgent audience."[44]

Draining Drury Lane's Coffers

In the last chapter, we compared the rationale for Kean's cast selections with predecessors such as David Garrick and John Philip Kemble. We might do the same here concerning Kean's repeated disregard for the financial costs of abandoning new plays and of discouraging new playwrights. Garrick was a playwright in his own right but unselfishly encouraged others to submit their works. Further, he co-wrote plays with the bluestocking novelist and poet Hannah More and the celebrated playwright George Colman the Elder. Even his successor, Kemble, while preferring old plays, allowed for a variety of new, light-hearted comedies.[45] It is true that Garrick upon occasion sunk or discarded plays. Out of "mixed motives," Garrick initially rejected John Home's *Douglas*, but he eventually allowed the play into Drury Lane's repertoire.[46] Kemble, too, sunk plays. On 2 April 1796, he worked in league with factions in the audience to destroy a supposedly lost Shakespeare play, *Vortigern*. In so doing, Kemble raised the ire of manager Richard Brinsley Sheridan, who, shocked by the actor's shoddy performance, stated that "he regarded that gentleman [Kemble] merely a servant of the theatre; and that it was consequently his duty to have exerted himself to the utmost for the benefit of his employers."[47] Kemble also wrecked Colman's *The Iron Chest*.[48] But Kemble paid for his temerity. Despite being at the height of his powers, after 1796, he lost his ability to select his own plays at Drury Lane and soon left that theater altogether. Again, we are left with the impression that Kemble normally did his best, normally worked in the interests of his employers, and when he did not, he suffered for it.

---

42 Henry Crabb Robinson, *The London Theatre 1811-1866*, 64. The order of the passages has been reversed.

43 Charles Lamb, *Plays and Dramatic Essays*, 189.

44 *The Times Review*, April 25, 1818; personal collection.

45 Kemble was romantically linked to the comedic playwright Elizabeth Inchbald.

46 Garrick did write a letter to Lord Bute, in which he outlined his reasons for refusing the play. Alice Edna Gipson suggests there might have been other (unspecified) motives at work. See her *John Home: A Study of His Life and Works*, 39.

47 William Henry Ireland, *Confessions*, 159.

48 The play was "coughed and plodded into purposeful ruin" (Jeffrey Kahan, *Reforging Shakespeare*, 187).

How different was Kean's approach. Kean shrewdly judged the value of each production in terms of his overall career and often discarded very expensive productions, even if they were going quite well. Take, for example, Byron's *The Bride of Abydos*, adapted for the stage by William Dimond.[49] Byron was at the time in exile. Nonetheless, Byron had been an active member of the Drury Lane Committee and was not shy in his praise of the actor. In a letter dated 2 July 1814, Susan Chambers, Kean's sister-in-law, aptly captures Byron's initial fascination: "Lord Biron is enchanted with Edmund, and is like a little dog behind the scenes, following him everywhere...."[50] I have a hard time imagining Byron actually acting this way, but Kean's influence was real. In Byron's poem "To Edmund Kean, Esq." The actor is seen as a kind of Promethean Tamburlaine, a god of fire who holds fast the chains of fate:

> Thine is the task, with mastery most perfect,
> To bind the passions captive to thy train.

In closing, the poet humbles himself. He is merely a choric angel, who venerates a theatrical god:

> Thou art the sun's bright child!
> The genius which irradiates thy mind
> Caught all its purity and light from heaven.
> ....a bold and burning mind,
> Whose impulse guides thee to the realms of fame,
> Where, crowned with well-earned laurels all thine own,
> I herald thee to immortality![51]

Byron's homage did not end there. He was so taken with Kean's portrayal of Richard III that it inspired the following verse from the first canto of *The Corsair*:

> There was a laughing devil in his sneer,
> That raised emotions of both rage and fear;
> And where his frown of hatred darkly fell,
> Hope withering fled, and Mercy sigh'd farewell![52]

---

49   Although Dimond adapted the play, he may have seen in Byron's poetry motifs that corresponded with Kean's acting. See Thomas C. Crochunis, "Byronic Heroes and Acting: The Embodiment of Mental Theater," esp. 74, 78.

50   See Jonathan Reynolds, *Dramatis Personæ*, 20 (1991):17. Harold Newcomb Hillebrand's Byron is only marginally less obsequious. "Byron," he writes, worshipped Kean, and was said to follow "him about like a small boy after a cricket hero" (*Edmund Kean*, 133).

51   The full poem, supposedly inscribed on a snuff-box, is found in F.W. Hawkins, *Life of Edmund Kean*, VII.

52   Raymund FitzSimons, *Edmund Kean: Fire From Heaven*, 69. John Clubbe has traced the influence of Kean on Byron's poetry. See his "Napoleon's Last Campaign and the Origins of Don Juan," 12-22.

Given Kean's love of sycophants, not to mention Byron's position on the Drury Lane Committee, it seems logical to assume that Kean would have done his best in the role. But this was not the case. The problem was not one of focus. The play ended with Kean, playing Selim, reviving his hitherto-thought-dead bride and cousin with Lear-like euphoria: "She lives!/ Delirious ecstasy! For me she lives!"[53] Nor was there a problem with the Bride herself. Kean made sure that part was paltry. The real sticking point was the spectacle of "camels and elephants and a castle in flames."[54] If you were busy looking at camels and elephants, would you or could you focus on that dwarf, Kean? The actor showed "his contempt for the piece," acted badly, and had it withdrawn 13 performances after its 5 February 1818 première.[55]

Rejecting Keats' *Otho*

As might be easily imagined, playwrights who worked with Kean faced great risk in having their works, even if commercially successful, suddenly withdrawn. Yet Kean's fame and skills were such that there was no shortage of playwrights to fashion something specifically for the actor. For example, when the poet and aspiring playwright Shelley wrote *The Cenci* (published 1819), he did so with Edmund Kean and Eliza O'Neill in mind for the principal roles.[56] Shelley was evidently thinking of an ideal cast. O'Neill had retired from the stage in 1817, and even if she hadn't, Kean would never have acted with her; she was far too competent. In O'Neil's final season, she proposed that she and Kean star in *Romeo and Juliet*. Kean declined because "to challenge a comparison with Miss O'Neill in her finest character was, he thought, an unfair expectation." He countered with an offer to have her star opposite

---

53 William Dimond, *The Bride of Abydos*, 73-4.

54 Peter J. Manning, *Byron and his Fictions*, 206. See also Manning's "Edmund Kean and Byron's Plays," 188-206.

55 Henry Crabb Robinson, *The London Theatre 1811-1866*, 82. Byron himself often asserted that he had no interest in having his works staged, but David V. Erdman doubts the poet's sincerity. "I believe it will be nearer the truth of the matter to say that far from considering his own plays unactable, Byron only feared they might be acted" ("Byron's Stage Fright,"220). Kavita A. Sharma also blames Byron's reluctance to have his works staged on "the fear of ridicule." See her *Byron's Plays: A Reassessment*, 17. Taking another vantage, Shou-ren Wang argues that Erdman's and Kivita's assertions are "unfounded," but does not suggest Kean as a possible explanation (*Theatre of the Mind*, 29). The evidence herein presented suggests that Byron might have abandoned the theater after a rational assessment of how likely it was that Kean would damn his plays. Margaret J. Howell also notes that in 1821, Byron exhibited a "veiled desire" to have *Marino Faliero* acted, but only by Kean (*Byron Tonight*, 204). The actor never complied. Kean's rebuff is discussed in Jonas Barish, *The Antitheatrical Prejudice*, 332. Byron's plays were staged successfully by both William C. Macready and Charles Kean, but only after Edmund Kean's demise. On this point, see Margaret J. Howell, *Byron Tonight*, 71-9, 161-2.

56 Jonathan Bate, *Shakespeare and the English Romantic Imagination*, 207.

him in *Macbeth*, but, when she agreed, he reneged on the deal.[57] In sum, Shelley could not have been surprised when Kean turned the play down. We can learn far more from Kean's rejection of John Keats' play, *Otho the Great*, which was tailored with Kean in mind for the character of Ludolph.[58]

Keats idolized Kean and wished "to make as great a revolution in modern dramatic writing as Kean has done in acting."[59] According to Jonathan Bate, the statement implied that Keats was interested in reviving "Shakespearean dramatic poetry as Kean had revived Shakespearean acting."[60] On this point, Bate is in sympathy with C.L. Finney who states that, in writing *Otho*, it was Keats' ambition to establish a "Shakespearean school of playwriting [*sic*]."[61] But there was no need for a revival; Shakespeare's plays had not disappeared, nor had Shakespearean acting. Before Kean, there had been Kemble, before Kemble, Garrick, a line of dramatic kings stretching back to Burbage. True, Kean had popularized his "natural" style, but there was nothing uniquely "Shakespearean" in it; indeed, the novelty of his delivery suggested that most audiences considered his approach unShakespearean. As for playwrighting, Shakespearean drama—which calls for a variety of strong characters and an ensemble approach to drama—inaccurately described what Kean was asking of his playwrights. Kean's productions were star vehicles; any attention that was not directed at him was a threat to his dominance. Keats might have wanted to revolutionize verse drama as Kean had done acting, but that in turn meant that Keats' plays would have to respond to Kean's monological approach to drama.[62] Keats, in lashing his dramatic craft to Kean's, couldn't so much start a new revolution as aid the one already in progress. To write for Kean, Keats had to write a Shakespeare play

---

57 It is just possible that Kean might not have been to blame. F.W. Hawkins writes that "the expected coalition never took place" (*Life of Edmund Kean*, II: 29). That being said, it seems clear that Kean was as reluctant as O'Neil was willing.

58 In a letter to George and Georgiana Keats, 17-27 September 1819, the poet noted there was no other actor who could play the principal character; "he [Kean] is the only actor that can do it." *The Letters of John Keats*, 430.

59 Jane Moody argues that Kean's acting incorporated aspects of illegitimate theatre such as pantomimic movements and operatic delivery. She suggests that *Otho* was designed to respond to Kean's skills. That being said, she seems unaware of Kean's tyrannical machinations at Drury Lane and further suggests that *Otho* was dropped simply because Kean went to America (*Illegitimate Theatre*, 241). If that were the case, why was it not revived upon his return? Independently, Jonathan Mulrooney suggests that Keats' revolutionary approach aimed at a more emotional and popular kind of Shakespearean entertainment (See "Keats in the Company of Kean," esp. 228). Again, no explanation is given as to why Kean dropped the play. In any case, it's doubtful that *Otho*, which is Neoclassical in tone and aristocratic in subject, would have appealed to working-class audiences.

60 Jonathan Bate, *Shakespeare and the English Romantic Imagination*, 165. For *Otho*'s Shakespearean parallels, see p. 187; also see Claude Lee Finney, *The Evolution of Keats's Poetry*, 662, and R.S. White, *Keats As a Reader of Shakespeare*, 204-8.

61 Claude Lee Finney, *The Evolution of Keats's Poetry*, II: 661.

62 Indeed, Etienne-Jean Delécluze called Kean's acting at the end of his *Richard III* "antiShakespearean" (*Journal de Delécluze, 1824-1828*, 492; translation my own).

as Shakespeare would have done if Shakespeare were forced to write a play that had only one developed character.

Most critics dislike the play. Their reasons, however, do not account adequately for Kean's direct influence. According to Clarence DeWitt Thorpe, *Otho the Great* "was written as no play ought to be written. It was written for money...."[63] Amy Lowell dismisses *Otho* as "dull beyond belief...hack work of the most glaring variety. ... dreary and stupid."[64] Francis Jeffrey is often quoted:

> There are brilliant images—and words of power—scattered thro it, no doubt—but the puerile extravagance and absolute bombast of most of the passionate speeches—([Kean's character] Ludolph's especially)—appear to me ... humiliating....[65]

True, Keats wanted to make money out of *Otho the Great*, but there is no indication that Keats felt any "humiliation" in writing it. As Charles Brown, Keats' own writing partner for the play, pointed out, Keats' name had "become a by-word of reproach in literature."[66] It's doubtful that Keats felt he was lowering himself. If anything, writing for Kean was probably seen as a great opportunity. Besides, removed of negative connotations, "hackwork" is really a compliment. After all, as Bernice Slote points out, it was standard practice for playwrights to customize their plays: "the limitations of a star system confined to a few licensed theatres naturally made a writer think in advance of his actors...."[67] More recent research, particularly by R.S. White, is coming round to see *Otho* as "an effective drama written in the vein of plays which had been enormously popular...."[68]

If some critics see Keats stooping to commercial concerns, they might take solace in the fact that his tailoring to such stringent specifications (the tilting of character over plot, the emphasis of tragedy, the constant courting of Kean's ego, etc.) was no small feat. *Otho* was carefully layered with all the standard Keanian conventions. This was no accident. The play was as much the result of creativity as it was of dogged research and first-hand experience. Keats had seen Kean in all of his principal Shakespearean roles, including Richard III, Othello, Hamlet, Macbeth, and Shylock. Further, Keats had written theater reviews for the *Champion* on Kean's performances in *Richard, Duke of York* and an adaptation of Massinger's *The City*

---

63 Clarence DeWitt Thorpe, *John Keats: Complete Poems and Selected Letters*, 396.

64 Amy Lowell, *John Keats*, II:294.

65 G.M. Matthews, *Keats: The Critical Heritage*, 209.

66 John Keats, *The Poetical Works*, V:3.

67 Bernice Slote, *Keats and the Dramatic Principle*, 107. We might further note that industry of this kind is not indistinguishable from Keats' other works; his sonnets, odes, etc. also follow and maintain convention.

68 R.S. White, *Keats As a Reader of Shakespeare*, 206. White prefers to see *Otho* as an imitation of seventeenth-century dramatic conventions, but there is no doubt that many plays of the era were star-driven. Oddly, although White states that Keats was zealously interested in Kean's acting (203), he does not connect Kean's acting or repertoire to the making of *Otho*.

Madam. Keats knew that Kean would only agree to play a madman, a passionate villain. In composing his Ludolph, Keats must have felt that his bloody, jealous and insane prince was perfect Keanian material. Keats also knew of the importance Kean placed on the fifth act. And, in writing his theater reviews, the poet had seen for himself that Kean preferred that the curtain fall directly after his last line. Keats wrote the first four acts of *Otho* with Charles Brown. But at the beginning of the all-important fifth act, Keats took total control.[69]

As the fifth act begins, Ludolph finds out that his wife, Auranthe, has betrayed him with Knight Albert and hunts them both. Albert, already wounded, is captured. Auranthe rushes to his aid. Ludolph has them now. His language is highly emotional:

> Ha! There! there!—He is her paramour!—
> There—hug him—dying! O, thou innocence,
> Shrine him and comfort him at his last gasp,
> Kiss down his eyelids! Was he not thy love?
> Wilt thou forsake him at his latest hour?
> Keep fearful and aloof from his last gaze.
> His most uneasy moments, when cold death
> Stands with the door ajar to let him in?[70]

The scene is only 32 lines. Of these lines, Ludolph has 15, or roughly 50 per cent of the scene. However, he only comes on at line 15, which means that after he appears, his dominance is so complete that other characters only interrupt him for a total of two lines.

In Act V.ii, there are 60 lines, Ludolph has 45 of them. In Act V.iii and iv, Ludolph is offstage but the dialogue concerns him directly. For example, we find out in scene iii that Ludolph, far from being satiated in his revenge, suffers from "Ghastly ravings."[71] In scene iv, Ludolph's father, Otho, and a physician discuss Ludolph's madness. When Ludolph does re-enter in Act V.v, he dominates the scene. After a series of fiery speeches, Ludolph demands that his wife be brought to him. While he awaits her entry, Ludolph goes mad, striking at the air with his dagger:

> Why do ye trouble me? out—out—out away!
> There she is! take that! and that! no, no—That's not well done—Where is she?

When news arrives that she is already dead, Ludolph, dies in painful epileptic convulsion. The curtain falls immediately after his death. Of the final scene's 192 lines, the supporting cast speaks just 49.5 of them. Ludolph accounts for the rest—

---

69 According to Brown, Keats "insisted ... that my incidents were too numerous, and, as he termed them, too melodramatic. He wrote the fifth act in accordance with his own view." See John Keats, *The Poetical Works*, V:3. The manuscript for Acts I through IV is stored at the Harry Ranson Center (HRC).

70 John Keats, *Otho: A Tragedy in Five Acts* V.ii.8-15.

71 Ibid., V.iii.16.

roughly 75 per cent of the scene's lines. Further, Ludolph's death is the only one the audience actually sees.[72] Death is a powerful dramatic moment, and Kean was not about to share it with other actors.

On 20 December 1819, the poet wrote excitedly to Fanny Keats with the good news: "Kean has perceived how suitable the principal Character will be for him."[73] The play was to be brought out the following session. Yet, by February 1820, the play had been rejected. Scholars remain puzzled by this sudden turn of events, though several theories have been put forward. C.L. Finney and Jonathan Bate have both pointed out that Albert and Conrad have Shakespearean speeches.[74] Did Kean think too many good lines were going to other actors? This is possible, but it doesn't explain why Kean didn't simply have the play re-cut to feature his part, as he had done in many other plays. Charles J. Rzepka sees in Ludolph a narcissistic quality that "attempts to poke fun at stage-play emperors and stage-play rhetoric."[75] Did Kean reject *Otho* because he felt Keats was making fun of him? Unlikely: Keats needed the money. Why would he take such care to please Kean in so many facets only to insult him in still others? Catherine Burroughs thinks the role of Auranthe "evokes the image of the dominant female performer of the period, Sarah Siddons."[76] Perhaps Keats wrote with Kean *and* Siddons in mind? If so, Kean might have rejected the play simply because he disliked appearing with star actresses. Again, this is unlikely: Sarah Siddons retired from the stage in 1812, seven years before Keats began writing the play, and Keats could not have expected that his play would coax her out of retirement. Besides, as the line counts suggest, the part of Auranthe hardly rivaled that of Ludolph. The fact of the matter is that Keats had done everything right. Not that it really mattered. Kean had his own mandate and did what he liked.

Bringing Experienced Playwrights to Their Knees

Inexperienced and financially distressed playwrights like Keats were easy prey for Kean, but he also toyed with well-known dramatists. Joanna Baillie, for example, was a successful and well-connected playwright, a friend of Sir Walter Scott, and known for her willingness to work with the piquant and manipulative practices of star actors. Take, for example, her *De Monfort*, which had been written as a closet drama but rewritten in 1800 to suit the stage skills of John Philip Kemble and Sarah

---

72 Auranthe's death is reported. Likewise, Ludolph's other enemies, Conrad and Albert, die offstage in Act V.iii.

73 John Keats, Letter to Fanny Keats, 20 December 1819, *Letters of John Keats*, 446.

74 R.S. White notes that, despite Ludolph's starring role, the plot turns on the actions of subordinate characters. Hence, Ludolph has "little room for active decision-making" — a stark contrast to Kean's other heroes, Richard III and Macbeth (*Keats As a Reader of Shakespeare*, 208).

75 Charles J. Rzepka, "*Theatrum Mundi* and Keats's *Otho The Great:* The Self in Society," 49.

76 Catherine Burroughs, "Acting in the Closet," 130.

Siddons; the latter was so pleased with the character of Jane that she invited Baillie to "Make me some more Jane De Monforts."[77] But writing with Kemble and Siddons in mind was far different than writing for Kean. Initially, Kean had been urged to play the lead in *De Monfort* and had only grudgingly acquiesced. Wisely, Baillie begged Kean for a meeting to discuss how she might tailor *De Monfort* to suit his talents. He agreed to the meeting, stating that he would be willing to do his best in the play, if the play were rewritten to further accentuate his genius. In a letter to William Sotheby, Baillie wrote:

> Kean was anxious to die upon the stage, but did not like the death which I had formerly provided for him, when Ld Byron wished him to act it, so after having had an interview with him which took place last saturday [*sic*] week, and hearing him explain his notions on the subject, I have written a new last scene where he is made to die of a broken spirit after having the chains put upon his limbs.[78]

Since she straitjacketed her muse to Kean's megalomaniacal demands, it's clear that Baillie wanted to oblige the star actor. Although she thought that sometimes he over-dramatized, she was taken with his "great power of expression."[79] Yet for all this, Baillie was sure Kean would damn her play.[80] On 4 December 1821, Baillie noted that Kean "wishes me & my Play at the bottom of the red sea."[81]

She was told by friends who had written plays for Kean to expect the worst. When the aforementioned William Sotheby submitted a tragedy, *Julian and Agnes*, to Drury Lane, Kean demanded rewrites to center the drama on him. Sotheby complied. In rehearsals, the Drury Lane Committee members reacted to the play enthusiastically, until Kean had a word with them; thereafter, the play was dropped unceremoniously.[82] On hearing the story, Baillie wrote to Sir Walter Scott that Sotheby was doomed from the start. If Kean did not like a play, it was madness to press it.[83]

---

77 Joanna Baillie, *Dramatic and Poetical Works*, XI.

78 Joanna Baillie, Letter to William Sotheby, 1821, *Collected Letters*, I:206.

79 Ibid., Letter to Mary Berry, 7 February 1814, *Collected Letters*, I:166. She saw his Richard III on 6 February 1814.

80 She seems unaware of the fact that Kean was also objecting to Mrs. West, a decent actress, playing opposite him. Drury Lane relented and had Mrs. Egerton play Jane De Monfort. See James Winston, 14 November 1821, *Drury Lane Journal*, 39. From another source, we learn that Kean "feared to stand beside Miss Kelly's *Page*" (*Oxberry's Dramatic Biography*, IV:189).

81 Joanna Baillie, Letter to William Sotheby, 4 December 1821, *Collected Letters*, I:207.

82 According to Byron, Sotheby withdrew this and other plays because of Kean's "tepidness"—i.e. lack of interest. See George Raymond, *The Life and Enterprises of Robert William Elliston, Comedian*, 259.

83 Joanna Baillie, Letter to Walter Scott, 26 February 1821. She further suggests that Kean only pretended to like Sotheby's play. See *Collected Letters*, I: 349.

Why, then, did Baillie submit her work to him? It might be that she thought she had several distinct advantages over Sotheby, Shelley, and Keats. She had friends in the theater, a loyal audience, and a strong track record. With these weapons in hand, she began an offensive against Kean's theatrical kingdom. Baillie enlisted Byron, a member of the Drury Lane Committee and a friend of Kean's, to give the play a fair trial.

Byron looked into the matter and was astonished. He knew that Kean had been rejecting plays, but he had no idea as to the extent of the actor's caprice. According to Byron's estimate, Kean had rejected about 500 plays. "Conceiving that amongst these there must be *some* of merit, in person and by proxy, I caused an investigation."[84] Thus, on a personal plea by Byron, Kean granted a hearing of the play and then insisted again that Baillie "with alacrity, carefully revise the play, bringing out the character of De Monfort in stronger relief."[85] Baillie complied; Kean's character was enlarged, and Jane, the other lead character, was diminished.[86] With alterations designed to promote—in the words of Macready—"the full splendor of his genius," Kean approved, and the play was duly brought out with great expense and fanfare on 27 November 1821.

Reviews stressed the audience's delight both with Kean and the play. *Drama* declared that in this "portrayal he was eminently successful"; the *Dublin University Magazine* noted that "the performance was one of his greatest efforts; he acted with all his tremendous energy"; *The Lady's Magazine* thought the play seemed "to harrow up the soul of the listening spectator."[87] After seeing the revival, Sarah Siddons wrote:

> I shall never forget the performance. There was a vast audience; among whom, I dare say, not three score persons were personally acquainted with the author of the play. ... There was so much silence, and so much applause, that ... I was impressed at the end with the belief that the play had now acquired and would henceforth for ever retain stage popularity.[88]

As the curtain came down on a ringing success, Kean told the stage manager that "it would never be an acting play."[89] After five performances, Kean withdrew *De Monfort* from Drury Lane's stage. Kean told Baillie that the receipts were disappointing, but it is clear that Kean had decided on withdrawing his support for

---

84 Quoted in George Raymond, *The Life and Enterprises of Robert William Elliston, Comedian*, 259.

85 Joanna Baillie, Letter to William Sotheby, 1821, *Collected Letters*, I:206. See also Margaret S. Carhart, *The Life and Work of Joanna Baillie*, 123.

86 Genest asserts that the character of "Jane was thrown into the background" (*Some Account of the English Stage*, VIII: 177).

87 Margaret S. Carhart, *The Life and Work of Joanna Baillie*, 125-6.

88 Ibid., 125.

89 Ibid., 127. Kean did revive the play for one performance in New York on 4 December 1826, his penultimate American performance.

the play well before Drury Lane could tally the gate. In fact, the numbers had been exceptionally good. The play sold out the first two nights. And, as Baillie was well aware, other Kean-endorsed plays had done far worse, yet Kean had allowed them to run.[90] We can, of course, only speculate as to why Kean abandoned the play. Was he angry at Byron for forcing his hand, or was he upset that one of the actors inadvertently drew too much applause, or was the stage artifice so grand that it detracted from Kean?[91] What we can say is that Kean's decrees were enforced immediately and without administrative dissent.

R.C. Maturin's *Bertram* was a rarity, a new play Kean actually liked.[92] The play builds on the plotline of *Cymbeline*, with an *Othello-King Lear* dénouement:

> She must not, shall not die, till she forgives me—
> Speak—speak to me—(*kneeling to the corse*)
> (*Turning to the Monks*—Yes—she will speak anon—
> (*A long pause, he drops the corse*)
> She speaks no more—Why do ye gaze on me—
> I loved her, yea, I love, in death I love her—
> I killed her—but—I loved her—

Bertram finds his life is meaningless. Grabbing a knife, he stabs himself, and, in dying, declaims that he:

> Died no felon's death;
> A warrior's weapon freed a warrior's soul![93]

After some hesitation, Kean staged the play at Drury Lane, where it ran for 22 nights and earned Maturin over £1000.[94] Yet the playwright was forced to watch helplessly as Kean sunk his new play, the equally Shakespearean *Manuel*, after just five showings—this, despite the fact that the Honourable Douglas Kinnaird, one of the members of the Drury Lane Committee, had personally commissioned the work.[95]

---

90 Joanna Baillie, Letter to William Sotheby, 29 December 1821. *Collected Letters*, I:208.

91 The *European Magazine* noted that the requiem in the fifth act was "very splendid … [and] well performed." See Margaret S. Carhart, *The Life and Work of Joanna Baillie*, 124.

92 Jane Moody suggests that Keats' *Otho* is in many ways similar to Maturin's *Bertram*. Since Kean liked the latter, this may also suggest that *Otho* was rejected for reasons other than performability (*Illegitimate Theatre*, 237).

93 John Doran describes *Bertram* as a play lacking all sense of morality, though he admitted the play had some "fierce sentiment and grotesque horrors." See *"Their Majesties' Servants." Annals of the English Stage*, II:374.

94 The printed version ran through seven editions within the year.

95 Kinnaird is also variously spelt "Kinnard." See letter by Mary Kean to Jane Porter, 27 May 1816, HRC. Inexplicably, Coleridge called *Bertram* a "senseless plagiarism" of *King Lear (Biographia Literaria*, VIII.ii:278). Its probable that Coleridge has confused the play with *Manuel*, which climaxes with a Learesque:

In a series of hitherto unpublished letters, the successful Gothic novelist Jane Porter appealed privately to Kean's wife Mary to have a word with her husband concerning her new play, *Switzerland*. Mary replied on 18 April 1816 with a promise to help her: "I should wish him to read [your play]." Mary was also thrilled to report that Kean was impressed: "he is partial to the plot & thinks, it *well* written—the Language *very Energetic would be a fine thing*." Nonetheless, Porter should expect, and Mrs. Kean hoped Porter would not be offended by, "Mr. Kean's *candid report*." On 15 May 1816, Mary wrote again, with bad news: although "Mr. Kean likes yours [the play] *exceedingly* & is most anxious it should be given," and "*likes the character in the play*," sadly, "*at present, He can't do it.*"

The correspondence continued. Porter convinced Mary to resubmit the play to the aforesaid Kinnaird, who said that "He knew the story & that it was very good," a reply that suggests that Kean had shown the play to him.[96] Mary wrote excitedly on 11 December 1816 that Kean was coming around: "he is confident when you make the alterations he proposed *it will do*." The main alteration concerns "one character[:] A Female you must alter entirely, he does not approve at all of it." Given Kean's directives, it's clear that the lead female part was too big or juicy in some way. On 28 February 1817, Mary reported that Kean had promised "that he will do all he possibly can with" his character; he "desires it to go [be performed] immediately." *Switzerland* finally premièred 15 February 1819 and survived just one night. Porter, who was there on opening night, registered her shock "when the Curtain drew up and discovered all this promised energy, transformed into an almost motionless Automation."[97] The details are amazingly prescient of Kean's near-identical entry for *Ben Nazir*. Not surprisingly, the play fell out of rotation because Kean acted lazily in front of a packed house.[98]

False!—false!—ye cursed judges—do ye hide him?
I'll grasp the thunderbolt!—rain storms of fire—
There—there—I strike! (R.C. Maturin, *Manuel*, 84. I have regularized some of the punctuation.)

Nonetheless, Coleridge stated accurately that *Bertram* was custom-made for Kean: "I am fully convinced ... that his mode of acting the part was in strict correspondence to the part itself ..." (*Biographia Literaria*, VIII.ii:260). Norman Fruman records that Coleridge's play *Zapolya* had been rejected by Drury Lane (*Coleridge, The Damaged Archangel*, 74). Might Coleridge's negative assessment of Maturin stem from professional jealousy? A similar motive may also explain his attack on Joanne Baillie (96).

96 Letter from Mary Kean to Jane Porter, 27 May 1816 (HRC). Mary later personally and secretly delivered the manuscript to Kinnaird, who resigned from the Committee, perhaps in protest of Kean's actions. See Mary Kean's letter to Jane Porter, 26 November 1816 (HRC).

97 Gordon Craig, *The Life and Theatrical Career of Edmund Kean*, 40.

98 See Harold Newcomb Hillebrand, *Edmund Kean*, 181. Charles Bucke thought that Kean walked through the part as if he were merely rehearsing it. "This was so palpable, that persons cried, 'shame!' upon him from the pit" (Preface, *The Italians*, XX).

The drama critic Leigh Hunt also submitted a play that he thought would flatter Kean's passionate style. He too had reason to hope for success: Hunt had been one of Kean's earliest and staunchest supporters. Further, critics were often feared; rejecting Hunt's play might draw his journalistic ire. However, Hunt made one fatal error:

> I unfortunately said that there were *two* characters in it, either of which, it was thought, would suit him: and it turned out just afterwards, that he had a mortal antipathy to having any second Richard in the field. He returned me a very polite answer, in which he said that his hands were full. …. You cannot suppose, of course, that I think my tragedy worse than those which are received. I know it to be a great deal better.…[99]

Kean's rejection of Hunt speaks volumes as to his confidence. Kean never worried that Hunt might retaliate with bad reviews, or that he might be reprimanded by the Drury Lane Committee.[100]

We can now see that Grattan's suspicions of foul play were well founded. Biographers, anxious to treat Kean sympathetically, reject this assessment, preferring to depict Kean as a failing actor, rather than a scheming Machiavel. Yet, the Machiavel-version is not without its charms. Indeed, it's difficult not to admire Kean's strategy, which was both ingenious and logical. Let us imagine, for example, that Grattan's play was a success. What was to stop Grattan from offering his next play to Covent Garden? Establishing Grattan's success now might add to a rival's success later. Kean's plan was, therefore, simple: fail the play and ruin Grattan's success and career now to hinder all upstarts later.

Of course, Kean was passing on a play designed to highlight him, but what had he really to gain? Very little. Kean's fame could not be heightened. He was the king of the stage. But what of the poor reviews of the plays he sunk? Surely, Kean was taking a great risk here? Not really. Commenting on *Ben Nazir*, *The Times* reviewer blamed the playwright for the theatrical debacle:

> In all the great attributes by which this lofty species of composition should be distinguished, *Ben Nazir the Saracen* is lamentably deficient. If the end of tragedy be to excite the passions of pity and terror, and some others nearly allied to them, the author of this play has wholly and entirely missed that end.[101]

Kean's first biographer, F.W. Hawkins, follows the logic of *The Times* writer:

---

99 Leigh Hunt, *Leigh Hunt: A Life in Letters*, 96.

100   There are yet other plays Kean may have sunk. In 1822, Frances Wright implied that it was Kean who refused to stage her play *Altorf* (1818): "The style of the first refusal was such as to destroy all hopes of attention from the theatrical committee, and that of the second, pretty much all anxiety for their approbation." She goes on to state that Drury Lane has no room for up-and-coming actors or dramatists: "perhaps the actor, as well as the dramatist, would do well to quit the field" ("To the Reader, *Altorf*, v).

101 F.W. Hawkins, *Life of Edmund Kean*, II:283. Grattan did, however, have the play performed in America, where it was tolerably received. See his *Beaten Paths*, II:221.

The tragedy itself ... failed both in conception and in execution; it was almost totally destitute of the qualities which constitute a thoroughly representable work; and the characters, with the exception of Emerance, were heavy, prosy, and soliloquizing.[102]

As for Kean's other biographers, only the sharp-eyed Hillebrand suspects that Kean did not do his best in *Ben Nazir* but excuses the fault as a minor one: "Poetic tragedy was not his [Grattan's] line, and certainly no harm was done either to him or to literature by the snuffing out of his first invention, however painful the experience may have been."[103]

Kean, doubtless, would be delighted to know that his biographers have been taken in. Yet, the plan was not perfect. Kean, for example, might be able to ruin plays and deflect any criticism for doing so, but nothing could stop a playwright like Grattan from thereafter taking a play to an established competitor such as Macready. The idea of succeeding in a play in which Kean had failed might have appealed to him.

On one occasion this actually happened. In 1820, James Sheridan Knowles custom wrote *Virginius* for Kean, but the actor rejected it. Macready then turned it into a star vehicle. Hillebrand writes that, by giving up *Virginius*, Kean "missed a chance at one of the most effective plays of the century. Hereafter the talents of the leading dramatist of his times were to be devoted not to him, but to his most dangerous rival."[104] Indeed, Macready's success with a Kean cast-off was the exception that proved the genius of Kean's rule. Actors, either fearing Kean's power or trusting the bad reviews of the critics, shied away from Kean's cast-offs. With the exception of Baillie's *De Monfort*, none of Kean's withdrawn plays ever made it back to the London stage, and even *De Monfort* spent more than twenty years on the shelf before being revived.[105] As for Knowles, when he offered Kean a new play, the actor refused to read it because the playwright had already worked with Macready.[106]

In the case of Baillie, the damage was minimal; a recognized author who had published four volumes of plays by 1812, she all but abandoned writing for the stage in favor of closet dramas. As long as Kean controlled Drury Lane, she knew that plays, no matter how good, how well received, or how well-suited to Kean, were still bound to be rejected. Hunt continued to write poetry, reviews, and essays; Shelley,

---

102 F.W. Hawkins, *Life of Edmund Kean*, II:282-3.

103 Yet, even here, despite what looks like Hillebrand's suspicions of Kean's efforts in the play, the biographer thereafter returns to the standard narrative set by Grattan. The play was fine; Kean had failed because his memory was ruined by drink:

> But Kean was irretrievably exposed in all his weakness, as a man half dead who could never hope to live again, as a man condemned henceforth to be a mere reflection of himself. His mind had suddenly hardened; it could retain what it had acquired while it was alive, but it could add nothing more. The realization must have appalled him. (*Edmund Kean*, 285)

104 Ibid., 192.

105 John William Cole, *The Life and Theatrical Times of Charles Kean*, I:128.

106 See James Winston, 6 February 1829, *Drury Lane Journal*, 141-2.

Maturin, Porter, and Grattan never wrote for the stage again; Keats tried but one more time, again unsuccessfully.

It's clear that Kean's power both within the playhouse and with his audience was such that he was able to control his own play selections. Yet, what was good for Kean was not necessarily good for Drury Lane. Kean had shelved a number of expensive productions, even when it looked as if they were about to become hits. In rejecting perfectly good plays and ruining still others, Kean discouraged new playwrights from offering their work to Drury Lane. If this went on indefinitely, Kean might destroy London's premier theater. But that was not Kean's concern: the actor understood that power, once gained, had to be maintained. Some are born great, some achieve greatness. Kean was of the latter camp, and he did everything in his power to maintain that greatness, even if it meant staging an occasional failure.

Chapter 3

Kean and the French (Sexual) Revolution

Edward Stirling's *Old Drury Lane* takes us back to those first days of Kean's fame and fortune. It's not all sunshine and holiday. In fact, our actor is depressed. Now that he is a star, Drury Lane tells Kean that he will no longer dress with the second rank actors. Without protest, the star sits alone in what had been John Philip Kemble's dressing room. Next door, he can hear his colleagues having conversations, laughing, commiserating. A lonely Kean decides that he shouldn't have to play along with the social distinctions imposed by his predecessor. Kean already realizes that he is, like Henry V, the maker of manners. Seeing his old friend Richard Hughes walk by, Kean decides to act:

> KEAN: Dick, I want to speak to you.
> HUGHES: Beg pardon, sir, I cannot enter the room.
> KEAN: What do you mean?
> HUGHES: I'm only a three-pounder; they are all tenners that are allowed to sit in the first green-room.
>
> *Kean sends for the stage manager, RAE, and insisted that his old friend should enter.*
>
> RAE: It's against the rules.
> KEAN: Well, then, you'll play "Richard" to-night without "Gloster."

Stirling concludes: "This settled a vexed question, once and for all time."[1]

No biography repeats the anecdote, which, we can assume is one of those inventions told of the famous. Certainly, given what we know of Kean's hiring practices, it's hard to image him as well liked by any acting company. But even if

---

1   Edward Stirling, *Old Drury Lane*, 142-3. I have taken minor liberties with the text. The original is in prose and reads:

'Dick, I want to speak to you.'
Beg pardon, sir, I cannot enter the room. 'What do you mean?'
Hughes: 'I'm only a three-pounder; they are all tenners that are allowed to sit in the first green-room.'
Kean sent for Rae, and insisted that his old friend should enter. The stage-manager hesitated; it was a rule.
'Well, then,' said the great tragedian, you'll play "Richard" to-night without "Gloster."

historically unverified, elements of Stirling's story gives us a plausible explanation as to why the masses loved this upstart actor. Edmund Kean, it seems, did everything he could to differentiate himself from John Philip Kemble.

Kemble and His Audience

William Hazlitt described Kemble as "the very still-life and statuary of the stage; a perfect figure of a man; a petrifaction of sentiment, that heaves no sigh, and sheds no tear; an icicle upon the bust of Tragedy."[2] A political and artistic traditionalist, Kemble's Shakespearean interpretations were aimed at curbing all rebellious tendencies and antisocial activities, including regicide and sexual license.[3] Even his tall, slim figure was a physical model of aristocratic self-restraint. Wrote Leigh Hunt: "He [Kemble] never rises and sinks in the enthusiasm of the moment; his ascension, though grand, is careful, and when he sinks it is with preparation and dignity."[4] Unsurprisingly, he excelled at playing calm, self-possessed heroes and well-mannered princes. Kemble played Hamlet "like a man in armour," impervious to the world around him, triumphant "with a determined inveteracy of purpose."[5] John Howard Payne vividly recalled Kemble's Coriolanus:

> His person derived majesty from a scarlet robe which he managed with inimitable dignity. The Roman energy of his deportment, the seraphic grace of his gesture, and the movements of his perfect self-possession displayed the great mind, daring to command, and disdaining to solicit, admiration.[6]

Anxious to distance his characters from any taint of working-class vulgarity, Kemble regularly bowdlerized words: country "whoring" gave way to urbane "wenching." Even inoffensive phrases were subject to his overly-severe prudery: "i'th' name of Venus" became "'th' name of wonder."[7] Offstage, Kemble lived, as it were, with "the

---

2   William Hazlitt, *Complete Works*, V:304. James Boaden, a noted theatrical critic of Kean's era, recalled that the "princely" Kemble looked as if he was "to the manor born" and was, "an abstraction, if I may so say, of the characteristics of tragedy" (James Boaden, *Memoirs of John Philip Kemble*, I:92). For a comparison of Kean and Kemble's physical characteristics, see C. Douglas Abel, " 'Alexander the Little': The Question of Stature in Edmund Kean's Othello," 100.

3   James Boaden, *Memoirs of the Life of John Philip Kemble*, I:92-3. Leo Braudy suggests that, prior to the American Revolution, theater was "part of the propaganda of tyranny" (*The Frenzy of Renown: Fame and Its History*, 455).

4   See sketches and criticism of Kemble in *Actors and Actresses of Great Britain: The Kembles*, 85.

5   *The Times*, 15 June 1817, in Press Clippings, Huntington Manuscript Collection, Huntington Library, 182799.

6   See sketches and criticism of Kemble in *Actors and Actresses of Great Britain: The Kembles*, 85-6.

7   Herschel Baker, *John Philip Kemble*, 115.

cloak of the 'noble Roman' around him."[8] As one praising theatergoer put it, "Who can like Kemble dignify the stage?"[9]

Kemble was also known for his distaste of the "lower orders." In 1796, audiences took exception to the text of his aforementioned *Coriolanus*, which contained "Certain sentences in this play [that] puts them [the working class] out of humour."[10] Having looked into the matter, John Ripley suggests that Kemble's modifications were as purposeful as they were antagonistic: Kemble, for example, restored Coriolanus' barbaric threat to "make a quarry ... of these quartered slaves as high as I could pick my lance." While the antagonism between Martius and the plebeians is apparent in Shakespeare's original, in Kemble's version the scorn he exhibited for "the 'voices' of the Roman mob"[11] seemed "more personal than political."[12] This *Coriolanus* exhibited an almost allergic rejection of the play's plebeians—Hazlitt said that Kemble's Coriolanus looked like a man "who is [always] just about to sneeze."[13] According to a *Times* review of 12 April 1796, the audience voiced its displeasure with a "laugh of contempt."[14] Nonetheless, Kemble refused to make changes to his text.[15] The real firestorm, however, began in 1809, when Kemble tried to raise theater prices.

To be fair, Kemble's Covent Garden had just gone through a costly refurbishment. Nonetheless, any raise in ticket prices were bound to affect lower income wage earners far more than the well-off—hence, the perception that this new Covent Garden had been rebuilt with a new, wealthier clientele in mind.[16] Shouts of "Old prices! Old prices!" greeted both Kemble and his sister, Sarah Siddons, each time they appeared on stage. The theater appealed to the government, which promptly sent 500 soldiers to protect the wealthier patrons and the theater itself from what would soon be know as the OP riots.

Kemble applauded the move and told his friend James Boaden that he would not placate the rioters: "he whose talent is prostituted to the amusement of a RABBLE, must, as a man either of sense or feeling, shrink in disgust from the meanness of his occupation."[17] There is something of Marie Antoinette's "Let them eat cake"

---

8   Linda Kelly, *The Kemble Era*, 103.

9   *Actors and Editors, A Poem By An Undergraduate* (1817), 33.

10   See Inchbald's edition, *Coriolanus or, The Roman Matron*, V:v. The text had actually been adapted for a production in 1789. See John Ripley, *Coriolanus on Stage*, 114.

11   George Taylor, *The French Revolution and the London Stage*, 55.

12   John Ripley, *Coriolanus on Stage*, 118, 121.

13   William Hazlitt, *Complete Works*, V:350.

14   *The Times* 12 April 1796, quoted in George Taylor, *The French Revolution and the London Stage*, 56.

15   He did, however, pull the play after just two performances. Thereafter, he did not perform the role for the next nine years. See John Ripley, *Coriolanus on Stage*, 114.

16   The perception may have been fueled by King George III, the Duke of York, and the Duke of Cumberland, who, combined, contributed roughly 15 per cent of the renovation costs, which in total exceeded £150,000.

17   James Boaden, *Memoirs of the Life of John Philip Kemble*, II:501.

in Kemble's dismissal. His scorn only intensified the poorer classes' resentment for the actor. For the next 67 nights, the theater devolved into political chaos, with governmental representatives reading the Riot Act, lawyers encouraging civil disobedience, and a once-attentive audience now demanding that its collective voice be heard.[18] To help quell the rebellion, Kemble hired professional boxers, among them the famed Mendoza, to awe and attack any rabble-rousers.[19] However, the hired muscle quickly sided with the audience.[20] Cried Mendoza: "Down down to H—l with all Ops & say t'was *Dan* that sent the[e] there."[21] The uprising ended when Kemble agreed to the old prices, but much of the audience never really forgave him. Kemble had to be replaced by an actor who was self-evidently a man of the people.

Kean and the Common Man

Jonathan Bate suggests that Drury Lane's audience embraced Kean because they saw him as an "embodiment of the rioting crowds who had triumphed over Kemble…."[22] Certainly, the *hoi polloi* could relate to Kean more than to Kemble: According to

---

18 See Julia Swindells, *Glorious Causes*, 28-9; Elaine Hadley, *Melodramatic Tactics*, 46.

19 John Doran, *"Their Majesties' Servants." Annals of the English Stage*, II: 364. There might be a further connection between Mendoza and Kean. If Mendoza was a man of the people, he was also pointedly Jewish, as were the other boxers Kemble hired. When Kean played Shylock, it was as if Mendoza and his kind had taken the stage. On Mendoza being compared, albeit in passing, to Shylock, see Pierce Egan, *Boxiana*, I:255. Mendoza compared himself to Shylock. See *The Memoirs of Daniel Mendoza*, 108.

20 According to John Doran, the pugilists began to allow "questionable looking people" into the boxes—to the infinite glee of the rioters (*"Their Majesties' Servants." Annals of the English Stage*, III: 366).

21 Marc Baer, *Theatre and Disorder in Late Georgian London*, 216.

22 Jonathan Bate, "The Romantic Stage,"110. Relatedly, Bryan Waller Procter encourages us to see the rise of Kean in political terms: Covent Garden's John Philip Kemble was of "the old dynasty" and Drury Lane's Edmund Kean was of "the opposite faction" (*The Life of Edmund Kean*, I:XVII). William Hazlitt described Kean as a "*radical* actor," analogous, if not identical to, a "radical politician" (*Complete Works*, XIX: 257). His "flashes of lightning" style was self-evidently similar to Whig politician Charles James Fox, who, according to Hazlitt, differentiated himself from the languid delivery of Tory counterparts by "speaking with the *rapidity of lightning*, and with breathless anxiety and impatience" (emphasis my own; William Hazlitt, *Complete Works*, XII:7.n.2). Jonathan Bate suggests that Kean's acting, at least in Hazlitt's mind, was aligned with the politics of Tom Paine and Joseph Priestley (*Shakespearean Constitutions*, 138-9). A.C. Grayling suggests that Hazlitt saw the rise of Kean as emblematic of revolutionary energies. Politics were very much in the air when Kean made his adult debut at Drury Lane on 26 January 1814. Only three and a half weeks before, on 2 January 1814, George III and the Duke of York had died. He further notes that the day Hazlitt first wrote about Kean he also wrote a column decrying English attempts to reinstate the Bourbons. See his *The Quarrel of the Age: The Life and Times of William Hazlitt*, 252 and 169.

Coleridge, Kean's trademark was the his ability to turn "the hyper-tragic" into the "infra colloquial."[23] Leigh Hunt said that his voice was like "a hackney-coachman's at one o'clock in the morning."[24] William Robson recalled: "Kean's person was mean ... no man, on the stage, was more ungraceful."[25] Even Kean's decisive marching around the stage separated him from his princely predecessor. Kemble's tall, steely form solidified the aristocratic *status quo*; Kean's flashing fits and starts gouged out a space of social unrest—characters who reveled in murders, delighted in seductions, and generally subverted the perceived limits of Shakespeare's supposedly conservative texts.[26]

In Kemble's view, what a falling off there was! Since the Licensing Act of 1737, only London's two patent theaters, Drury Lane and Covent Garden, were allowed to perform plays; the rest had to make do with pantos, musicals, and melodramas. However, increasingly, both theaters were now willing to allow the public to exercise greater control over the price and, more significantly, even the type of entertainments and entertainers. When the patent theaters began adding "low" entertainments to their evening fare, they had also to hire like-minded performers. Kean, who had come up through the rankest of rank provincial theaters, was the kind of actor London's patent theaters had tried to banish.[27] Now the barbarian was at the gate, and he was quoting Shakespeare.[28]

---

23 S.T. Coleridge, *Table Talk*, 27 April 1823, XIV:ii.40.

24 Leigh Hunt, *Dramatic Criticism*, 114.

25 William Robson, *The Old Play-Goer*, 112-13.

26 Julia Swindells, in her study of English politics and theater from 1789 to 1833, writes that the stage was often used as a way of loosening perceptions of hierarchical control. Oddly, she does not mention Kean. She does note that in 1832 George Colman objected to plays that had adultery, murder, and parricide (*Glorious Causes*, 1-5). I'm not sure that these acts are necessarily less hierarchical; nonetheless, Colman might have been objecting to the violent aesthetic of Kean's repertoire.

27 After seeing him act, Charles Mayne Young wrote, "no man oftener violated the canons of good taste" (quoted in Julian Charles Young, *A Memoir of Charles Mayne Young, Tragedian*, 56-7).

28 Julia Swindells argues that the growing variety of performance offerings was designed to entice a new clientele, perhaps one sympathetic to French Revolutionary tendencies (*Glorious Causes*, 43-4). Jane Moody writes "Kean's celebrity threatened to dissolve the generic and, by implication, the social and political distinctions between Shakespearean tragedy and illegitimate theater. His performances seemed to challenge the myth of Shakespeare's aristocratic politics ..."(*Illegitimate Theatre*, 235). Jonathan Mulrooney writes,

> Kean imported an 'illegitimate' grammar of representation onto the Drury Lane stage, rendering the traditional relation between performer and audience uncertain and exposing the legitimate theater's increasing commercial reliance on lower-class modes of consumption. His presence—not only in the theater but in London society—called attention to those 'low' aspects of middle-class life that aspirants such as Smith, Hill, and Du Bois would have wanted to mask. ("Keats in the Company of Kean," 229)

Unsurprisingly, the old guard was bewildered by the sudden change in tastes:

> Oh Kemble, pshaw!
> Thy Eagle eye, must feel this Lion's paw,
> Thy skill is mocked at, and thy reading spurned,
> Be silent Judgement, let our books be burned,
> The man's a genius! Watch his sidling mien,
> The man's a Genius! For the man is Kean!
> ....
> You ope my eyes, and now my wonders grow
> That Kean's adored, while Kemble is forlorn,
> That fits, and starts should charm an audience
> When hard-earned judgment, is but mere pretend.[29]

Their outrage was directed not only at Kean, but also at his supporters—a "knot of numbskulls" who exercised "the most conceited, insolent, filth, and ignorant dominion" over the theater. But these "numbskulls" were Kean's people, and his voice was their own.

Exhibitions of Power

All well and good—Stirling's story embodies the broad outlines as to why audiences tired of Kemble and were ready to embrace Kean. But, on second reading, Sterling's story is troubling. After all, this Kean might easily solve the problem other ways. He might give all the actors £10 a week, in effect, making wages a useless determiner of talent. He might himself refuse to use the room. (Legend has it that after Drury Lane hired Kean to play Shylock, he refused to use the star dressing room because he had been treated so badly by the managers.) Besides, if he wanted to talk to Hughes, he could always chat with him in the hallway or go directly into the other dressing room.

What is clear is that the story has very little to do with the "little guy" at all. This Kean is more interested in getting Hughes to cross the doorway in front of Drury Lane's conservative managers. It's an exhibition of his power. Kean pulls rank. In effect, he demands: "Allow me to rewrite rules, or I walk." True, Kean does create a level playing field, one in which actors are raised to the level of managers and managers are lowered to the level of actors, but all must be pressed down equally by the whims of the tyrannical Kean. Even the title to Stirling's book, *Old Drury Lane*, smacks of the political: *Old* Drury Lane might receive its sanction from the Crown, but *New* Drury Lane takes its orders from England's most popular actor.[30]

---

29 *Actors and Editors, A Poem By An Undergraduate* (1817), 15-16.

30 James Winston notes that Kean was actually upset when someone else used his dressing room. See his entry for 5 January 1827 (*Drury Lane Journal*, 138). As for wanting to spend time with the minor actors, Kean did order that a bust of himself should be placed in their dressing room (Ibid., 7 September 1820, 17).

Plate 4:   Kean as Napoleon, seizes absolute power over Drury Lane. Reprinted from Personal Collection

Kean's Brutus: The Reluctant Tyrant?

A more reluctant, though no less tyrannical, Kean is presented in Pierce Egan's novel, *Life of An Actor* (1824), a work dedicated to Edmund Kean. The novel concerns the rise of an actor of genius, Proteus,[31] who finds—after becoming manager of an unnamed, though famous, London theater—that Napoleon and Wellington would have had their hands full at Drury Lane: "It is much worse than the commander of an army; the order of the general must be obeyed without a murmur, or punishment enforces the decree; but not so with the manager of a great theatre, he is frequently insulted

---

31 A caricature (ca. 1820) of The Wolves' Club identifies Kean as Proteus. See Gordon Craig, *The Life and Theatrical Career of Edmund Kean*, 60.

by the actors, and rank or superiority of talent goes for nothing."[32] Thus, against his conscience, Kean finds himself ruling with an iron hand, if only to stave off "a complete rebellion in the theatre."[33]

Stirling's Kean enjoys bullying managers; Egan's Kean is an egalitarian constrained by institutional realities. Perhaps both versions had some validity, but only one carried Kean's official position on the matter. Egan's novel, written with Kean's consent, if not his decree, was almost certainly part of a self-promotional campaign the actor launched soon after seizing power over his play selections. Appropriately, this was a campaign waged not just in newspapers and theatrical magazines, but also, and primarily, in fictions, beginning with the only commissioned play he added to his permanent repertoire: *Brutus*, which premièred 3 December 1818.

The focus is on Kean's character, Brutus, a Hamlet-like figure who feigns madness. When the death of Lucrece incites the people to revolution, Brutus steps forward to lead them. Here, we have all the trademarks of the French Revolution: the overthrow of a corrupt monarch and the promise of a new republicanism. But, after the revolution, Tullia, Rome's queen, now under house arrest, sees clearly that Brutus' coup is a success, but that the revolution is already a failure. Mocking Brutus' call for liberty, even as he rounds up more aristocrats for execution, Tullia suggests that Brutus, who yearns for a republic, has taken the role, if not title, of king:

TULLIA: But, tell me, doth the king know of this kindness?
PRIEST: What king?
TULLIA: What king? Brutus, the King of Rome,
Knows he of this?
PRIEST: He does.

Kean's Brutus finds, after all, that Tullia was right. The Republicans might be able to plot the murder of a king, but that murder merely teaches bloody instruction. At

---

32 Pierce Egan, *Life of An Actor*, 246. According to Egan, Kean owed his initial success to the Freemasons. The theory has spawned some serious research. According to C. Douglas Abel, Kean joined the Freemasons in 1810-11 and was presented, at an unspecified date, with a Masonic Jewel. Further, Kean attended meetings at the local lodge when in Scotland, "not far from Kean's country retreat on the Isle of Bute." Samuel Arnold, the manager of Drury Lane who first signed Kean to a contract, was a Freemason. He had seen Kean perform at the Dorchester Theatre, on the advice of Henry Lee, the manager. Lee was also a Freemason. See C. Douglas Abel, "Edmund Kean's Masonic Career," 69-70. Abel may have built a stronger case had he known that Samuel Whitbread and John Cam Hobhouse, both shareholders in Drury Lane, were also Freemasons. Kean's son, Charles, was also a Mason.

33 Pierce Egan, *Life of An Actor*, 246. After Kean's meteoric rise, he played the Coburg for £50 a night but complained that the audience was filled with "ignorant, unmitigated brutes." At the conclusion of the performance, he "folded his mantle majestically, made a slight, contemptuous obeisance, and stalked off, with the dignity of an offended lion" (John William Cole, *The Life and Theatrical Times of Charles Kean*, I:162). Kean's reaction, as well as Cole's description, suggests that, soon after coming to power at Drury Lane, Kean renounced his radical politics.

the climax of the play, Kean's Brutus[34] has all the Royalists executed, including his own son, Titus:

> BRUTUS: Well, Titus, speak, how is it with thee now?
> Tell me, my son, art thou prepared to die?
> TITUS: Father, I call the powers of heaven to witness
> Titus dares die, if so you have decreed.
> The Gods will have it so?
> BRUTUS: They will, my Titus:
> Nor heav'n, nor earth, can have it otherwise.
> It seems as if thy fate were pre-ordained
> To fix the reeling spirits of the people,
> And settle the loose liberty of Rome.
> 'Tis fixed; oh, therefore, let not fancy cheat thee:
> So fixed thy death, that 'tis not in the power
> Of mortal man to save thee from the axe.

After the death of his son, it is clear that Brutus' regime is to be far more restrictive than the tyranny it sets out to destroy. Brutus' government—new as it is—is already bathed up to the elbows in blood and conspiracy.

The passage has a strong whiff of Edmund Burke, who wrote that the recent French revolutionaries had merely "contrived no better remedy against arbitrary power than civil confusion."[35] By implication, Kean's Brutus argues that the same is true for the French Revolution. However, *Brutus* does not simply look back to the executions of the French Revolution; it also discusses the rise of Napoleon—and of Kean. Brutus, like Napoleon, may want a republic, but, in the political anarchy that ensues, he has no choice but to rule through tyrannical despotism. While the play may look at the democratic virtues of Republican Rome, Brutus' actions reaffirm the inevitability of an autocracy. No matter who rules, be it Tarquin or Brutus, all political roads in the play lead to a historically unrepublican Rome or, to use a Napoleonic model, a royalist France. Thus Kean's custom-made *Brutus* ends up stamping republicanism, even imaginings of republicanism, as unworkable, if not unthinkable.

The link to Kean's own management of Drury Lane is obvious. As we have seen, the rise of Kean initially promised a new kind of actor for a new kind of audience: of the people, by the people, for the people. Yet, as discussed in Chapter Two, very soon after coming to Drury Lane, Kean seized power and began to rework his plays to serve his own vaulting ambition. Was Kean arguing that he was a kind of Brutus/Napoleon, trapped reluctantly in a position of absolute power? It can be no accident

---

34 All quotes from *Brutus* are derived from the third volume of *Shakespeare Imitations, Parodies and Forgeries 1710-1820*. This study refers to Kean, rather than to Payne, because Payne wrote the play under Kean's direction. Writes Payne, "it was for the interest of the theatre that the great tragedian [Kean] should be the cynosure of attraction in every new piece, in which his extraordinary talents were to be called into requisition" (Introduction, *Brutus*, IV-V).

35 Edmund Burke, *Reflections on the Revolution in France*, 115.

that Kean exhibited the very monarchical tendencies his custom-made character comes to see as inevitable.[36]

Plate 5: **A Depiction of a drunken Kean presiding over a meeting of The Wolves' Club. On the far left, one member explains to a new recruit that Kean is a revolutionary with dynastic ambitions: "I am very Intimate with the Gemman, and I know his Motter is naught Caesar Naught Nullus and I says Caesar for ever." Reprinted by kind permission of the Harry Ransom Humanities Research Center; The University of Texas at Austin.**

---

36 Relatedly, one supported of Booth wrote: Kean's "Plodding dullness… could not brook a rivalship from a boy who snatched the chaplet of fame from the brow of age and experience almost without effort…" See *The Actor; Or, A Peep Behind The Curtain*, 13. The passage suggests that by the time Booth presented himself as a rival to Kean, the latter had already repositioned himself as the consummate insider. Certainly, we can say that this anonymous writer, and, by inference, all of Booth's supporters, were on some level dissatisfied with Kean, who was now the King of the Stage, rather than the upstart challenger. (On this point, see footnotes 22 and 33, above.) Booth was not merely a copy of Kean, he was, in the minds of Booth's supporters at least, the "real" revolutionary Kean of "the opposite faction." It was now Booth who threatened to replace Kean as the premier antiestablishment maverick of his age.

Kean's Political Platform

In addition to launching his *Brutus*, Kean founded a number of social clubs and held many of his meetings at bars like The Coal Hole. In Chapter One, we saw that one of his clubs, The Wolves, was first put together to stop actors from challenging Kean's genius but, as public opinion shifted against the actor, so too did the officially published versions of the club's proceedings. Before quoting from Kean's printed Wolves' Club speeches, it's important to point out that Kean himself may never have spoken them. He may merely have had someone else write them and then had them published under his name to give the impression that he wasn't always, as his biographers later asserted, legless at the Lyceum. That being said, fictional or otherwise, these printed speeches suggest Kean's savvy manipulation of the media to shape and to sharpen his public image. The first and most important of them was published in the news journal *Monthly Mirror* (1818). Addressing The Wolves, Kean thundered that club members had a duty to perform on the world stage:

> Courage, the only distinction our ancestors were acquainted with, must be one of the first principles of our body, and to what better end can we employ that magnificent ingredient, than in defence of our friends, against the foes of the general cause?

What was that cause? Liberty:

> When men consider they were created for each other, not only for themselves, the interest of mankind must be blended with individual speculation, and every one that bears the human form, each must see a *brother*; and it is my wish to instil these sentiments into the minds of our little community; that no insignificant distinctions shall have weight, when we can (with personal convenience) serve a fellow-creature; or worldly exaltation prevents us from mixing with worthy men ... no one, I hope, will enter this circle of *good fellows* without the pride that ranks him with the courtier, or philosophy that levels him with the peasant.[37]

Here is a speech perhaps not worthy of Washington, Lincoln, or Jefferson but engaging, nonetheless, in political revolution, attacking class rigidity and the prancing, self-justifying traditions it rides upon.

However, Kean's early biographers refuse to see these clubs as vehicles for social responsibility.[38] They either have Kean ordering his Wolves to attack an up-and-coming-actor, or they present him engaged in frolicsome foreplay before a visit

---

37 *Oxberry's Dramatic Mirror*, 149.

38 Kean was aware that many were blaming him for setting The Wolves upon his rivals. In a letter to an editor of a daily newspaper, Kean noted the charge and countered that The Wolves were dedicated solely to "*universal philanthropy.*" See *The Actor: Or, A Peep Behind the Curtain*, 30. The newspaper remains unspecified.

to a brothel.[39] His biographer Hillebrand (*Edmund Kean*, 1933), describes a typical soiree:

> night after night, he drank, cracked jests, sang, argued, and beat the table. And from there, night after night, he was brought home and put to bed. ... it was a harmless club of scalawags, a little too low for his station, a little too liquorous for his health, but still harmless enough.[40]

The perception is not discouraged by Giles Playfair (*Kean*, 1943), who writes: "These organized gatherings gave a purpose to his carousals and made the tavern more surely his kingdom. ... seemingly, they provided him with the excuse to finish many bacchanalian nights under the table, he regarded them, in his sober moments, with monarchical gravity."[41] This is quite odd. As we have seen, when presented with the option, biographers, particularly Kean's early biographers, usually tried to portray Kean sympathetically or, at least, poignantly. It seems that his biographers preferred a smashed clown to a sober revolutionary.

Dumas' Kean

Both Keans are found in Alexandre Dumas' play, *Kean* (1836), written only three years after the actor's death. As the play opens, our actor, at the height of his success, is an altruistic narcissist, preoccupied with helping the poor and with bedding as many well-bred women as possible. We see him seducing the wives of aristocrats, drinking cognac with the Prince of Wales, and reciting Shakespeare before adoring legions of fans. Life is good. But the actor never forgets his working-class roots. In one particularly nauseating scene, Kean meets a friend from his youth, Pistol, a tumbler and comedian. Seeing the great Kean, he begins to grovel, but Kean orders him to stand tall:

> KEAN: On your feet! You need your hands to shake mine.
> PISTOL: (*Shaking his hand*) Oh, Mr. Kean, this is an honor.
> KEAN: For me, boy. Tell me—how is the troupe?
> PISTOL: It gets along.
> KEAN: And Kitty?

---

39 Many men's clubs were places of debauchery. For an overview of the off-color proceedings of men's clubs, see Geoffrey Ashe, *The Hell-Fire Clubs: A History of Anti-Morality*. In his pamphlet entitled, "Serious Thoughts on the Miseries of Sedition and Prostitution" (1783), Charles Horne railed against these clubs, which were only interested in accepting men who frequented houses of prostitution. "I belong to no club; I am sure; if I did, I should, on the publication of this defense of virgin honor, be immediately expelled, and used with all manner of opprobrious language" (39).

40 Harold Newcomb Hillebrand, *Edmund Kean*, 152.

41 Giles Playfair, *Edmund Kean*, 145.

PISTOL: She loves you, poor girl. But that's not surprising—you were her first.
KEAN: And old Bob?[42]

And so it goes, Kean inquiring as to the health and welfare of his quondam friends, touched that he is still remembered, gratified that he is still loved. He makes plans that evening to have a reunion of sorts in his favorite bar, The Coal Hole. Arriving at the bar, he hears bad news. The cackhanded Bob has injured himself:

KITTY: Is he hurt badly, Pistol?
PISTOL: (*Almost crying*) They think he's dislocated his shoulder. And all because he wanted to kick my ass.
KEAN: Did you send for a doctor?
PISTOL: Yes.
KEAN: What did he say?
PISTOL: He said he'll have to stay in bed six weeks, without budging. That means the troupe will starve. ... Tomorrow, if our sign is gone, people will think we've gone bankrupt, and they won't come.
KEAN: Is starvation the worst thing you expect?
PISTOL: Isn't that enough? Fasting six weeks when it isn't even Lent. Fasting makes you hungry.
KEAN: Peter! Peter Patt!
PETER: Here I am!
KEAN: A pen, ink, and paper!
KITTY: What are you going to do?
PETER: (*Bring articles*) Here they are.
KEAN: (*Writing*) Have this letter sent to the director of Covent Garden. (*Finishes it, hands it to PETER*) I'm informing him that I will play the second act of Romeo and the role of Falstaff tomorrow night for the benefit of one of my old comrades who has dislocated his shoulder.
KITTY: Oh, Mr. Kean!
PISTOL: (*Joining KITTY in embracing KEAN*) There's a real friend, Kitty.[43]

Dumas made the scene up, of course, but the themes of charity, fraternity, and sexuality, all repeated in prior anecdotes concerning the actor, suggest that he knew, or had heard, quite a bit about Kean. Certainly, some of his knowledge came first hand.

Kean, Drunk in Paris

In 1827-28, a troupe of English actors, including Charles Kemble and William Macready, performed at the Odéon in Paris.[44] The English press noted that the French

---

42 Alexandre Dumas, *Kean*, 97. All citations, unless otherwise stated, are from his play *Edmund Kean*, in *The Great Lover and Other Plays*, trans. Barnett Shaw.

43 Ibid., 111-12.

44 This was not the first time Kean had been to Paris. *The Times* (22 September 1818, [p.2]) reported his visit and his meeting with the French actor Talma, in Press Clippings,

were only interested in Kean: "the fact is, they are angry at Macready's preceding Kean, about whom there is great anxiety; they are afraid he'll die before they see him; his name is in everyone's mouth as the '*only Shakesperian*.'"[45] Throughout the winter of 1828, illnesses—catalogued in the concluding chapter—had stopped him from joining his fellow actors. By the spring of 1828, Kean was healthy enough for the journey and performance. The star found Paris to be much like London; that is to say, he found the bars in Paris and frequented them as often as he had in London. On 12 May 1828, Kean made his first Paris appearance in the role of Richard III.

Because of public demand, the orchestra was cleared out for more stall seating. Still, the theater was completely sold out. The artistic elite of France came to see the great Kean perform: among them, the novelist Victor Hugo, the composer Hector Berlioz, the Romantic playwright Alfred de Vigny, and the talented and versatile writer Alexandre Dumas. But moments before the curtain rise, Kean was nowhere to be found. The manager knew enough of the Englishman's reputation to know where to send messengers in search. One found him utterly drunk at the Café Anglais. On being told that the audience awaited him, he replied superciliously, "I do not care a fig" (a euphemism for our modern "F" word). He was then told that the Duchess of Berri was in the audience. Said Kean groggily, "I am not a servant of the Duchess. More brandy."[46] Returning to the theater in his own good time, he performed poorly and drunk. Stories of this kind concerning Kean's 1828 Paris trip were common. Kean, it was said, cursed the aristocracy "with all the vigour of a sincere hater"; Procter writes that, after the performance, he was invited to meet the Duke of Wellington at a large party, an invitation the tragedian rejected instantly.[47] "I'm not invited as a guest but as a wild beast to be stared at," explained Kean.[48]

Kean as Rebel, If Not Revolutionary

Harold Newcomb Hillebrand dismisses virtually all of this, noting only, "The fictions that have been told of this visit [to Paris] by the biographers of Kean are amazing."[49] Certainly, it's not impossible to imagine Kean drunk or giving the Duke the royal raspberry. Whether factual or not, the story survives because it serves a communal function, in this case, explaining the actor's licentious excesses as a form of farcical social rebellion. Kean was fond of ambiguously framing himself as an aristocrat, while irreverently poking fun at the whole notion and value of the aristocracy. Claiming to be alternatively Irish and the illegitimate son of the Duke

---

Personal Collection.

    45 Quote found in the undocumented Harold Newcomb Hillebrand, *Edmund Kean*, 294.

    46 J. Fitzgerald Molloy, *The Life and Adventures of Edmund Kean* II:199. On another occasion, Kean wrote, "I kick all such pests to the devil, for I hate a lord" (Ibid., II: 99).

    47 Bryan Waller Procter, *The Life of Edmund Kean*, II:156-7.

    48 Eleanor Ruggles, *Prince of Players*, 32.

    49 Harold Newcomb Hillebrand, *Edmund Kean*, 295, n.10.

of Norfolk—the Duke denied the claim[50]—Kean performed in England, Scotland, Wales and Ireland.[51] Geographically, Kean's empire extended over all of the United Kingdom. And to impress this point further, the actor staged a variety of elaborate displays of power. As *mise-en-scène*, he bought Bute Castle in Scotland, one of the most historically significant seats in that country—the Third Earl of Bute, John Stuart, had been the Prime Minister during the reign of George III and was royally descended from James I.[52] And Kean often thought of himself as a king. On planning his first trip to America, Kean instructed the Drury Lane Committee that even while in exile, he would be "making arrangement for the restoration of Drury's monarchy...."[53] He did not disappoint in regal pageantry. Returning from America, his coffers rich with gold, he arrived at Drury Lane in a huge carriage, pulled by six horses with a troop of horsemen bringing up the rear. He was met by a hand-picked (and presumably prepaid) "heterogeneous rabble"[54], "including fifty soldiers [who] ... gave him three cheers."[55] He instituted boat races on the Thames, founded, as noted, various social clubs, and even bought himself a lion—a long-standing symbol of the British crown.[56]

The Drury Lane Committee paradoxically complained that his recent behavior, while theatrical, was unsavory and undesirable.[57] They had long talks with him,

---

50 On the Duke of Norfolk as Kean's father: "One day in the lobby of Drury Lane Theatre, Lord Essex openly accused his Grace of the fact, and asked him why he did not acknowledge his son. The Duke protested his friend was mistaken, and added that if it were so he should be proud to own him" (Henry Barton Baker, *Our Old Actors*, II.i.165-6).

51 John Doran had heard that Kean's grandfather was the bastard son of George Saville, Marquis of Halifax. See *"Their Majesties' Servants." Annals of the English Stage*, II: 377. If so, Kean could claim connections to two aristocratic houses.

52 The fourth Earl, also named John Stuart, died in 1814, only ten years before Kean's purchase.

53 George Raymond, *The Life and Enterprises of Robert William Elliston, Comedian*, 263. In the meantime, he ordered that Drury Lane place a bust of himself in the Green Room, as a "monumental *simulacra* of departed greatness." The ceremony for its placement included a procession, speeches, and a dinner in his honor (287-8). See also footnote 30, above.

54 Undocumented newspaper testimonial in Giles Playfair, *The Flash of Lightning*, 97.

55 James Winston, 23 July 1821, *Drury Lane Journal*, 35. Yet other presentations of fealty were more spontaneous: at the 7 April 1816 performance of *Merchant of Venice*, crowds, impatient for Kean's entrance, drummed, "Kean, Kean." Hazlitt noted that this chant soon morphed into "God save the *King*" (William Hazlitt, *Complete Works*, V:294). It's possible that many thought of Kean as a king. On this point, see Jane Moody, who writes that Kean's attempt to destroy Booth suggested a monopolistic system that "precisely corresponded to that being practiced in post-Waterloo Britain" (*Illegitimate Theatre*, 76).

56 William Hazlitt described the beast as an "American lion, a pumah, a sort of a great dog. But still it shews the nature of the man, and the spirited turn of his genius" (*Complete Works*, XX:111).

57 George Taylor notes that actors who were employed by the "Royal" Theatres Covent Garden and Drury Lane were expected to act as if they were royal servants (*The French Revolution and the London Stage*, 192).

pointing out that David Garrick, to whom Kean was often compared, had performed before King George II and King George III and had been a close friend of Lord Chancellor Camden and the Lord Chief Justice, the Earl of Mansfield.[58] Likewise, John Philip Kemble, who had reigned supreme in London prior to Kean's sudden ascension, was a cultivated and well-read man, one who discussed the finer points of elocution. Once, he even politely corrected the Prince of Wales for his "Frenchified" pronunciation of "oblige." His manners were so impeccable that on another occasion he challenged an actor to a duel for being rude to him at dinner.[59] Despite this conduct, which many might call pompous, Kemble never overstepped his position, was deferential and polite, was always a man who "offstage faded into the respectability of the middle-class."[60] Why shouldn't Kean follow Garrick's and Kemble's respective—and respectable—examples? But he wasn't really like either of these actors. Kean's characters died in tragic glory and were praised for their passion and physical vigor. Why should he be expected to be anonymous when his audacity had made him rich, famous, and—if not respectable—sought?

Kean ignored the committee members of Drury Lane. Sometimes, he openly contradicted them. Told to act more like the sexually-staid Kemble, Kean seduced his sister.[61] As for drinking, said Byron: "[Lord] Essex has endeavored to persuade Kean not to get drunk; the consequence of which is, that he has never been sober since."[62] Similarly, after receiving a letter from the Drury Lane Committee chastising him for his whoring, Kean told his wife, Mary, "This is all my fault, d—d fool that I am!" Yet, when asked by the Committee if Kean needed anything before a performance, he replied, "Give me bread and cheese and a couple of whores."

Kean and the English Aristocracy

To be sure, Kean had reason to despise his moneyed and aristocratic masters. Early on, Kean had, in fact, tried to join their afternoon teas and dinner parties, always with disastrous results. As a star and a minor shareholder of Drury Lane Theatre (a position gained within a year of his stardom), Kean was expected to banquet with the Drury Lane Committee and their elitist friends: businessmen, politicians, nobles, even royals. They expected an *entrée* of fine, deep eloquence, accompanied by honeyed anecdotes and delicious jests, a *digestive* of lightness and delicacy. Instead,

---

58 On Garrick's royal performances and friendships with Lord Chancellor and the Lord Chief Justice, see Clement Parsons, *Garrick and His Circle*, 257-60; 262-4, 264-5.

59 James Aickin, a fellow actor, fired his revolver and missed; Kemble fired his shot into the air. As far as Kemble was concerned, honor had been served. See James Boaden, *Memoirs of John Philip Kemble*, II:60. Aicken's name is also spelled "Aiken" in some texts. I here follow Boaden's spelling.

60 Raymund FitzSimons, *Edmund Kean: Fire From Heaven*, 90.

61 On Kean's seduction of the novelist Ann Kemble, see Frederick S. Frank, *The First Gothics*, 78.

62 Byron, letter to Thomas Moore, 12 June 1815, *The Selected Letters*, 82.

they found a man of indigestible manners and conversation who pugnaciously disputed with lords; a man who loathed affectation but loved to quote half-chewed Latin. Drury Lane Committee member John Cam Hobhouse summed up Kean's limitations: notwithstanding his best efforts, Kean remained "a simple man" who ate "most pertinaciously with his knife."[63]

Kean did make attempts to be less vulgar. Even his sexual shenanigans might have been an attempt to fit into Regency elegance. It was an era, writes Venetia Murray, during which keeping an inamorata "was positively respectable."[64] Even Whig members of Parliament Charles James Fox and Richard Sheridan openly kept mistresses.[65] Yet, not everyone was so thrilled with this state of affairs. William Hazlitt sarcastically remarked that seducing married women had become princely *de rigueur*. In his essay, "On the Spirit of Monarchy," he wrote, "If however there is any foundation for the above insinuation, it throws no small light on the Spirit of Monarchy, which by the supposition implies in it the *virtual* surrender of the whole sex at discretion; and at the same time accounts perhaps for the indifference shown by some monarchs in availing themselves of so mechanical a privilege."[66] Further, the press had a field day uncovering scandal after scandal, delving into who slept with whom, how much a royal paid for his mistress, and how much of the money came from public funds. The most famous sex scandal of the era involved the Regent, the future George IV, who was secretly married to a Catholic woman, Maria Anna Fitzherbert, while publicly married to his cousin, Princess Caroline of Brunswick, and notoriously cheating on both of them. No less scandalously, the aforementioned third Earl of Bute was rumored to be the lover of the Dowager Queen.

Perhaps this conduct was appropriate for a peer, but when Kean, a common player, did the same, society banished him. As Harriette Wilson, one of the Regency's most notorious courtesans, noted, "beyond all doubt, a man ought to be of royal blood before he presumes to commit adultery, except in private...."[67] Thus, when Kean flamboyantly flashed his new-made money and claimed he was the illegitimate son of the Duke of Norfolk, society merely observed that this tawdry actor was denigrating the reputation of a peer of the realm and was encouraging the notion that adultery was acceptable.[68] When visiting even the finest households, the public perception

---

63 Quotations found in the undocumented Raymund FitzSimons, *Edmund Kean: Fire From Heaven*, 77-8. Joseph Farington recorded one dinner conversation concerning the actor: "He is an *Humbug*: His acting is often false, & without anything like classical taste. He is a *Pot-House* Actor" (*The Diaries of Joseph Farington*, VII:228).

64 Venetia Murray, *An Elegant Madness*, 134.

65 By way of comparison, Jonathan David Gross argues that Tories were "seemingly uninterested in seducing women or keeping mistresses" (*Byron: The Erotic Liberal*, 33).

66 William Hazlitt, *Complete Works*, XIX:263.n.1.

67 Undocumented quotation, found in Venetia Murray, *An Elegant Madness*, 141.

68 If whoremongering is a genetic trait, it is possible that the eleventh Duke of Norfolk, who died in 1815, at the age of seventy, sired Kean. Ill-educated, and unhygienic, the Duke sired many bastards, particularly to lower-class women, including poverty-stricken gypsies, Negroes, and Jews. To give the Duke credit, he did leave legacies for all of his progeny. Food,

was that Kean probably debauched every woman in it, whether she was a duchess or a scullery maid. For reasons, then, ranging from silverware to seduction, from crass manners to class warfare, the doors to high society were eventually shut on Kean.

Embarrassed by this turn of events, the actor created a heroic narrative in which he turned his back on the nobility. According Kean, all the aristocrats loved him, until he was seen walking down Bond Street with the vocalist Mr. Incledon. Lord Essex took Kean aside and explained to him that, while he was fond of Mr. Incledon, he clearly "never did belong to our '*set*,'" and, since his "popularity is now quite *passèe* [*sic*], it is a duty which I conceive I owe you, as well as myself and our friends, to say, that your continued intimacy with him may militate against your own reception in the circles in which you have hitherto been a most welcomed guest." Given the choice of remaining friends with the old actor or joining this new clique, Kean told Essex: "if I could now desert him in the decline of his popularity, or the fall of fortune, I should little deserve the friendship of any man, and be quite unworthy of the favorable opinion your Lordship has done me the honour to entertain of me." So saying, he left the stunned Essex and continued on.[69] On another occasion, during a dinner party held in Kean's honor, the actor, bored by his aristocratic company, quietly asked the butler to fetch his coat. As he dressed, Kean told the servant, in a whisper just loud enough for Lord William Pitt Lennox to overhear: "Six months ago not one of these great lords would have noticed the poor stroller; now their adulation is unbounded, Pshaw! I prefer a quiet glass with a friend like you, to all their champagne, effervescent, frothy as themselves!"[70]

Kean's Bastard Warfare

Whether these stories were factually true or not, the Tory Press was none-too-thrilled by Kean's supposed thumbings at Essex and other English aristocrats. If the Whigs attacked the Prince of Wales for his affairs, the same weapon might be drawn to decapitate this lecherous dragon. On 14 September 1820, Kean was in court because he had, allegedly, debauched a young girl, who was now with child. She admitted that she was unsure who had sired the child, and Kean was excused from paying damages.[71]

---

particularly beef, was another of the Duke's passions. He was a member of the "Sublime Society of Beef-Steaks," a group of gourmands who insisted their steaks weigh at least three and as much as four pounds each. The Duke, at one sitting, might devour as many as fifteen of them (Ibid., 169). The time-frame for this feat is not specified, though it does indicate that eating itself was one more pleasure seen as increasingly indistinct from other stagings of physical excess.

69   Theodore Norton, *Kean, A Poem*, Appendix, 24.

70   Lord William Pitt Lennox, *Plays, Players, and Playhouses*, I:230.

71   At least James Winston makes no mention of a fine. See *Drury Lane Journal*, 18. *Oxberry's Dramatic Mirror* mentions the case. The destitute girl thought that Kean would make "an indulgent papa" but admitted that she was unsure who was the father. Kean, who "often relieved her as he passed at night," was certainly a candidate (147).

With this story in hand, Tory writers claimed that Kean's sex life was more than simple, lewd behavior; it was a deliberate act of class warfare. Writing on the miseries of sexual license, Charles Horne warned:

> If, I say, they [cheating men] only debauched the wives and daughters of their own rank, and it extended no further, the evil would not be an object of magnitude, or indeed of any consideration; but the debauching of each other is by no means sufficient for the gratification of their unbounded appetites, increased to the most unnatural rapacity by every artifice that can be devised.[72]

Going on, Horne argued that the real danger was not that rich were sleeping with poor, but that their union might create a brood of bastards—a class to which Kean belonged—which would be inherently predisposed to further acts of sexual license. Bastards would mate with prostitutes, daughters would become prostitutes, devastating, eventually, all sense of class structure. "If it is suffered to continue, prostitutes will become so numerous, that they may by their superiority of numbers, rise up and destroy all the modest women in the nation."[73] Numbers were on his side. The author calculated that in 1783 more than 40,000 women were engaged in London prostitution.[74] In 1812, William Hale put the number of London prostitutes at 50,000—roughly one in five London women between the ages of 18 and 50.[75] Unless something was done to stop this process, bastards would have to be allowed into polite society.[76] Already, one could see this phenomenon: the Duke of Clarence fathered ten bastards with the actress Mrs. Jordan, acknowledged them all, set up legacies for them all, even gave them a title: FitzClarence. His eldest son, George, was even given an earldom. (He was the Earl of Munster.)

While the Duke might be lauded for paying for his bastards, very few had his financial wherewithal.[77] What of the other unprovided illegitimates? A generation of starving children would inevitably rise with justified hatred for their fathers. It was

---

72 Charles Horne, "Serious Thoughts on the Miseries of Sedition and Prostitution," 59.

73 Ibid., 53.

74 Ibid., 48.

75 William Hale, "Considerations on the Causes and the Prevalence of Female Prostitution," 84. In 1843, Ralph Wardlaw disputed these claims: "It *is not*, — it *cannot be*, true, nor even an approach to truth" but, nonetheless agreed that prositition annihilated "all bonds of kindred, all the sweet and blessed charities of domestic life, and all the possibilities of regular government…" (*Lectures on Female Prositution*, 28, 15).

76 William Hale anticipated Reverend Thomas Malthus' *Essay on the Principle of Population* (1798), in which he argued that poor people were more sexually active that rich people. Hazlitt pointed out the sexual scandals among the rich were common enough. For an overview, see A.C. Grayling, *The Quarrel of the Age: The Life and Times of William Hazlitt*, 112-16. Oddly, Malthus assumes that even among the extremely sexual active, all children would be born in wedlock and that all fathers would at least attempt to support their offspring.

77 Similarly, the Prince of Wales' mistress, Mrs. Fitzherbert, was given an allowance of £3000 a year for life (Saul David, *Prince of Pleasure*, 154).

only a matter of time before this lustful and hateful litter attempted to take what it could not legitimately inherit. Sexual intercourse with mistresses and peasant girls, argued Horne, led directly to social anarchy and the worst excesses of the French Revolution.

Hazlitt's Counterargument: Frailty, Thy Name is Genus!

By copulating with housewives, whores, and duchesses, Kean's theatrical seductions would transform society, one drunken night and four ruined women at a time[78]—this outrageous number, as will be made explicit, was fairly accurate. But not every one was willing to condemn Kean. William Hazlitt, always (it seems) a Kean apologist, reacted to such arguments in an essay entitled "What is the People?" in which he urged Kean not to adopt any "hereditary pretensions." While not openly advocating bastardy, Hazlitt did argue that the aristocratic obsession with lineages was nothing more than a blue-blooded excuse to maintain social privilege. He made his point by exploring a fiction: "Suppose Mr. Kean had a son... [and] what if Mr. Kean should take it into his head to empower him and his heirs for ever, with this hopeful commencement, to play all the chief parts of tragedy?"[79] No, it was self-evident that Kean would have to go one day, but his successor would be chosen on the basis of his talent, not his name or wealth.[80]

As for Kean's social excesses, Hazlitt played devil's advocate.[81] Since Kean generated joy and pain for his audience, it was the actor's duty to hone his skills by indulging himself in sensuous entertainments. A successful actor "requires some corresponding physical excitement … and not a little to allay the ferment of the spirits attendant on success."[82] Surely there is a similarity between the seduction of a lone woman and the seduction of an audience, whether literary or theatrical?

Hazlitt sees Kean as an artist who gave pleasurable sensations (terror, tragedy, pathos, and, for his selected partners, sexual delight) and was paid in kind (applause, cheers, worship, and of course, money, which allowed him to purchase other forms of

---

78 This thesis is in basic agreement with Paul Friedland who notes that "The French Revolution ... stands at the threshold of an era in which theatrical and political forms became virtually indistinguishable" ("Parallel Stages," 250).

79 Not all such arguments revolved around Kean: "we see no more reason why Mr. Stephen Kemble should play Falstaff, than why Louis XVIII is qualified to fill a throne, because he is fat, and belongs to a particular family" (William Hazlitt, *Complete Works*, V:340).

80 Ironically, Kean's successors were obsessed with claiming his name. See Chapter 5.

81 It should be noted that Hazlitt liked to visit prostitutes, so his defense of Kean may have been self-serving.

82 William Hazlitt, *Complete Works*, V:293. Hazlitt was quick to add that he found such thinking wrongheaded: "If there is any tendency to dissipation beyond this in the profession of a player, it is owing to the state of public opinion, which paragraphs like the one we have alluded to are not calculated to reform" (Ibid., V:293-4). Thus, Hazlitt would have been horrified to learn that his defense has stood the test of time.

sensuous gratifications). Kean—who was raised by a part-time whore—sold himself night after night. Indeed, his demand that managers provide him with prostitutes before each show suggests that Kean saw sexual encounters as raw material for his own art, a necessary preparative for performance. Practicing the art of seduction may explain (though not excuse) Kean's most outrageous sexual antics: copulating *between* acts within the theater itself.

In Kean's day, the main feature (i.e. the Shakespeare play he was performing that evening) was preceded by a variety of sketches and musical pieces. More entertainments often took place between acts. After the play proper, yet more entertainments followed. Though not designed for the purpose, these breaks allowed Kean opportunity to have sex. James Winston, a member of staff at Drury Lane, recorded the following:

> **JANUARY 17 [1820]:** ((Kean)) requested the rehearsal might not be till twelve as he should get drunk that night—said he had frequently three women to ((stroke)) during performance and that two waited while the other was served. Penley said he had [formerly] seen ((Storace)) waiting her turn. This night he had only one woman (Smith) though he was much ((infected)) [with syphilis]. [83]

> **JUNE 5 [1820]:** On ((Kean)) being asked … whether he would require to wait long between acts [i.e—would his between act 'quickies' take long], he said, "No, not now, his *bubo* [syphilitic sores] was ((broke))"—same night a woman waiting.[84]

> **FEBRUARY 26 [1825]:** Kean came into my room. I asked him what sort of house he had at Brighton. (He had been playing there for three nights.) He said, good, but not so good as the whore [he] had….[85]

Kean wasn't utterly irresponsible. On July 19, 1830 after a particularly feeble performance of *Richard III*, Kean stated in a letter to W. Dunn Esq. that he felt "almost ashamed to ask for payment … not would I but for Doctors Bills—for Lancets & Boluses—however I hope all will soon be better than ever, these little casualties of nature teach us to be cautious."[86] But the relationship between his early success and his sex-life cannot be discounted. Perhaps Kean's sex life was an experimental scenario wherein he could test his powers again and again, and then measure his abilities against his theatrical performances, but these acts were far

---

83 James Winston, *Drury Lane Journal*, 4. An anonymous reader of this manuscript points out that this may have been Nancy Storace, a major singing star of the era. In 1816, her fiancé, John Braham ran off to France to pursue an affair with a Mrs. Wright. The affair generated a fair amount of satire, but none of it suggests that Storace was promiscuous. See Jonathan Reynolds, *Dramatis Personæ*, 88 (2005):11.

84 James Winston, *Drury Lane Journal*, 11.

85 Ibid., 106.

86 Gordon Craig, *The Life and Theatrical Career of Edmund Kean*, 39.

from private.[87] The audience could not have been oblivious to what was going on. Women who fainted, or pretended to faint, were taken to Kean's (un)dressing room. Those aware of their fate presumably volunteered; others may have been raped. The interval, then, served as yet another kind of theater, one in which patrons imagined the sexual acts taking place behind the curtain.

Kean's Audience and the Theatre of Social Transgression

Word of sexual improprieties at Drury Lane spread quickly. Prostitutes and sodomites flocked to the theater, eager to meet like-minded participants. One man complained, "It is impossible that individuals can visit our theatres with safety; the avenues leading thereto are nightly thronged by such [prostituted] wretches."[88] But was this Kean's fault?

Prostitution in London was nothing new, nor was its association with the theater. When Casanova came to London in 1763, he was impressed with the game: "a rich man can sup, bathe and sleep with a fashionable courtesan, of which there are many in London. It makes a magnificent debauch and only costs six guineas...."[89] What had changed during Kean's reign was its open advertisement. When Jane Austen saw Edmund Kean soon after his rise to fame—she said he was "too short"!—she made no mention of seeing prostitutes in and around Drury Lane.[90] Further, she had no qualms taking her sister, Cassandra, to the theater, which she did a few months later in November, again without remark. Unless we're going to radically rewrite Jane Austen's propriety, we can infer that Drury Lane, at least in 1814, was still perfectly respectable. In 1816, a constable noted that Drury Lane prostitutes were beginning to congregate regularly both in and around the theaters. Being near so many theater patrons, he wrote, made it "quite handy for them to go on with their purposes."[91] By 1822, Kean had fully transformed Drury Lane and the very notion of going to the theater from a social convenience to a sexual transgression:

> The galleries, generally visited by the industrious part of the community, are frequently polluted by gangs of well-dressed scoundrels, who situate themselves in various places to

---

87 Certainly, Kean's interval rituals did not differ markedly from his offstage activities. When not in the theatre, Kean spent most or all of his free time in the bars, with what FitzSimons calls the actor's "drink-swilling toadies" or copulating with whores (*Edmund Kean: Fire From Heaven*, 88).

88 "The Bishop!!" 353.

89 Giacomo Casanova, *The Memoirs of Jacques Casanova*, VI:258.

90 Austen first saw Kean on Saturday, 5 March 1814. See *Jane Austen's Letters*, 377-8, 380-81. This is not to say that there were no prostitutes in or around the theater. Austen might have been fooled by their elegant dress. In 1813, *The Christian Monitor* reported that there "were a number of well-dressed prostitutes doing business in the foyer" of Drury Lane for the premiere of Coleridge's play *Remorse*. See Richard Holmes, *Darker Reflections*, 335.

91 Tony Henderson, *Disorderly Women*, 59.

insult decent individuals; boys and simple looking clowns are the object they look for, in order that they may more easily assault them....[92]

Local enforcement tried to intervene but found it powerless to stop prostitutes in the theater itself. The dividing lines between the parishes of St. Martin's, St. Paul's, and Covent Garden ran right through the center of the Drury Lane lobby, hence it was outside of parish jurisdictions. Kean was now free to turn Drury Lane into a Georgian Club Med of social taboo.[93]

Fact and Fiction

Yes, Dumas' Kean might have engaged in backstage canoodling, but how close was he to the aforementioned social activist who helps Kitty, Bob, and Pistol in Dumas' play? As stated, Alexandre Dumas had seen the actor Edmund Kean in 1828, but the title character of his *Kean* play differs from that Kean in many ways: the real Kean was married with two sons and was known for his Richard III, Iago, Othello, and Shylock; he was a known failure as Romeo. Dumas' Kean, on the other hand, is single, childless, and famed for his Romeo. In Dumas' play, Kean is a friend of the Prince of Wales and vies with him for female prey; in reality, there is no record of Kean having ever mixed with the Prince Regent, and he would certainly have to be careful in what he did with, and said about, him.

It is true that the Regent was a notorious womanizer, particularly in his youth, but that was in the 1790s. By the time of his death in 1830, George weighed 308 pounds, and his stomach reached his knees.[94] Even without the Prince's money and power, it's difficult to imagine the Prince of Wales, or as he was sometimes called, the Prince of Whales, hanging out—much less competing—with Kean. Their social stations were just too far apart. It would be like Prince Charles and Kid Rock hitting on married women at a Walmart.[95]

---

92 "The Bishop!!" 353. The Duke of Newcastle noted that the stage had degenerated into "actual obscenity" and then praised Kean's son Charles for helping raise the moral standards of the theater. See *The Kean Banquet*, 12.

93 Tony Henderson, *Disorderly Women*, 73.

94 Venetia Murray, *An Elegant Madness*, 187. Ironically, the Prince did spend time with Kemble, but the two certainly did not go about prowling for virgins.

95 Robert J. Nelson writes that Kean as an actor "is paradoxically almost forgotten in Dumas's play." See his *Play Within A Play*, 95. Though not concerning Kean, there is one historical vignette that does bear some resemblance to Dumas' play. In 1781, the Prince of Wales had an affair with the wife of Count Karl von Hardenburg. They first met at a concert given in the Queen's apartments in Buckingham Palace, and the Prince noted that she was "a very sensible, agreeable, pleasant woman, but devilish severe." After their second meeting at one of the Queen's card parties, the Prince was entirely captivated: "From that moment, the fatal though delightful passion arose in my bosom for her, which has made me since the most miserable and wretched of men." Eventually, they became lovers. The Count, outraged by his wife's conduct, ordered her to break off the affair. Instead, she secretly proposed that the

Flirting with the Porno-Political Tradition

But Dumas' play was not meant to be read as a literal history of the actor. Rather, the play flirts with the French porno-political tradition.[96] According to Jean-Marie Goulemot, pornography as a metaphor for political inequality came into its own around 1765.[97] The growth of pornographic writings, the critic declares, was "without doubt a product of those uncertain and troubled [pre-Revolutionary] times."[98] As Lynn Hunt points out, while pornography might be traced back, in various guises, thousands of years, the "French Revolution marked a turning point in the history of Western pornography, not only in France but elsewhere in the Western world."[99] Politically motivated pornography reached its zenith in the 1790s and only lost its association with subversive philosophy and politics in the 1830s.[100] Dumas' play, then, was a bit late to the party but determined to go out with a bang.

Surprisingly, the play is (comparatively) sexually sedate. There is none of the vulgarity found in the anonymous and unperformed French play, *The Patriotic Brothel* (1791), which begins Act Two with the following stage direction: "Barnave fucks Théroigne's cunt, while Bailly fucks Barnave's arse; Lafayette mounts the queen again and gives her another good fuck." While this closet play depicted the aristocracy as sexually depraved, other works called for equality on the basis of sexual power, a key feature of Dumas' *Kean*. For example, the anonymous French play *The Royal Dildo* (1789) has "Juno" or the Queen of France, Marie Antoinette, rejecting soft aristocratic phalluses in favor of hardier peasant stock. *The Royal Dildo* was not designed for mere titillation; rather, it subversively linked sexual taboos to established social hierarchies.[101] The play's sex parties rearrange the aristocratic

---

Prince run away with her, an appealing romantic gesture. However, the boyish Prince soon revealed all to his mother and "cried excessively." The Queen informed the King, who ordered the Count to take his wife and return to Germany. The Count divorced his wife and ended up becoming State Chancellor (Saul David, *Prince of Pleasure*, 28-31).

96 Dumas had recently written a number of political history plays which touched on many of the themes of the French Revolution, including *Henri III* (1829), *Charles VII* (1831), and *Trente Ans* (1832), but they had been only politely received. His more successful plays were sexually-stewed dramas: *Christine* (1828) was a thinly disguised drama about Napoleon's ex-mistress; his play *Antony* (1831) centers on a bastard who attacks his society by ruining the reputations of virgins. The subject of *Kean* allowed Dumas to combine both aspects in one play.

97 Jean Marie Goulemot, *Forbidden Texts*, 22.

98 Ibid., 25.

99 James Grantham Turner notes that England had a similar political pornography, but it died out around 1685. See *Libertines and Radicals In Early Modern London: Sexuality, Politics, and Literary Culture, 1630-1685*, 252.

100 Lynn Hunt, "Pornography and the French Revolution," 302-3.

101 The Queen of *The Royal Dildo* differs from traditional depictions of erotically energized French queens. In the medieval era, the sexually unfaithful queen was considered "evil" and might have even questioned the logic of a woman's political power. See Peggy

divisions of master and servant upon a principle of sexual vigor.[102] For instance, when demanding her maid bring her a group of men to have intercourse with, the Queen warns her procurer:

> Take care you don't bring back that pack of turds,
> Mooning pimps, fake marquis,
> Who spend half their time gazing at their reflections,
> Those splendid specimens called fops;
> At the signal to advance, they turn traitor:
> Their cocks at first seem hale and hearty,
> But the bugger shoots his load in a second and scurries off!

As a class, the Queen prefers mindless, working-class studs: "I want cocks whose shaft/Knows neither rest nor measure in fucking."

If this Kean is related to French revolutionary pornography, his endless sexual liaisons might even be seen as a Rousseauian paradigm for cultural succession. In his *Discourse on the Origins of Inequality*, Rousseau writes that the ideal man should "not even know his own children."[103] In place of blood-ties, displaced sexual passion should rule as society's chief hegemonic force. The idea is central to his *Confessions*, in which the author discusses all the women he has enjoyed or longed to enjoy, and all the women and men who longed to enjoy him. To Rousseau, political porn was not an act of literary escapism, but an attempt to turn desire into physicalized action, literally a call to masturbatory and emancipatory arms.

Rousseau's ideas of sex as revolutionary practice became the philosophical basis for much of the sexually explicit and anarchic literature of the period. Sade's *Eugénie*, for example, espouses the value of sex as an act of social freedom:

McCracken, *The Romance of Adultery*, 146-7. But such depictions and queries carried with them no imputation on the logic of royalist rule.

102 According to Robert Stam:

> Sex at its worst is an exercise in power, a clash of languages and mistranslations of linguistic, gestural, and proxemic codes, an epidermal juxtaposition of monologues, dialogue gone awry. Sex at its best is an 'ideal speech situation,' a communicative utopia, a microcarnival (just as carnival is macro-*jouissance*) characterized by 'free and familiar contact' and transindividual fusion. (*Subversive Pleasures*, 182)

103 Jean-Jacques Rousseau, *Discourse on the Origin of Inequality*, in *On the Social Contract and Discourses*, 137. Rousseau further argues that there are no natural bonds between fathers and sons:

> …. the son, completely independent of the father, then owes him merely respect and not obedience; for gratitude is clearly a duty that must be rendered, but not a right that can be demanded. Instead of saying that civil society derives from paternal power, on the contrary it must be said that it is from civil society that its power draws its principal force. (Ibid., 153)

Therefore, all men possess an equal right to enjoy all women; according to the laws of nature, no man can claim a woman for his sole, personal use. …. I therefore decree that these women, being much more drawn to the pleasures of lust than we, will be able to indulge their desires to their heart's content, entirely free from the bonds of matrimony…. Fair sex… cast off your shackles; nature wishes it so. Let your tastes be your only limits, your desire your only laws; let nature be your only morality. [104]

If the French saw sex as a libertarian force, phallically rising up to challenge the forces of oppression, who better than Kean, the ultimate masculine, ever-snatching, ever-roving, ever-sexually-erect conqueror, to put the dominant, ruling class in a weakened, feminine, supine, and dependent position? Dumas' Kean was more than an actor of revolutionary principle, he was a metaphor of where to hit the aristocracy: in the genitals.[105]

Dumas' Revolutionary Hero

Pedigrees and property have no place in Dumas' *Kean*, a sexual play-world where the old ways are abandoned, but only after being treated like whores, endlessly exploited, enjoyed, raped, exposed.[106] For example, in the play, Kean's foe, a titled member

---

104 Donatien-Alphonse-François de Sade, *La Philosophie dans le boudour*, in *Oeuvres Complétes du Marquis de Sade*, 3:515. Scott Carpenter sees de Sade's character Eugénie, the heroine of *La Philosophie dans le Boudour* (1795), as the complement to Rousseau's Emile. See his *Acts of Fiction*, 51. John Phillips connects Sade's *La Philosophie* to the serious revolutionary pamphlet: *Français, encore un effort, si vous voulez être républicains* [*Frenchmen, do it one more time if you want to be republicans*]. He further suggests that *La Philosophie* might have been meant ultimately to be performed as a play. See *Sade: The Libertine Novels*, 63 and 84. More likely, Sade's novel was meant for the imagination, like the closet play, *The Patriotic Brothel*. Timo Airksinen, a philosopher who has made a detailed study of de Sade's fiction, interprets *Justine* in the following political terms: "Meals of excrement symbolize hard work, with all the effort that goes into it and the waste which comes out. Silling is a parody of the Hobbesian social contract. The great drunken homosexual orgies at Silling are parodies of Socrates in the *Symposium*" (*The Philosophy of the Marquis de Sade*, 103). Objecting to Sade as a revolutionary, Lucienne Frappier-Mazur argues that Sade's pornography ridicules the idea of social inversion. His "porn" is not an attack upon traditional hierarchies, but a parody of the supposed new order of post-revolutionary France (*Writing the Orgy*, 125). The idea is intriguing but supposes that parody cannot further the ideology it subverts. As we will see with Twain, parodying Shakespeare can also bolster his reputation.

105 Descriptions of sex were used by royalist propagandists as well. Burke's *Reflections on the Revolution in France* implied the Queen had been raped when her private bedchamber was stormed by the peasant class: Has the Queen "really deserved these unvowed but unavenged murderous attempts, and those subsequent indignities more cruel than murder [?]" (178-9)

106 Presumably, Rousseau would have been horrified to see his ideology espoused in a play. In his "Letter to M. d'Alembert on the Theater" (1758), Rousseau argued against the use of theater as a moral agent on the grounds that actors had no core personality: "What is the

of the aristocracy, Lord Melville—sometimes translated as "Mewill"[107]—should be noble; instead, he disguises himself as Kean and attempts to rape an orphan girl. He fails because Kean confronts him, rips off his mask, and exposes him publicly. Kean's exposure of Melville is, in effect, a rape of a rapist.

Ethically, however, we do not see Kean and Melville as equals. Kean's acting, in which he plays a villain on stage and a hero off, is contrasted with Melville, who masquerades as Kean but remains a coward and a fool. This point is further emphasized when Kean challenges Melville, a peer of the realm, to a duel. The latter refuses on the basis that their stations are too disparate. Kean agrees, but with a remarkable distinction: it is Melville who has attempted to kidnap a defenseless girl and Kean who has protected her; it is Melville who wears disguises and Kean who acts without pretense. It is Kean, the actor, who is too good for this lord of England:

> Lord Melville has eaten away all the fortune of his ancestors with cards and dice, and betting on cock-fights and horse races. It's true that his coat-of-arms is tarnished by his own debauched life, and that instead of rising higher, he sinks lower.[108]

Dumas' point, surely, is to expose the dissipation of the aristocracy by noting that Kean, not Melville, is the nobler man. The point is re-emphasized when Count Koefield invites Kean to a party, and the actor turns him down. The Count is astonished and remarks, "We're living in a strange age, you'll have to admit. A mountebank refuses the invitation of an ambassador."[109] Kean himself notes that his only equal or "rival" is the Prince of Wales. Sartre suggested that this friendship of actor and prince is a sign of Dumas being carried away with pomp and royalty.[110] Without question, this is to misread the play. Kean may allow the Prince to be his equal, but he does not court him. Indeed, it is the Prince who courts Kean. When Kean shows his displeasure with the Prince, the latter whines, "Isn't my purse always at [your] service?"[111] However, Kean weighs the Prince's actions, not his assets.

This is rather inequitable of Kean. After all, is the Prince to give up his money simply to be on an equal footing with the actor? What else can he do but fund Kean so that he seems part of his millionaire set? Not only is Kean holding the Prince to an

---

talent of the actor? It is the art of counterfeiting himself, of putting on another character than his own, of appearing different than he is, of becoming passionate in cold blood, of saying what he does not think as naturally as if he did think it, and, finally, forgetting his own place by dint of taking another's." Rousseau's fears only reaffirm the actor as an agent for alternative social structures. Yet, when the French philosopher visited London in 1776, he was delighted to be fêted at the Theatre Royal, Drury Lane (J.H. Huizinga, *Rousseau: The Self-Made Saint*, 238).

107 See, for example, *Edmund Kean: Or, The Genius and the Libertine* (London: G. Vickers, 1847).

108 Alexandre Dumas, *Kean*, 120.

109 Ibid., 86.

110 Jean-Paul Sartre, "Kean," 241.

111 Alexandre Dumas, *Kean*, 132.

impossible standard of friendship, he doesn't even value the attempt on the Prince's part to establish or maintain that friendship. Kean is, quite simply, ready to do without any and all alliances with the rich and powerful. He has already exposed Melville as an abductor, but now, publicly, he will attack both Melville and the Prince—the former for trying to ravish Anna, the virgin orphan, the latter for hindering Kean's own attempt to ravish Elena, the married Countess of Koefield:

> ….to the health of the Prince of Wales, the most dissolute, the most indiscreet, the most egotistical of us all. To the health of the Prince of Wales, who loves every female, from the girl who serves sailors in a tavern, to the lady-in-waiting who places the royal cloak on his mother's shoulders. To the Prince of Wales, who cannot look at a woman without seducing her with his look. …. And who has a stick for Lord Melville? …. a stick for that miserable abductor of young girls, who carries a sword at his side, but refuses to fight with a man whose name he has stolen. And why will he not fight? Because he is a lord, and a peer![112]

After Kean denounces the Prince and Melville, the actor's protean powers are at an end. Kean is to be tried for his remarks against the Crown. This trial will not be in the theaters, nor will it be judged by the force of Kean's personality, but by the cold, unyielding weight of the law. That humiliation is avoided when the Prince intervenes privately to save Kean from jail; publicly, however, he is silent. His quotidian part, his acting the role of the Prince of Wales, is at odds with his personal beliefs, and, thus, like Kean, he is isolated, trapped by social constraints. Kean, too, is ultimately defeated by the social system he braved; he is forced to leave England.

The Failure of Dumas' *Kean*

At first blush, Kean is a powerful champion of the working class. Repudiating the notion of Shakespearean nobility and beauty as synonymous with a conservative agenda, Kean becomes a working-class hero, transcending the narrow social boundaries that inevitably contain him; he becomes, if only temporarily, the embodiment of the social possibilities of success denied to the lower classes.

Or does he? Despite Dumas' best attempts, elements of Kean's reluctant tyrant find their way into his play. If Kean is a hero of the lower-classes, in many ways he demonstrates why their revolution must fail. Firstly, Kean shows no real intellectual gifts. Dumas' Kean never prepares for his roles; his acting is artless, spontaneous; his movements, while powerful, are lacking in dignified grace—all of which imply a lack of cognitive skills and requisite mental concentration. Like the contemporary actor Russell Crowe, this Kean's one overriding appeal is his animal magnetism. His power resides in his phallus, not his intellect. As such, the image of the potentially superior Kean validates the notion that the lower classes can never be more than packhorses or studs.

---

112   Ibid., 143.

Secondly, if *Kean* is transgressive porn, it fails because it does not offer any practical options. At the close of *Kean*, no one seriously believes that Kean can change the political framework of the government.[113] Melville might enter the Coal Hole in temporary *dishabille*, but he remains a lord; it is Kean, in his aristocratic stage garb, who retains the title of servant. He says he is "the first actor of England," and that he "wouldn't change [his] place for that of the Prince of Wales," but admits that he is little more than a slave to his audience:

> If our heart is breaking, we have to play Falstaff—if full of joy, we must play Hamlet. Always a mask—never a face! .... What a torture! And if I go on stage with all the horrors of hell in my heart, I must smile when I'm supposed to smile, I must say every word as it should be said, or the audience will hiss.... They take us for machines, with no feelings but our roles.[114]

More than just failing to transform his society, Kean's acceptance of exile confirms just who is boss. To Anna and to Elena, Kean is Hamlet, Othello and Romeo, but to much of the nobility, he is a court jester, unable to bridge the gap between genius and status.[115] When Count Koefield invites Kean to his dinner party, it is "as one invites such people—in the quality of buffoon. We'll have him play us a scene from *Falstaff* after dinner"; "*it* will amuse us—we'll laugh."[116] Such passages help reinforce social regimentation. Kean is seen as a clever circus animal, no more.

Thirdly, what is best about Dumas' Kean is hardly worthy. It's true that Kean sees himself as better than Melville, but the actor assesses the lord's intellectual and moral shortcomings by Melville's ability to stage sexual misconduct. To be sure, Dumas' Kean is not championing a virgin because he believes in virginity—the play, after all, teems with sordid backstage business. Kean's main contention is that he has just as much a right to deflower virgins as any aristocrat. Out of context, Kean's defense of Anna seems wholesome; in context, it is merely to argue that the spoiled have no monopoly on despoiling. Kean is better than Melville because when he sets up a rape, he doesn't get caught. Melville is an amateur rake; Kean is a master whose art is indissolubly linked to gambling, adultery, and fiscal irresponsibility.

It's possible, of course, that Dumas is arguing here that a representative of the people can be just as good (or bad) as any aristocrat. But the longer the play goes on, the less worthy Kean is of our trust and even our interest. His attempts to seduce Elena, the Prince's mistress, seem clownish. Why is he unable to give over his interest in this married woman? The answer, of course, is that *Kean* is not so much story of

---

113 On this point, a return to *The Royal Dildo* will be helpful. Despite the Queen's dependence upon working-class men for sexual satisfaction, once the orgy is over, no one disputes that the Queen of France is more powerful than the men who service her.

114 Alexandre Dumas, *Kean*, 136.

115 On this point, see Richard S. Stowe, *Alexandre Dumas père*, 56.

116 Alexandre Dumas, *Kean*, 85; emphasis my own. Rather than *Falstaff*, the Count means either *1* or *2 Henry IV*. The second quotation is from Alexandre Dumas, *Kean*, 85; emphasis my own.

one man realizing his own self worth, as realizing that he is just as worthless as those he despises. Thus, Kean epitomizes the worst consequences of social change and represents ways in which revolutionary energies of social conscience are drained by undisciplined behavior, illicit desire, and personal narcissism.

Even Kean's sexual powers are implicitly questioned. If Kean uses sex as a revolutionary weapon, its discharge seems to backfire more often than not. If Kean is such a great lover, then why does Elena cheat on him? If his sexual prowess makes him superior to the Prince, then why does Elena prefer the Prince's company to Kean's? If he undermines hierarchies, then why is he the Countess' toy-boy? Why isn't she his mistress? And why, at the play's end, does he follow Anna to America? Shouldn't she be following him? Lastly, Dumas' play comes too late to make a difference. The play champions the democratic principles of equality, even while French equality itself was no more than a nostalgic enterprise. The French Revolution had ended with the rise of a tyrant, and even that tyrant, Napoleon, had been defeated, and replaced, in turn, with a monarch. The idea that all men were (and are) created equal coming from the mouth of a vulgar actor only suggests that the idea was (and is) a theatrical illusion. All this actor can do is play to the crowd and pretend that there is a better world elsewhere.

Chapter 4

Kean as Comedy

On 19 November 1825, the American newspaper, *The Courier* counseled the public not to buy tickets to any of Kean's upcoming shows:

> For his vices and crimes committed in Europe, it does not belong to us to inflict any other punishment than neglect. He sets up no claim to innocence, to purity of moral character. … No one can sincerely respect him; no one can love him. But every one can pity while he condemns, and no one can carry his resentment so far as to drive from the face of the earth the wretched fallen creature on whom the Almighty seems to have set the seal of his displeasure.

The advice was ignored. When Kean arrived in Boston for a scheduled performance on 21 December, the manager of the theater expressed his fears. Kean gave an *impromptu* interview with the *Columbian Centinel*, in which he asked the citizens of Boston for clemency. "The first step toward the Throne of Mercy is confession," said Kean, and "I have suffered for my errors and indiscretions, my loss of fame and fortune is but too melancholy an illustration."[1]

If anything, the apology merely intensified their rage. "Kean! Kean!" chanted the mob, as they ripped chairs out of the pit and smashed them into makeshift bats; iron hand railings were pulled from their moorings and carried as clubs. Kean exited stage right, pursued by an angry mob.[2]

Four days later, on Christmas Eve 1825, *The Christian Register* published this rather uncharitable assessment of the actor:

> Whilst we deeply regret the lawless conduct of the mob violently entering and mutilating the building [the Richmond Theatre], we feel constrained to say, in relation to Mr. Kean, that, with men of correct moral feelings it cannot be esteemed a subject of regret that this corrupt and degraded man, after having been publicly exposed as an adulterer in his own country, and driven, as it were from society by the force of public sentiment,—should be allowed to insult and dishonor our city by showing himself publicly among us.[3]

---

1   Quoted in Harold Newcomb Hillebrand, *Edmund Kean*, 263. Charles H. Shattuck suggests that Bostonians were still harboring a grudge against Kean for his 1820-21 tour. See his *Shakespeare on the American Stage*, 42.

2   J. Fitzgerald Molloy, *The Life and Adventures of Edmund Kean*, II:160-61. For a secondary and somewhat differing account, see Harold Newcomb Hillebrand, *Edmund Kean*, 264-5.

3   *Christian Register* 24 December 1825, in Press Clippings, Personal Collection.

On 18 January 1826, Kean appeared again, this time in Philadelphia. "The tragedy [of *Richard III*] then began, and was continued in pantomime, the noise drowning all sound of the players' voices...."[4] Four months later, on 13 March, he was in Charleston. Kean was now in fear for his very life. In broken tones, he pleaded with the manager, "For God's sake, I entreat you not to let me play if you think the audience will not receive me. I have not strength of mind and body ... to undergo a continuance of the suffering and persecution I have already endured." After the performance, Kean said, "Hear them moving out—how they would like to fall upon me like a pack of famished wolves!"[5] The last quotation comes laced with irony. Kean, who maintained his own power over London theater by releasing his Wolves, now found himself to be similarly victimized. Yet, even with the fear of attack, he remained in America and earned a fortune wherever he went. Kean sent £2550 to his London bank in the first five months of this supposedly disastrous American tour.[6] If Kean was paying for his sins, it was coming at a handsome profit.

Why Did Kean Go to America in 1825?

The answer was sex. It began as so many of Kean's affairs had. During one of Kean's soliloquies, a woman fainted and the star stopped the play to have her carried to his private dressing room. Her name was Charlotte Cox, wife of Alderman Cox, a member of the Drury Lane Committee, and she became one of Kean's mistresses almost instantly. Charlotte was perfect for Kean, young, vulgar and over-sexed, but her relationship to the nexus of Drury Lane's authority cannot be overlooked. Kean may have bedded her as a way of asserting his power.

Kean Re-Pressed

Biographers do not dispute the fact that Kean had an affair with Charlotte Cox but prefer a less petty motive. For example, Giles Playfair's solution is to explain Kean's sexual infidelities as a form of melancholy consolation:

> No wonder his affair with Charlotte Cox began about this time. It was the perfect psychological moment. What was there left for him but to fall in love? He, who could not survive without adulation, fled to a woman who was prepared to give it to him unstintingly. Charlotte had become 'essential to his happiness.' In her arms he found an exhilarating refuge from his wounded pride.[7]

---

4   J. Fitzgerald Molloy, *The Life and Adventures of Edmund Kean*, II:168.
5   Harold Newcomb Hillebrand, *Edmund Kean*, 268.
6   Gordon Craig, *The Life and Theatrical Career of Edmund Kean*, 48.
7   Giles Playfair, *Edmund Kean*, 193.

Yet other Kean biographers improbably describe his dalliance with Charlotte as an expression of his innocence. Molloy, for example, blames Charlotte. Kean was simply not sophisticated enough to see that she was using him:

> That he was thoroughly fascinated by this woman there is no doubt, and that she, a heartless coquette, used his blind passion for her own and her husband's benefit was evident to all. The sums she received from him, whose generosity amounted to extravagance, can only be guessed from the occasional reference to money which their correspondence contained, and from evidence given. James Newman remembered handing an envelope containing notes to Miss Wickstead for Mrs. Cox one evening at the theatre; and Kean writes to her, 'What money you want you shall have at three hours' notice.' When in Londonderry, he tells her, 'I cannot send you the money, for there are no banks here, or in any other town that I have been acting in, but write to Holton,' and he encloses a note for Holton, saying he was to let her have 'whatever money she may ask you for in my name.' [8]

The affair generated a significant amount of press and with good reason: Kean was an easy and legal target. There were libel laws protecting the royals and the peers of the realm, none for commoners. When Leigh Hunt wrote of the Prince of Wales' sexual dalliances, he went to jail for two years; attacking Kean carried no such danger.[9]

Besides, this was a good, juicy story: Mr. Cox had found the love-letters Kean had written to his wife. The affair between the two was now over. Charlotte had left both men for a clerk. Kean took his revenge by sleeping with two whores and then sent them to Mrs. Cox to tell her of it.[10] But there was also Mr. Cox to consider. Now destitute, he sued Kean for compensation and published the papers in Whig presses. The trial was a circus, the court room noise "exactly resembled that of the over-crowded pit of the theatre."[11] Kean's letters were read aloud in court and published in the papers. They swing wildly from the romantic:

---

8   J. Fitzgerald Molloy, *The Life and Adventures of Edmund Kean*, II:114. Raymund FitzSimons, on the other hand, argues that Kean's acts were both selfish and vengeful. Seducing Charlotte:

> gave a wonderful boost to his [Kean's] self-esteem. Although he claimed to have rejected high society, his love-hate attitude towards it still remained; he scorned it because he wanted to be a part of it. Mounted on Charlotte's hot, exciting body, he was not only entering most intimately into that society but also proving his dominance over it. To his delight, he found her to be a lady at table and a harlot in bed. (*Edmund Kean: Fire From Heaven*, 142)

9   In 1811, the British government sued Hunt over a story in the *Examiner* concerning the brutality meted to British soldiers. The government charged that the article implied French soldiers were better treated than English soldiers, a libel which might undermine morale at a time of war. The Judge thought him guilty, but the jury found his innocent of the charges. He was eventually imprisoned for slandering the Prince of Wales. See Ann Blainey, *Immortal Boy*, 43-44, 58-59.

10   James Winston, 30 June 1824, *Drury Lane Journal*, 90.

11   *Cox V. Kean*, 31.

**Plate 6:   Charlotte Cox, an unlikely femme fatale. Kean's friend Grattan said
                    of her "she was so little remarkable in any way that I can scarcely
                    remember her appearance." Reprinted by kind permission of the
                    Harry Ransom Humanities Research Center; The University of Texas
                    at Austin.**

> O God! Charlotte, how I love you. If such a feeling is a crime, why are we given it? I did not
> seek it. The power that will condemn has placed you in my way; the same inspiring hand
> that framed my better qualities pointed to you as the object of my love—my everlasting
> love. I must not doubt the justice of the great Being, and have little or no faith in the
> general Tempter. Whate'er it be, 'You are my fate—my heaven or my hell.'

to the lewd:

> My dear, dear, dear, little B***h,—I do declare, when next I see you, I will whip *   *   *
> *   *   * .   .... Be a good girl, and do not fret, or remember the whipping.[12]

The immoral words are veiled, but we can assume Kean was promising some playful
S & M. In the end, Kean was found guilty and ordered to pay Mr. Cox £800.

Kean's penance was more than financial; his very mind seemed to crack. On stage,
the actor confused lines from one play with another and, even more alarmingly, often

---

12 Ibid., 25. The reader may see some parallels between Kean's scandal
and the 1993 Royal Scandal in which the British press published transcripts of an
alleged telephone conversation between Camilla Parker Bowles and the Prince of Wales. The
conversation featured, among other intimate comments, the Prince's declaration that, if only
he were a tampon, he could be closer to Camilla.

drifted from Shakespeare altogether and began talking to himself about the his recent troubles.[13] One friend wrote:

> I never saw a man so changed .... he had all the air of desperation about him .... The day I saw him, he sat down to the piano, notwithstanding the agitated state of his mind, and sang for me 'Lord Ullin's Daughter' with a depth and power, and sweetness that quite electrified me. ... I could not repress a deep sentiment of sorrow at the wreck he presented of genius, fame and wealth. At this period I believe he had not one hundred pounds left of the many thousands he had received. His mind seemed shattered; he was an outcast on the world.[14]

The crowds, hypocrites all, still paid to see him, if only to gaze at the actor they now considered a monster.

All this he could manfully stomach, but a new form of attack had caught him unaware and had crippled him more than any physical blow. The Kean-Cox letters had become the talk of the town, and Kean was comically roasted. They were writing satirical pamphlets about him; he was being recast as a clown, and there was nothing he could do. George Daniel poked fun at Kean's Richard III, who, rather than plotting deaths, now lolled about drinking with his friends:

> Plantagenet, with heart so stout,
>   This joyful greeting sends;—
> My boys, we'll have a merry bout—
>   King Richard and his friends![15]

Similarly, an anonymous satirist penned *The Poetic Epistles of Edmund*, which included the following verse mouthed by Kean in Macbeth-dress:

> O sweet Little Breeches! Wherever I wander
> Thou still art my theme—still on thee do I ponder!
> My heart has discarded all other b—s
> To love only thee, most becoming of witches![16]

"Othello *Little* Breeches" as he was now called, became a clownish foil of his own tragedies. The "discovered evidence"—his letters written to Mrs. Cox and read in court—intriguingly parodied the tragic scenarios of his stage dramas.[17] As Richard III, Kean complained that some tardy cripple was late in delivering the letters needed to save Clarence; as the comedic Kean, those letters were discovered and delivered too soon to do him any good. As Othello, he gave Desdemona a handkerchief; as the

---

13 J. Fitzgerald Molloy, *The Life and Adventures of Edmund Kean*, II:132.

14 Quote found in the undocumented work of Raymund FitzSimons, *Edmund Kean: Fire From Heaven*, 205.

15 George Daniel, *Ophelia Keen!!! A Dramatic Legendary Tale*, 8.

16 *The Poetic Epistles of Edmund*, 10.

17 See *Ballad: Little Breechs* in Kean, Edmund C. Newspaper Articles Messmore Kendall Collection, HRC.

comedic Kean, the lover gave his mistress tokens of affection, usually money, which she frittered away.

This comedic recasting was so omnipresent that the actor even stopped one performance of *Othello* in order to reason with the crowd: "Ladies and Gentlemen, my personal life is my own. I am only a representative of Shakespeare's characters and it is on this sole basis the public has a right to judge me."[18] Even Kean could not believe this feeble defense. After all, he had made himself into a public spectacle and had made his living off marketing himself; his loss of privacy was the price of his fame.[19] Mocked, jeered, and pilloried for his affair with Charlotte Cox, Kean packed his bags and headed for America.[20]

Kean's First American Tour

Kean had been to America once before, with mixed reviews. According to Harold Newcomb Hillebrand, the impulse behind the first American tour (1820-21) was strictly monetary: "the main impulse arose from the opinion, growing stronger in England with every year, that the American market must be attended to."[21] If, in fact, Kean's first American tour had nothing to do with art and everything to do with

---

18 The original narrative of Kean's speech is in the second person, found in *Cox V. Kean.*

19 Jean-Marie Apostolidès' analysis of Molière's Don Juan comes perhaps closest to explaining why British and American societies needed to attack Kean: "Although the market structure is in place, the economic vocabulary is not yet well-established…. By participating in the elimination of Don Juan, the group of protagonists (and the spectators) … economizes its collective guilt by finding a scapegoat for the transgressions which have thrown society out of joint…."("Molière and the Sociology of Exchange," 490). See also E.P. Thompson, who argues: "while deviant behavior might be tolerated up to a point, beyond that point the community [Georgian England] sought to impose upon transgressors its own expectations as to approved marital roles and sexual conduct" (*Customs in Common*, 8).

20 In Bryan Waller Procter's biography, we learn that the juvenile Kean once ran away from home with the intent of going to America:

After the lapse of three weeks, however, during which time many vain inquiries were made after him, he was brought back by a man who lived in an adjoining mews, having been found there sleeping on a dunghill, in a state of exhaustion, ragged and foot-sore, and altogether in squalid disorder. He shewed much remorse, and being called upon to explain where he had been, answered that he had resolved to go to America, and had actually travelled on foot as far as Bristol. None of the seafaring men, however, to whom he applied would receive him into their vessels, on account of his being so little, and apparently so weak. (*The Life of Edmund Kean*, I:32)

The anecdote suggests that in Kean's mind America was a place where one could always start again.

21 Harold Newcomb Hillebrand, *Edmund Kean*, 200. According to George Raymond, Kean needed the money. He was planning on buying Drury Lane outright. See *The Life and Enterprises of Robert William Elliston, Comedian*, 261-8.

money, his first visit was initially a great triumph. Theaters that usually grossed about a thousand dollars a week were now grossing a thousand a day. He was so popular that some box-offices began auctioning off tickets to the highest bidder—the first instance in American history of ticket scalping.[22] On leaving Boston, a "crowd of seven hundred people cheered him as he drove out of town." From Boston, he returned to New York, then on to Baltimore. It was the same wherever he went. Money poured in, the crowds filled the theater and shouted, "Bravo, Kean!" Working on percentages of the house, Kean made a "mountain of American gold":[23] $5,454 in his first 16 nights. In addition, he did a few shows for charity, raising $2,999.75. Despite his altruism, the impression of Kean is that he was a marauder, plundering American gold while keeping an eye on his kingdom back in England. Kean had no intent on staying.

But at least he was putting on a good show. Appreciative audiences held him in reverence and terror. One American reviewer said that Kean hovered "just on the edge, sometimes quite over the edge of madness.... [It] blinded and stunned the beholders, appalled the imagination, and chilled the blood."[24] His grace period with American audiences and critics was not to last. On 25 May 1821, Kean canceled a Boston performance because the house was only half-full. He had sufficient reason to expect little return for his effort. Although most nights he had been drawing huge crowds and equally large receipts, Boston had been a disappointment. On 23 May, he had played his Lear to a half empty house; the 24 May house for his Jaffier in *Venice Preserved* was emptier still. Checking with the box office some hours before curtain call, Kean announced that "he had positively declined to play on account of the lack of patronage."[25] The crowd, which actually turned up in large numbers by the time of the performance, was outraged.[26] The following morning the papers published the now notorious "One Cent Reward" for Kean's whereabouts:

Run away from the 'Literary Emporium of the New World,' a stage-player calling himself Kean. He may be easily recognized by his misshapen trunk, his coxcomical, cockney manners, and his bladder actions. His face is as white as his own wroth, and his eyes are as dark as indigo. All persons are cautioned against harbouring the aforesaid vagrant, as the undersigned pays no more debts of his contracting, after this date. As he has violated his pledged faith to me, I deem it my duty to put his neighbors on their guard against him.

PETER PUBLIC.

---

22 Esther Cloudman Dunn, *Shakespeare in America*, 151.

23 Bryan Waller Procter, *The Life of Edmund Kean*, II:192.

24 Anonymous American account of Kean, quoted in Lawrence Levine, *Highbrow/ Lowbrow*, 38.

25 Giles Playfair, *The Flash of Lightning*, 94.

26 Esther Cloudman Dunn reports that the Boston managers had warned Kean that the crowds would be thin, owing to the fact that "people were away"—presumably on vaction (*Shakespeare in America*, 151).

After this bad press, Kean hastily returned to England. Now, four years later, with English ticket-buyers hostile, America, with its huge paydays, didn't seem so bad. Even indifferent audiences would be preferable to the comic eruptions of his London audiences. Kean even toyed with the idea of permanently relocating in the United States.[27]

The Pursuit of Happiness

If Kean really were planning on moving to America, he may have done so because he believed that this new land was more sexually liberated than England. Yes, he had been chased from American shores for not caring about his audience, but the Americans had never once questioned his lifestyle. As he well knew, the American press reported all his speeches and all his scandals, but the actor had good reason to expect some compassion, even empathy. Kean was (and is) in many ways America in the flesh, an industrious, self-made man too vigorous for the rigidities of English culture. In a land where parlors of the flesh were common, where masters might copulate with slaves, a land whose constitution specifically enshrined the rights of its citizens to "the pursuit of happiness," Kean's sexual energies might be winked at, if not applauded.[28]

If this was Kean's thinking, he was being blindly optimistic. A surprising number of Americans were hostile to Kean, even before his British audiences turned on him. The drama critic for *The American* (18 September 1821) stated that it was a wonder that anyone could enjoy Kean's acting. One day, he hoped, his readers would awaken from their tasteless slumber and:

> with impartial eyes and ears, ... choose independently to distinguish eloquence, grace, and talent, from vulgarity, deformity, and ignorance. We believe such a golden age to be far distant, and think Mr. Kean may, therefore, carry on the great game of *humbug* for sometime to come, in perfect security.[29]

Now, with Kean coming to America because he couldn't face a scandal at home, a large body of Americans expressed their outrage for this profligate, who presumed that America would welcome him with open arms and open legs. On 14 November 1825, Kean appeared as Richard III at the Park Theater, New York. Instead of "bravos!", cheers, and adoration, the actor was showered with fruit and drowned with

---

27 J. Fitzgerald Molloy, *The Life and Adventures of Edmund Kean*, II:131.

28 America's need to allow sexual pleasure legally is integrally related to its economic system. See Lawrence Birken's *Consuming Desire: Sexual Science and the Emergence of a Cultural Abundance 1871-1914*, which connects sexual practice to "a wider society in which idiosyncratic consumers freely enter into erotic relations with each other"(49); "As economic man realized his freedom only by submitting to the law of the market, so psychological man and woman realize their sexual freedom only by submitting to the law of the sexual market" (49).

29 *The American* 18 September 1821, in Press Clippings, Personal Collection.

catcalls. Kean continued. Someone threw an orange at him. Kean continued. During the wooing scene, a noose made from a piece of heavy rope was thrown at him. It missed but nearly hit the actress Mrs. Hilson. The leader of the orchestra was so alarmed that he leaped onto stage and escorted her to the wings, leaving Kean to face the crowd. He tried to reason with them. They drowned him out. "Off with his head!" they cried.[30] The press, arbiters of good taste, applauded the crowd's actions: "We think that no manager should allow such a lump of moral pollution to contaminate the boards. Every female must stay away and males hiss with indignation."[31] Worse than even the threats of violence were the jeers. When his Othello so much as went near his Desdemona, American audiences began to whoop intolerably.

Why Pick on Kean?

The behavior of Kean's audiences is hard to fathom. Sexual scandals were hardly novel to the English. The Prince of Wales, as stated in the last chapter, had his well-publicized problems. And Americans had a habit of forgiving actors who had fallen on hard times. Kean's rival Junius Brutus Booth was a bigamist, but Americans were happy to let him start his life over in this land of second chances. Why, then, was Kean alone singled out for such abuse? *The Champion* suggested that turning on Kean was in some way related to his theatrical skills, not his public scandals:

> Mr. Kean! Mr. Kean! tho' the summit you've trod
> > Of greatness theatric at Drury,
> The very same mob that now hail you a god
> > Will stone you to death in their fury.[32]

The intimation that Kean was sacrificed, symbolically stoned to death, is worth bearing in mind. As Michael Bristol explains, the comic butt or scapegoat is a common figure in drama because of his symbolic ability "to ward off a more terrifying, indiscriminate violence among members of the same community. This sacrificial murder [or in this case, the unstated need to make Kean into a clown] is the partly hidden meaning of all religion and thus of all social life."[33] In a letter to his London banker, Kean wrote that American audiences revered him, even as they stoned him; he was, as he put it, "really not the people's actor—but their Idol."[34] In layman's terms, Kean was treated comically, not because his audience sensed

30 Harold Newcomb Hillebrand, *Edmund Kean*, 260.

31 Giles Playfair, *Edmund Kean*, 255.

32 F.W. Hawkins, *The Life of Edmund Kean*, II:244.

33 Michael Bristol, *Carnival and Theatre*, 33. This line of reasoning is further legitimated by the following London *Times* editorial: Mr. Kean's "very disgrace is calculated to excite the sympathies of the profligate, and to fill the theatre with all that numerous class of morbidly curious idlers who flock to a play or an execution to see how a man looks when he is hanged, or deserves to be hanged" (quoted in Giles Playfair, *Edmund Kean*, 244).

34 Gordon Craig, *The Life and Theatrical Career of Edmund Kean*, 48.

something in Kean's offstage behavior that was ignoble or debased, but because they had to shun Kean ritualistically for the acts they as a society had promoted and engaged in.

His American audience was not merely upset by Kean's pagan sexuality but by the rise of Kean himself. As we saw in the first chapter, democratic and economic trends raised the curtain on the age of Kean. But it was by no means certain that the era would call upon the skills of a tragedian. As Shelley discussed in his *Defence of Poetry*, the rise of Caroline comedy correlated with the political turmoil of the era; comedy was a mark of political dissatisfaction.[35] By this logic, it was only natural that Georgians also embraced the lowest forms of comedy. The period was mired by costly wars in America and France, a ruling family seemingly addicted to excessive expenditures and sexual scandals, a parliament stewed in corruption, and a growingly politicized citizenry voicing its discontent in work stoppages, mutinies, and riots.[36] In short, the rise of Kean should have signaled the deathblow of tragedy. (He had,

Plate 7:   **Mr. Cox Versus Kean: Kean and Charlotte on the couch, with the cuckolded Mr. Cox outside, holding in his hand Kean's letters. Note Kean's theatrical pants and Mr. Cox's balcony view of the seduction, private moments staged as comic encounters. Reprinted by kind permission of the Harry Ransom Humanities Research Center; The University of Texas at Austin.**

---

35 Percy Bysshe Shelley, *A Defence of Poetry*, 37-8. Raymond Williams agrees, stating that the role of tragedy is to depict the sufferings of one great man, not an entire society; hence, the "idea of tragedy … has been explicitly opposed by the idea of revolution…" (*Modern Tragedy*, 63).

36 Georgian discontent is well mapped in Saree Makdisi's *William Blake and the Impossible History of the 1790s*, 64-5 and 115. George Steiner argues that in Kean's era the audience was increasingly at odds with neoclassical tragedy (*The Death of Tragedy*, 110-11).

after all, first achieved fame in the comedy *The Merchant of Venice*.) Instead, Kean became a tyrant and performed nothing but tragedies.

Audiences in England and America would no longer be told what was tragic merely because Kean said so; they would now decide if Kean's life was tragic, or whether his Othello, given their opinion of Kean, was now unproblematically comic. Kean, or at least the tragic side of Kean, had to die and be reborn in comedy for his audiences to know for certain that they, not Kean, were firmly in charge. When Kean was on stage, his audiences were powerless to choose his roles; they accepted that only Drury Lane and its principal star had control over his choice of characters. But off stage, Kean was their clown, a jester in the court of public opinion and, after the Cox affair, this comedic view of the actor began to empower the ways they saw him on stage.[37] His Shakespearean tragedy became comic when his life became contemptible. Kean became carnival.

Enter *Huckleberry Kean*

Making their way upriver, the protagonists of Mark Twain's *Huckleberry Finn* meet a social and political exile, an English Duke no less. As the novel progresses, he shows Huck and Jim how to make some easy money. All they have to do is stage a Shakespearean fleshy carnival. He should know what the people want. This Duke was also a theatrical star back in England. His name is Edmund Kean. In his first of four Shakespearean renditions, the actor gives us a taste of his Hamlet:

> To be, or not to be; that is the bare bodkin
> That makes calamity of so long life;
> For who would fardels bear, till Birnam Wood do come to Dunsinane,
> But that the fear of something after death
> Murders the innocent sleep,
> Great nature's second course,
> And makes us rather sling the arrows of outrageous fortune
> Than fly to others that we know not of.
> There's the respect must give us pause:
> Wake Duncan with thy knocking! I would thou couldst....[38]

Twain knew many actors who had either performed with Kean or who knew yet other actors who had done the same. One of his best friends was Edwin Booth, whose father had acted with Kean in 1818. Certainly, scholars have commented

---

37 Simon Williams writes that "while Kean's stage *persona* was an embodiment of tragic suffering, his *persona* as a public man was closer to that of the jester of English society of this time." See "Actorial Representations of the Self in the Romantic Age: Edmund Kean and Ludwig Devrient," 109. Relatedly, Kim C. Sturgess argues that Americans saw *Richard III* as an anti-monarchical piece (*Shakespeare and the American Nation*, 56-7). Certainly, turning the play from tragedy to farce would have aided in that emphasis.

38 Mark Twain, *Adventures of Huckleberry Finn*, 179.

upon Kean's appearance in the novel. Twain editors Blair and Fischer point out that Twain incorrectly refers to Kean as "Kean the Elder"; Michael Patrick Hearn, editor of the *Annotated Huckleberry Finn*, identifies the Twainian Kean's acting partner as Charles Kean but notes that Charles never toured with his father in America.[39] Twain scholar Anthony J. Berret corrects Kean's soliloquy, which he describes as "a hodgepodge of lines from different parts of *Hamlet*, *Macbeth*, and *Richard the Third*."[40] In sum, these scholars studied what Twain got historically right or wrong about Kean's Shakespearean performance.

It's true that literary theorists, armed like violent cupids, their literary arrows dipped in the magic of Foucaultian analysis and delivered in the arching beauty of feathered Deriddian quotation, are on target when they say that since all narratives are constructed, there is no real difference between a history and a fiction. Hence, even Twain's fictions are histories, just as all histories are fictions. We have seen that in the case of Dumas' play, *Kean*, we could discuss Dumas' use of Kean in ways that were fairly independent of the historical figure. The aim here is not to use one text to correct another, but to suggest that stories that get repeated serve cultural functions above and beyond those of telling straight biographical or historical facts. What Twain has to say about Kean seems far less important than what Twain uses Kean to say.

That being said, there are startling connections. The aforementioned pastiche of Shakespearean verse broadly recalls Kean's own performances after the Cox affair, in which he garbled lines from different Shakespeare plays. In sum, it would be inaccurate to say that Twain's use of Kean is utterly devoid of historical application. Indeed, there would be little point in Twain using the name Kean, unless it retained some cultural signification. Twain must have expected at least some of his readers to know something of Kean's two tours of America.

Clearly, Twain was playing with Kean here, but to what end? We might begin by looking at Shakespeare's inkhorn verbosity, which Twain rendered seemingly nonsensical; "seemingly" because Twain had a purpose here. James Hirsh suggests that the overt function of Twain's Shakespearean pastiche was to point out the coarseness and obtuseness of Americans, at least as compared with the eloquence and profundity of authentic Shakespeare.[41] Agreed, but we can vehemently oppose his conclusion that Twain "Shakespeareanized America by giving American experiences Shakespearean patterns."[42] Twain's Keanian appropriations suggest the converse: it was Shakespeare's fancy words that were a threat to the democratic future because it was Shakespeare that represented the British concept of a feudal and undemocratic

39 Michael Patrick Hearn, (ed.), *The Annotated Huckleberry Finn*, 245-6.

40 Anthony J. Berret, *Mark Twain and Shakespeare*, 81.

41 James Hirsh, "Samuel Clemens and the Ghost of Shakespeare," 255.

42 Ibid., 267. We can similarly disagree with Michael Bristol, who reads America's interest in Shakespeare as an expression of "communal solidarity with the past" (*Big-Time Shakespeare*, 233).

past.[43] Shakespeare had to speak like a typical American to be embraced by typical Americans.[44]

The issue of Shakespeare's language, and its suitability for American tastes, returns time and again in Twain's writing. Among Twain's earliest pieces was a journalistic account of *Othello*, in which Shakespeare's poetry is flattened into prose: "Mr. O. requested that in our account ... we should speak of him as he was, nothing extenuating, nor setting down aught in malice. At the close of a few well chosen remarks he suddenly stabbed himself."[45] Likewise, in Twain's unfinished burlesque of *Hamlet*, Basil, Hamlet's foster brother, complains that Elizabethan English, "ain't *human* talk; no body that ever lived, ever talked the way they do. Even the flunkies can't say the simplest thing the way a human being would say it."[46] According to Basil, Shakespeare, at least as represented on the printed page, has no place in American society because he doesn't speak the language.

To the above cited, we might also add Twain's discarded play *1601*, in which Shakespeare and Queen Elizabeth, rather than engaging in long-winded speeches, mischievously engage in passing wind.[47] Twain was going to include this fart-joke drama in his novel *The Prince and the Pauper*. Similarly, in the early draft of his first book, *Life on the Mississippi*, Twain included a *Hamlet* parody. Both passages were excised in the final versions of these respective books because the author considered

---

43 As William Leggett, himself a Shakespeare adapter noted, "What a vast and godlike influence he [Shakespeare] might have exerted in molding the public mind and guiding the upward progress of nations, if his great genius had not been bedazzled by the false glitter of aristocratic institutions, and blinded to the equal rights of the great family of man!" See Thomas Cartelli, *Repositioning Shakespeare*, 38.

44 I should here note that the American Shakespeare editor Richard Grant White suggested that one of the reasons Americans liked Shakespeare was that their language had somehow preserved more Shakespearean words than contemporary British dialects. This novel idea might have justified Americans seeing Shakespeare as their own but is certainly not supported by Twain's parodies. For more on White, see Kim C. Sturgess, *Shakespeare and the American Nation*, 78-9.

45 Undocumented quote found in Anthony J. Berret, *Mark Twain and Shakespeare*, 75. Twain also wrote another flat prose version of Shakespeare: "The Killing of Julius Caesar 'Localized.'" See *Early Tales and Sketches*, 2:113. I am indebted to James Hirsh, who looks at parallels in *Huck Finn* to *Comedy of Errors*, *Henry IV*, *Richard III*, *2Henry VI*, *King Lear*, *Hamlet*, and *Macbeth*. However, many of these echoes take place outside of Kean's appearances in the novel. Hirsh also notes parallels between Twain's *The Prince and the Pauper* (1811) and *King Lear*, and passages from "The Mysterious Stranger" (1897-1908) which resemble lines from *The Tempest*. See "Samuel Clemens and the Ghost of Shakespeare," 261-2 and 256.

46 Lawrence Levine, *Highbrow/Lowbrow*, 74.

47 Twain confided to the Reverend Joseph Twichell of Hartford, Connecticut, that he considered the work "dreadfully funny." Twain's letter is reprinted in "Jeff DeMarco's Twain *1601* Page."

any direct critique of Shakespeare to be "a sort of sacrilege."[48] Ironically, the sacred Shakespeare Twain wished to protect had little to do with the plays audiences paid to see performed.

Shakespeare as Lewd Diversion

In *Domestic Manners of the Americans* (1832), Fanny Trollope discusses her encounter in Cincinnati with a "serious gentleman." She mentions her interest in Byron, but the American dismisses the poet as immoral; she then mentions Pope, who is dismissed as equally ribald. With no other avenue of discussion, she asks, "and Shakspeare, sir?" The gent replies, "Shakspeare, Madam is obscene, and, thank God, WE [Americans] are sufficiently advanced to have found it out! If we must have the abomination of stage plays, let them at least be marred by the refinement of the age in which we live." No doubt, Shakespeare was ubiquitous in the popular culture of the era. "Performances of Shakespeare were ... a common occurrence along the Mississippi in the mid-nineteenth century," but the above-cited anecdote suggests that what people experienced in the theaters was a radically more lurid product than what they allowed and enjoyed in their homes.[49]

Even in England, critics such as Bowdler admitted the need to clean up Shakespeare: "although the writings of Shakspeare possess greater merit than those of any other dramatist, they are, nevertheless, stained with words and expressions of so indecent a nature, that no parent would chuse to submit them, in an uncorrected form, to the eye or ear of a daughter."[50] He, therefore, urged that "IF ANY WORD OR EXPRESSION IS OF SUCH A NATURE, THAT THE FIRST IMPRESSION IT EXCITES IS AN IMPRESSION OF OBSCENITY, THAT WORD OUGHT NOT TO BE SPOKEN, OR WRITTEN, OR PRINTED; AND IF PRINTED, IT OUGHT TO BE ERASED."[51] To do otherwise was to "employ his [the Critic's] talents and his pen in defense of obscenity."[52]

---

48 See Lawrence Levine's undocumented *Highbrow/Lowbrow*, 74. In "About Play-Acting" (1898), Twain acknowledged that low comedy had a place and function in American entertainment. However, Twain, complained that it was incongruous to think of Shakespeare as just another form of sleazy amusement: "Comedy keeps the heart sweet; but we all know that there is wholesome refreshment for both mind and heart in an occasional climb among ... the intellectual snow-summits built by Shakespeare" ("About Play-Acting," in *The Complete Essays of Mark Twain*, 207). See also See Anthony J. Berret, *Mark Twain and Shakespeare*, 53.

49 Louis Marder, *His Exits and His Entrances: The Story of Shakespeare's Reputation*, 303.

50 Thomas Bowdler, *The Family Shakespeare*, I:12-13. Thomas Bowdler's *The Family Shakespeare* (1807) was not printed in America until 1840, but was available through British importation.

51 Thomas Bowdler, *A Letter to the Editor of the British Critic*, 17.

52 Ibid., 32.

Plate 8: **A tragic farce: Kean pelted with fruit. Kean made a name for himself playing tragic roles, but, after the Cox affair, audiences in England and America turned his tragic performances into unmitigated farce. Twain's Edmund Kean meets a similar fate. Image from private collection.**

Fig-leafed, Shakespeare became an object of veneration. Said Walt Whitman, "If I had not stood before [Shakespeare's] *poems* with uncover'd head, fully aware of their colossal grandeur and beauty of form and spirit, I could not have written Leaves of Grass"; Ralph Waldo Emerson thought of Shakespeare as "inconceivably wise."[53] Others, such as James Fenimore Cooper, combed through Shakespeare for pious aphorisms.[54] John Bartlett's *Familiar Quotations* quoted from Shakespeare twice as often as from the Bible.[55] Rhapsodizing on the centrality of Shakespeare to a wholesome and happy life, Gary North recalled that "Families spent quality time

---

53 Robert Falk, "Shakespeare in America: A Survey to 1900," *Shakespeare Survey* 18 (1965): 103, 115. I have silently added the italicization. Alan L. Ackerman, surveying American nineteenth-century theater, concludes that wholesome-minded people abandoned the playhouses for reading groups and closet drama (*The Portable Theater*, 1-41; esp. 1-10). For Shakespeare's standing among British intellectuals, see Alfred Harbage, *As They Liked It*, 186-7.

54 Louis Marder, *His Exits and His Entrances: The Story of Shakespeare's Reputation*, 297.

55 Ibid., 27.

together … making hand-cranked ice cream, milking the cows, reading Shakespeare by firelight. Local people depended on each other for help…. Public opinion kept moral standards high."[56]

Given Shakespeare's high moral character in print, Twain's reluctance to publish his parodies is understandable. But his parodies might easily have been staged, seeing as they were so in keeping with contemporaneous theatrical tastes. After all, parodying Shakespeare was not only popular, it was venerable. The first parodies of Shakespeare date from the eighteenth century, but the apogee of Shakespearean parody was during Twain's era.[57] Even as parodies go, many of these works were tasteless. In some parodies, Hamlet was actually played by a dog.[58]

Why Use Kean at All? Carnival Audiences and Criminal Actors

Granted, staged Shakespeare publicly debased the mind it privately improved.[59] But Twain could have made this argument without including Kean, couldn't he? Certainly using the name of a famous actor had its benefits in signaling to his readers that his parodies were aimed at the stage, not the page.

Kean, and actors like him, performed in the same houses that charged variously for minstrel shows, magic shows, burlesques, displays of educated pigs and monkeys, staged sexual enactments of women with other women or women with animals, and contests to see how many rats a terrier could kill in a given time.[60] In St. Louis, until 1837, the theater was an abandoned blacksmith's shop; in Cincinnati, the first

---

56 Gary North, in Susan Wise Bauer, "Y2Krazy."

57 Lawrence Levine, *Highbrow/Lowbrow*, 13.

58 Elizabeth Reitz Mullenix, "The Sublime or the Ridiculous?" 1. For more on Shakespeare burlesque, see also Kim C. Sturgess, *Shakespeare and the American Nation*, 87-9.

59 Shakespeare as smut is by no means a new conception. The business holdings of Renaissance entrepreneur Philip Henslowe included the Rose Theatre—a place where Shakespeare's plays were often performed—and a number of brothels. Indeed, Joseph Lenz states that a "predominant metaphor for the practice of the theater in Shakespeare's age was prostitution, an image the professional actor, playwright, and theater-owner helped to define and were defined by and to which they responded with ambivalence"("Base Trade: Theater as Prostitution," 833). He goes on to note that: "by definition the professional theater is a fabricator of pleasurable illusions for profit, in a culture that conceives the act of seeing as copulation and the transaction of trade as base. The more it succeeded at attracting, pleasing, and profiting from audiences by making a spectacle of itself, the more it resembled a prostitute" (845). What can be said of Shakespeare's theater in this regard might be extended and magnified to Kean's Drury Lane and the various theaters Kean toured in America.

60 Gene Smith, *American Gothic*, 51-7. Some argued that these carnivalesque events were more "Shakespearean" than traditional, formal theater in that the variety and earthiness of these entertainments captured the essential atmosphere of Shakespeare's bankside. See Kim C. Sturgess, *Shakespeare and the American Nation*, 79.

theater was a stable-loft.[61] Much of the audiences were well-suited to their "low" surroundings. According to an account dating to 1837, the St. Louis audience was known for chewing apples and tobacco, eating peanuts and loudly sucking candy during performances. Many theatergoers were described as rivermen, "who were half horse, half alligator and could whip their weight of bull-dogs."[62] On 15 April 1844, William Macready, hoping to find a fortune similar to the one that Kean had mined on his first visit to America, played St. Louis. He later recorded, "the *continued* vulgar speeches, ejaculations, and laughs of some ruffians in the second tier quite overcame my patience. I threw up the attempt and walked right off."[63] Audiences on the west coast were no better: San Franciscans of the Gold Rush decade viewed drama as merely an alternative to the tedium of drinking, gambling, and whoring.[64] If a player stumbled over a line, gunmen in the audience often showed their irritation with performers by discharging their revolvers in the theater.[65]

It wasn't just audiences that needed polish. Most American actors were little more than homeless vagrants. Edgar Allan Poe's father, David, an actor, was usually in debt and the family relied, as did most actors, upon theatrical benefits. The system is no longer in place and therefore may require brief explanation. The benefit system allowed an actor or the entire company to receive the profits from a performance after all the expenses of the run had been paid. It was a way for actors to increase their wages, certainly, but benefit is akin to charity or begging.[66] Farmers and blacksmiths made things, created wealth; but actors, like vagabonds, created nothing of substance. They merely fleeced money in exchange for an insubstantial dream. Other critics suggested that actors were little better than criminals. Said John Quincy Adams said: "since I entered upon the third of Shakespeare's seven ages, the first and chief capacity in which I have read and studied him is as a teacher of morals; [yet] I had scarcely ever seen a player of his parts who regarded him as a *moralist* at all."[67]

If theater were akin to criminal deception, it came as no surprise that many actors were also practiced criminals. Kean's own mother was a prostitute; Junius Brutus Booth had attempted to kill a fellow actor; one of his actor-sons was an assassin. Even the subject matter of their Shakespearean performances reinforced the actors' sensual and criminal characteristics. Shakespeare's plays are filled from the tip to the crown with criminality and cruelty: vagabonds and conmen such as Feste, Falstaff,

---

61 On the history of early American theater, see William G.B. Carson, *The Theatre on the Frontier*, 4-5.

62 William G.B. Carson, *Managers in Distress*, 261.

63 *Diaries of William Charles Macready*, II:269. See also Nancy Webb and Jean Francis Webb, who noted that in 1849 New Yorkers pelted Macready with rotten eggs and "dubious vegetables" (*Will Shakespeare and His America*, 150).

64 Joseph Gaer, Introduction. *The Theatre of the Gold Rush*, 4.

65 Gene Smith, *American Gothic*, 54.

66 The *OED* cites "benefit" as a form of "pecuniary help" from 1755 onwards.

67 John Quincy Adams, "The Character of Desdemona."

and Autolycus, thieving brothers such as Oliver and Edmund, rapists such as Chiron and Demetrius, and, Kean's specialty, murderers.

Saving Shakespeare from The Americans

Looking at *Huck Finn*, we can see how Twain uses Kean to parody American theater without undermining Shakespeare's power as a privileged and morally appropriate text for both innocent children and civilized adults. In his staging of the famous balcony scene in *Romeo and Juliet*, for example, Twain uses Kean to expose the audience's preference for adulterated Shakespeare. Instead of listening to the poetry, the audience simply falls about laughing at Kean, who appears as Juliet in a frumpy negligée.

Another criticism of Kean's Shakespearean performances and what they represented is found in the Twainian Kean's decision to stage *Richard III*. The actor explains, "The first good town we come to, we'll hire a hall and do the sword-fight in *Richard III*."[68] Richard's medieval world is turned into a get-rich-quick scheme in which the rule of kings gives way to overhead and market share. The language of swords is reduced to a verbal, contractual agreement, summed up in Kean's phrase, "How does that strike you?"[69]

Signaling that this fight will be a burlesque, their practice turns literally from pathos to bathos:

> Well, next they got out a couple of long swords that the duke made out of oak laths, and begun to practice the sword-fight—the duke called himself Richard III; and the way they laid on, and pranced around the raft was grand to see. But by and by the king tripped and fell overboard, and after that they took a rest.....[70]

Comedic dunking of dukes aside, Twain's pun, "How does that *strike* you?" may have hit upon an essential feature of staged Shakespearean—and by Shakespearean read "Keanian"—drama. After seeing Kean, American theatergoers demanded that their actors often dispense with Shakespearean verse altogether and get down to the business of "duking" it out with swords. As the American paper *The Champion* pointed out:

> Every personator of *Richard* must fight like a madman, and fence on the ground, and when disarmed and wounded, thrust with savage impotence with his naked hand.... Mr. Kean has passed this manner into a law and woe unto him who breaks it.[71]

---

68 Mark Twain, *Adventures of Huckleberry Finn*, 169.

69 Ibid., 169.

70 Ibid., 177.

71 Quoted in Blair and Fischer, notes to *The Adventures of Huckleberry Finn*, 409:169.8.

MR KEAN AS RICHARD THE THIRD
Act V. Scene last.

Plate 9: **The highlight of any Kean performance was his sword fight. As stated in Chapter Two, the first time Kean played Richard III at Drury Lane, he allowed himself to be killed by Alexander Rae, the actor playing Richmond, but not before chasing Rae "round and round the stage."[72] One spectator, who saw Kean's Richard III at Bath, on 18 July 1815, noted: "Kean ... overdid his death—he came up close to Richmond, after he had lost his sword, as if he would have attacked him with his fists—Richmond, to please Kean, was obliged to stand like a fool, with a drawn sword in his hand without daring to use it." On another occasion, one actor playing Richmond, deferentially asked Kean, "Where shall I hit you, sir?" Kean replied scornfully, "Where you can, sir."[73] Reprinted by kind permission of the Harry Ransom Humanities Research Center; The University of Texas at Austin.**

Given the popularity of Kean's swordsmanship, it's not surprising that, out of the many dozen theatrical renderings of Kean still extant, only a handful show him without a knife or sword. The depiction of Kean's Hamlet shows the actor with

---

72 J. Fitzgerald Molloy, *The Life and Adventures of Edmund Kean*, I:150.

73 Otis Skinner, "Three Madmen of the Theatre II," 630.

a book open and eyes blazing; one depiction of his Sir Giles Overreach shows Kean attempting to break through a crowd and attack his enemies. More typical are depictions of Kean as Richard III, Iago, or Othello with a sword or dagger; even his Romeo is armed and ready for combat. James Henry Hackett, an American who saw Kean in London, paid attention to how Kean used his sword throughout the play. When describing love scenes, for example, Hackett recorded how Kean entered, "Sword under arm. ... Left arm raised & struck with his right several times in anger," then "draws his sword while advancing and knocks the guard's halbert with his sword and then comes down to Lady Anne left hand in a supplicatory manner."[74]

Kean did more than use his sword as a walking stick. The Frenchman, Etienne-Jean Delécluze observed Kean's Richard and was both shocked and impressed by the careful choreography:

> Richmond and Richard's sword-fight lasts for *five or six minutes*, and ends with the latter receiving a deadly thrust from his opponent. Kean, playing the king, does not fall but staggers at the blow, still gripping his sword, which finally clatters to the ground. His unarmed hand makes a last unavailing effort, mimicking a sword thrust, until Kean at last falls backwards to the ground.[75]

The theatrical record suggests that Keanian tastes were still in place long after the actor left American shores. In December 1832, Junius Brutus Booth, famed for his ability to copy Kean, played Richard III at New York's Bowery Theater. When Richmond and Richard engaged in single combat, the audience went onto the stage and "made a ring round the combatants to see fair play, and kept them at it for nearly a quarter of an hour."[76] His youngest theatrical son, John Wilkes Booth, took the swordfight in *Richard III* so seriously, savagely slashing at his Richmond, that one or both actors were often wounded during these stage combats.[77]

Critics applauded Wilkes Booth's efforts. On 7 January 1862, the theater reviewer for *The Daily Missouri Democrat* effused: "the fight between Richard and Richmond in the last scene is terrific; indeed, we have never seen it equaled upon the stage."[78] According to one theatergoer:

> he [John Wilkes] was the only Richard, after his father. His fifth act was terribly real, while his fight with Richmond was a task that many a good swordsman dreaded. John Wilkes, as Richard, never knew when he was conquered, consequently he was never ready to die, until it was evident to him that his death was necessary to preserve Richmond's life according to the story and the text of the tragedy. In many instances he wore poor

---

74   James Henry Hackett, *Oxberry's 1822 edition of Richard III*, 26-8.

75   Etienne-Jean Delécluze, *Journal de Delécluze, 1824-1828*, 492; translation my own.

76   Lawrence Levine, *Highbrow/Lowbrow*, 29.

77   John Wilkes Booth was wounded on four separate occasions playing Richard and once while playing Romeo. He also wounded his Richmonds quite often. See Gordon Samples, *Lust for Fame*, 59-60, 78-80, 90-91, 132-3.

78   Ibid., 66-7.

Richmond out, and on one occasion Richmond was compelled to whisper, 'For God's sake, John, die! Die! If you don't I shall.'[79]

Shakespeare's tragic heroes were honorable, pious, generous, often marriage-minded, and always ready to settle their problems in single combat, but Keanian swordplay had nothing to do with chivalry, romance, or even furthering Shakespeare's stories.[80] His skill with a sword was more akin to gymnastics with knives, the popularity of which threatened to turn Shakespearean drama into a commercial and potentially deadly sport.[81]

Shakespeare or Sodom?

A similar trumping of the visceral over the intellectual is found in the final Keanian performance in *Huck Finn*. After rehearsing *Romeo and Juliet*, Twain's Kean decides to preempt the play in favor of the "Thrilling Tragedy of The King's Camelopard or The Royal Nonesuch!!!" As Kean explains, "these Arkansas lunkheads couldn't come up to Shakespeare." They decide, therefore, to stage a "low comedy and maybe something ruther worse than low comedy."[82]

Shakespeare is bumped from the bill to make way for a more commercially viable enterprise: a "bump-and-grind" nude review; bare bodkins give way to bare bottoms. Kean parades before his all-male patrons: "a-prancing out on all fours, naked; and he was painted, all over, ring-streaked-and-stripped, all sorts of colors, as splendid as a rain-bow." Shakespeare's text is overturned in favor of vivid colors and naked flesh. Indeed, Kean's dumbshow describes the I.Q. level of the patrons, who obviously enjoy mindless comedy:

> it was just wild, but it was awful funny. The people killed themselves laughing; and when the king got done capering, and capered off behind the scenes, they roared and clapped

---

79 Ibid., 81.

80 This is to disagree with Charles Edelman's suggestion that swordplay is carefully designed "to enhance the audience's appreciation and understanding of characters and themes" (*Brawl Ridiculous*, 192).

81 In general, it seems that American audiences attached little importance to Shakespeare's words. On the other hand, they understood the chivalric ethos of the plays. In 1856, F. McDermott undertook Cibber's *Richard III*. In Act I, Richard kills Henry VI with a sword thrust. McDermott added to the killing a "thrust, *a posteriori*, after Henry had fallen." The audience reaction to this disdain for chivalry was as swift as it was severe. They pummeled the stage with cabbages, carrots, pumpkins, potatoes, a wreath of vegetables, a sack of flour, a pot of soot, and even a dead goose. As in Shakespeare's version, the play includes a supplication scene with Lady Anne, Richard's future wife. He places the sword in her hand and demands that she love him or kill him. When McDermott placed the sword in the actress' hand, "one half of the house, at least, asked that it might be plunged in his body." See Lawrence Levine, *Highbrow/Lowbrow*, 28.

82 Mark Twain, *Adventures of Huckleberry Finn*, 194.

and stormed and haw-hawed till he come back and done it over again; and after that, they made him do it another time.[83]

Twain portrays American audiences more satisfied by sword than by soliloquy, more captivated by sex than by Shakespeare. But the mood turns ugly. The audience complains: "What, is it over? Is that *all?* Is that it?" In a subsequent performance, the ticket-buyers come armed, ready to attack Kean and his co-actor. "I smelt sickly eggs by the barrel, and rotten cabbages, and such things."[84] This attack on Kean is not for the show's content, or even for a poor performance, but for the brevity of a fine performance.

Twain's attempt to ridicule American tastes is not a total success. Huck's enjoyment of the parodies ("it was awful funny")—and our identification with Huck—enable us to feel that we are, at moments, like Twain, aware of both the authority and subversiveness of Shakespeare, testing, in effect, the proposition that Shakespeare is good for you. At issue is not only the contrary desires and expectations of American audiences, yearning for both sexual titillation and high culture, but also the ways in which Shakespeare's texts naturally yield to such entertainments. Americans did remake Shakespeare in their own image, but, ironically, they had to create two Shakespeares. Readers, who might be deemed the new cerebral aristocrats of America, demanded a highbrow Shakespeare, not vastly unlike the version British intellectuals celebrated; but, for the growing working class, the refuse of Shakespeare took another shape, one of sensuous delights and outrageous stage antics.

Twain's Kean, a P.T. Barnum lord of misrule, is willing to expose himself to any humiliation for a fast buck. And, like P.T. Barnum, Twain's Kean is an idiosyncratic seer, a visionary showman, and salesman, and what he sells is not theater but debasement. Twain's joke was not aimed at Kean but at his crowd. The real Kean had been chased from America because the Americans were outraged by his sexual peccadilloes. In Twain's version, American audiences roar their approval when Kean comes on as the lewd, vulgar sexual deviant they imagined him to be and only complain when the striptease is abridged. The real Kean was attacked for his indecency; Twain's Kean is attacked for not going on with the show.

---

83 Ibid., 196.
84 Ibid., 198.

Chapter 5

Kean and Mr. Keene

Kean's mostly Victorian biographers almost always overlook the actor's bold explorations of race. When the issue comes up, it usually is for a comic turn. Hawkins, for example, writes:

> After the tragedy Kean gave a specimen of tight-rope dancing, and another of sparring with a professional pugilist. He then played the leading part in a musical interlude, and finished with Chimpanzee the Monkey in the melodramatic pantomime …[and] in one his mischievous pranks … went home in the dress of the ill-favoured animal, threw himself on the bed, and went to sleep as he was![1]

Humor aside, this anecdote suggests something naturally savage, even feral, about Kean, at home in his monkey suit. The image is not radically distant from the bestial images often associated with black men sleeping with white women. ("Making the beast with two backs," as Iago describes it.) The implication, later picked up by John Doran, is that when Kean lay down with his wife in his monkey suit, he was mentally imagining Othello's seduction of Desdemona.[2]

The story is a powerful one and is a prime example of how biography and appropriation works. Once the story is in place, we can't help but see Kean's Othello as somehow bestial. Yet, like so many other facets of Kean's biography, this is merely one story based on a selection of details, placed in such a way as to (dis)orientate the reader to a guided conclusion. A different—and possibly more dramatic—story might be spun using not just the facts Hawkins selects, but others he leaves by the wayside.

---

1   F.W. Hawkins, *Life of Edmund Kean*, I:93. The monkey suit story, though not its relation to Kean's tragic roles, is also mentioned in the earlier Procter biography: "It is a fact, characteristic of the man, that he went home after the play, in his transformed state, and swore, *ore rotundo*, that he would remain thus all night; and he *did*! The remonstrances of his wife, who complained bitterly of the execrable odor arising from the undressed skins (the monkey costume), and from the paint and varnish that encrusted his face, were of no avail" (Bryan Waller Procter, *The Life of Edmund Kean*, I:131). Procter also notes that Kean's early, provincial roles included "a Savage" and "SAMBO, the Black" (Ibid., I:198, 74).

2   John Doran suggests that the monkey suit aided Kean in playing tragic roles: Kean's "deep tragedy in the monkey's death scene … made the audience shed tears." See *"Their Majesties' Servants." Annals of the English Stage*, II:384. The anecdote is unknown to Hawkins. James Winston notes that on one occasion Kean played Othello and left the theater with his face paint still on (15 January 1827, *Drury Lane Journal*, 139).

Mr KEAN as OTHELLO,
Yet I'll not shed her Blood.

**Plate 10: Aspects of Kean's tawny Othello blurred into his Iago. Reprinted by
kind permission of the Harry Ransom Humanities Research Center;
The University of Texas at Austin.**

    In point of fact, there is no visual connection between Kean's simian roles
and his Othello. Indeed, what differentiated Kean from other Othellos was his
comparative whiteness. Kean did not so much black up for black parts as bronze
up. Given the murkiness of gas lighting, some of the actor's critics went so far as to
complain of the difficulty in visually distinguishing between his Othello and Iago.
Further intertwining the parts, Kean played Othello one night, and Iago the very
next, tacitly suggesting that Iago and Othello somehow "smudged" into each other.
Audiences for a performance of Kean's Iago almost certainly brought associations
from the previous night's performance of Othello with them. Kean was both Iago
and Othello, both villain and hero, good and evil, black and white. On the nights he

played Othello, audiences could still see or hear him acting Iago; when acting Iago, the memory of his Othello answered.

In his ability to be both Othello and Iago, Kean suggested a cross-cultural exchange by which racial and cultural "differences" were increasingly rendered fictional; Kean's ability to act "black" without looking "black" inadvertently deconstructed the "natural" facade of race.[3] During a performance of his near-white Othello, one audience member shouted out: "*Your face is black, but your heart is blacker.*"[4] Similarly, the *Edinburgh Literary Journal* wrote that the genius of Kean's Othello lay not in his ability to act like a black man, but in his heredity: "a great deal of Mr. KEAN's best acting lay in his blood."[5]

The inappropriateness of Kean's method was spelled out by *The Champion*:

> An actor may be very well able to sustain both these characters, but there are many objections to his playing in both within the course of a few days. ... The method to which we object, forfeits these advantages, only, as it would seem, to incur... several disadvantages [the actor] cannot avoid....

The danger, the paper suggested, was that in switching back and forth between roles, Iago's whiteness somehow lightened the character of Othello and, thereby, made the olive-skinned Moor less odious. A standard Othello "is connected, in the minds of us *white men*, with characters of ignorance and inferiority." But "if *Othello*'s appearance be in every respect calculated to disgust a female, it [Kean's Othello] will not." Why? Because Othello should be black as night, and, as such, work under "the disadvantage of a complexion." But Kean's olive-skinned Othello won not only the heart of Desdemona but of his audience as a whole because the lighter make-up allowed the audience to see "Mr. KEAN'S countenance... [which] yet haunts our mental vision."[6]

The aim of Kean's doubling may not have been to expose some hidden meaning in the play. Doubling Iago and Othello allowed Kean to display the full range of his talents. It was a showcase for his genius. The process, nevertheless, explored the interdependency of the roles. Kean could play an Othello who bullied Iago around the stage, or an Iago who bullied Othello. But having devalued the idea of color as a signifier of difference, Kean could only substitute in its place the idea of "star" actor; for it was evident that whoever played opposite him that night was to play second fiddle. On the nights Kean played Iago, Othello was played by a person named Sowerby, a "dull, literal plodder who no doubt did his best," or by Alexander

---

3   "Mr. Keene" also played with other definitions of color by appropriating minstrel songs into his repertoire. See Nicholas M. Evans, "Ira Aldridge: Shakespeare and Minstrelsy," 165-87.

4   *Cox V. Kean*, 74.

5   See Edmund Kean playbills in Huntington Manuscript Collection, Huntington Library, 182799.

6   "Mr. Kean's OTHELLO," *The Champion* 15 May 1814, in Huntington Manuscript Collection, Huntington Library, 182799.

Rae, an actor of "ordinary talent," or by Alexander Pope, a "mediocre actor" or, on occasion, by Robert Elliston, a good comedic actor but hopeless at tragedy.[7] These negative notices were inevitable. Kean's audiences dreamed of their hero playing both Othello and Iago at the same time. Only then could both sides of Iago and Othello come alive; when Kean could answer Kean; when Othello could look into Iago's eyes and see himself.[8]

The Black Kean

On 10 October 1825, at London's Royal Coburg Theatre, a "Mr. Keene" performed in the lead role in Thomas Southerne's play *Oroonoko, The Royal Slave.* The poster for the performance describes the event:

> its principal character [is played] by a *Man of Colour*, and one of the very race whose wrongs it professes to record; being the first instance in which one of that Complexion has displayed a striking degree of Histrionic Talent, and which has secured him the rapturous Approbation of an enlightened Public on the other side of the Atlantic.[9]

The use of the cognomen "Keene" was an obvious attempt to trade on Edmund Kean's reputation. Sometimes he even billed himself and was referred to by others as "The African Kean."[10] It seems clear that Kean's reputation included an enlightened philosophy concerning race. We have already looked at his Othello/Iago combination, but it is important to grasp how habitually and insistently black (or in Kean's case, olive) characters appear throughout his oeuvre. Like Mr. Keene,

---

7   Harold Newcomb Hillebrand, *Edmund Kean*, 130, 30; on Robert Elliston see *Actors and Actresses: Kean and Booth*, 50-51.

8   Hazlitt noted that Junius Brutus Booth copied Kean down to "the most trifling *minutiæ*" (*Complete Works*, V:356). Kean's hybridity has survived in a variety of critical arguments: E.A.J. Honigmann argues that Iago and Othello are two sides of Shakespeare's artistic mind (Introduction, *Othello*, 79, 105).

9   Herbert Marshall and Mildred Stock, *Ira Aldridge, the Negro Tragedian*, 54. Aldridge at the Coburg was a good fit; the theater was known for its exotic spectacles. See Jim Davis and Victor Emeljanow, *Reflecting the Audience*, 34. Southerne's play was based on the Aphra Behn novel, *Oroonoko; or The Royal Slave, A True Story* (1688).

10   Ira Aldridge, *Memoir and Theatrical Career of Ira Aldridge*, 14. It should be further noted that Kean himself was indifferent to the spelling of his surname. In 1814, for example, Kean was advertised as "Mr. Keane of Theatre Royal, Exeter." "Mr. Keene" used the same phraseology; in 1827, the same year Charles was billing himself as "Mr. Kean," Aldridge promoted himself as "Mr. Keene of Theatre Royal, Newcastle." Another poster from the same year advertises "the Celebrated Mr. Keene, the African Roscius"; even as late as 1831, Aldridge billed himself as "F.W. Keene Aldridge, the African Roscius." "Roscius" refers to the Roman actor, Quintus Roscius (c.126 B.C.-62 B.C.), a slave who became the greatest thespian of his time. Roscius' slave status is not of direct concern here. Many white actors, when reaching the summit of their art, were referred as "Roscius." Of more interest is Aldridge's adoption of the names "Keene" or "Kean."

Plate 10 (left, close up): Kean as Othello. Plate 11 (right): Mr. Keene (Ira Aldridge) as Othello. Reprinted by kind permission of the Harry Ransom Humanities Research Center; The University of Texas at Austin.

Edmund Kean played the tragic lead in Thomas Southerne's stage version of Aphra Behn's novella, *Oroonoko*. The play also features another black character, Aboan. On the nights when Kean wanted to rest himself, he often chose to play this minor role. To this, two more variations of Othello may be added, the murderous Zanga in Edward Young's *The Revenge* (1719) and the lead role in John Brown's *Barbarossa* (1755). And there was the ill-fated and previously discussed *Ben Nazir*, with yet another Moorish role. Cataloguing Kean's parts, Edward Ziter estimates that eleven of Kean's 57 roles were non-Caucasian. Although this number does not take into account Kean's purposeful ruination of all but a handful of these characters, there is no doubt that Ziter is correct when he writes that Kean's Africans and Moors "ultimately obscured the 'natural' antipathy whites feel for blacks."[11]

Who was this black man attempting to use Kean's name? Mr. Keene's real name was Ira Frederick Aldridge, born in Bel Air, Maryland, in 1804. Nothing is known of Ira's mother. Ira's father, Joshua, was a slave who claimed to be an African prince.[12]

---

11 Edward Ziter, "Kean, Byron, and Fantasies of Miscegenation," 610-11. This calculation does not include his pre-Drury Lane role of chimpanzee. There is a lone voice of dissent on Kean's radical recoding of Othello. Charles B. Lower looks at some of the same evidence and suggests that a bronze Othello was no more or less objectionable than a black one. See "Othello as Black on Southern Stages, Then and Now," esp. 202-5.

12 In his memoir, Aldridge or his proxy, writes that: "His [Aldridge's] forefathers were princes of the Fulah tribe, whose dominions were Senegal, on the banks of the river of that name, on the west coast of Africa, to which shore one of our early missionaries found his way, taking charge of the father of Mr. Aldridge...." We learn that during a civil war, Ira "then a promising youth, was taken to America by the missionary, and sent to Schenectady College, near New York, to receive the advantages of a Christian education." See Ira Aldridge, *Memoir and Theatrical Career of Ira Aldridge*, 8.

How did Aldridge become interested in theater, in Shakespeare, and in Kean? To pick up that part of the story, we must return to the night Kean humiliated his other double, Junius Brutus Booth.

The Exile of Mr. Booth

As we recall, Junius Brutus Booth, once a darling of the English stage, had been trashed by Kean. Thereafter, Booth's career went into a slow but inexorable decline. On 25 February 1817, a riot broke out in the pit of Covent Garden because Booth dared to appear in one of Kean's most famous parts: Richard III. Kean's Wolves drowned him out with shouts of "Liar! Pretender! Imitator of Kean!" Despite this reaction, Booth appeared soon after in another of Kean's principal roles, Sir Giles Overreach, but could not match Kean's histrionics and resorted to "a manœuvre which was severely commented upon. One of the attendants who held him was furnished with a sponge filled with blood (pink rose), which he, unseen by the audience, squeezed into his mouth to convey the idea of his having burst a blood-vessel."[13] The play was a success and prompted the management to try Booth in now-forgotten roles in now-forgotten plays: Fitzharding in Tobin's *The Curfew*, Mortimer in Colman's *The Iron Chest*. Both parts were potentially star vehicles for Booth. True, John Tobin's *The Curfew* is an absurd revenge play concerning a villain (Booth's Fitzharding) who is unhappy that his life has been saved and sets out to punish his rescuer. Nonetheless, the part allowed Booth to display a sullen, savage sensuality:

> ... I should kill thee with extremest torture:
> To 'suage the burning thirst of my revenge—
> Drink thy blood life-warm; tear those trembling limbs,
> And scatter them as whirlwinds strew the dust....[14]

The Wolves howled their contempt.

Similarly, in George Colman's *The Iron Chest*, Sir Edward Mortimer's death speech allowed Booth the opportunity to create an impressive spectacle of bombast, violence and tragedy:

>   One fatal, fatal turn,
> Has poison'd all! Where is my honour now?
> To die!—To have my ashes trampled on,
> By the proud foot of scorn! Polluted Hell—
> Who dares to mock my guilt? Is't you—or you?
> Rack me that grinning fiend! Damnation!
> Who spits upon my grave? I'll stab again—
> I'll—Oh!   *Falls* [*dead*].[15]

---

13 William C. Macready, *Macready's Reminiscences*, 106.
14 John Tobin, *The Curfew*, 50.
15 George Colman the Younger, *The Iron Chest*, III.iii.p.81.

But this too failed to re-ignite interest, except among The Wolves, who wished to humble the actor yet further.

On 11 February 1818, the man who once commanded a huge salary and dictated terms to Drury Lane, the man who was the prize in a bidding war between London's two principal theaters, the man who had once rivaled the great Kean, was now playing Shylock in St. Albans, earning £3.11s. On 7 March 1818, Booth wrote to the theatrical manager of a company of actors in Stamford, Mr. T.W. Manley, asking for travel expenses. Manley refused. Moreover, he insulted Booth, who had been billing himself as "the great Mr. Booth, the fearful rival of Mr. Kean." According to Manley, Booth was nothing but a "Weak little man." Worse yet, he wrote:

> Acknowledged genius and admired talent may have its pardoned weaknesses, but an actor of your humble kind can have no pretence for giving himself the airs of a popular favorite: when he does, it becomes provokingly ridiculous .... your actions were full of unmannerly and coarse arrogance....[16]

In the 1818-19 theatrical season, Booth was given one last chance: Gloucester in Nicholas Rowe's *Jane Shore*. The part was not huge, but it did allow for some scene-stealing rants. An expected highlight was Booth's confrontation with Jane, who refuses to give up her belief that Edward's children should rule:

> GLOU. Ha! Dost thou brave me, minion! Dost thou know
> How vile, how very wretched my pow'r can make thee?
> That I can place thee in such abject state,
> As Help shall never find thee; where, repining,
> Thou shalt sit down and gnaw the earth for anguish,
> Groan to the pitiless winds without return;
> Howl like the midnight wolf amidst the desert,
> And curse thy life in bitterness and misery?[17]

Although the production was a hit and filled the house for 13 of its 14 nights, Booth "was so ineffective that he quitted the theatre after the first night, and Egerton filled his place."[18] The following year at Covent Garden, Booth appeared as Lear, with Macready as Edmund. Macready blamed the failure of the play on Booth, noting with some scorn that with Booth as Lear, "It could not be a success."[19] When Covent Garden discovered the growing drawing power of Macready, Booth was relegated to secondary parts.

Some time in summer 1821, Booth deserted his wife and son. He and his mistress, Mary Anne Holmes, boarded a ship bound for the West Indies. At Madeira,

---

16 Quoted in Stephen M. Archer, *Junius Brutus Booth: Theatrical Prometheus*, 49.

17 Nicholas Rowe, *Jane Shore*, IV.1.171-8. The text is derived from *Shakespeare Imitations, Parodies and Forgeries*, Vol.1.

18 William C. Macready, *Macready's Reminiscences*, 131.

19 Ibid., 156.

he changed his mind and boarded another ship, bound for Norfolk, Virginia.[20] Along the journey, Booth began to refer to his mistress as his "wife," and, by the time they arrived in America, the sham took hold.[21] The newly arrived actor bought some land in Bel Air, Maryland—the same town Ira Aldridge, the future Mr. Keene, lived in—and employed farmhands among the local Negro population to build him a huge log cabin and, thereafter, to work his land.[22]

Aldridge's Early Career

Was Aldridge one of those workers? Indirect evidence suggests he was. Booth's chief farmhand was Joe Hall, who claimed to be a descendant of the Royal House of Madagascar.[23] Unless we envision Bel Air unique in that a disproportionate number of her workmen were descended from the bluest of African blood, Joe Hall and Ira seem to have traded stories.

It is attractive to imagine that Ira Aldridge worked for Booth. It would certainly explain his interest in and knowledge of Shakespeare. In his recent study of John Wilkes Booth, Gordon Samples noted that all the Booths regularly recited passages from Shakespeare, and that "[m]any of the workers heard the recitations so frequently that they were able to join in and recite along too, being able to prompt each other."[24] Chief among those workers was the abovementioned Joe Hall, who would cue the Booths when reciting their lines.[25] Is it too much to imagine that Aldridge glimpsed Junius Brutus Booth, or that he overheard from other farmhands stories concerning

---

20 J. Fitzgerald Molloy, *The Life and Adventures of Edmund Kean,* II:135. A more sympathetic version of Booth's relationship with Mary Anne Holmes is presented in their daughter's account. See Asia Booth Clarke, *Booth's Memorials*, 64-5. James Winston records that Junius Brutus Booth's father promised Mary Anne Holmes' mother £50 a year to hush up the matter. See 14 March 1821, *Drury Lane Journal*, 28.

21 Gene Smith notes with some sympathy that Junius Brutus Booth did send his British wife, Adelaide, money for their son, Richard (*American Gothic*, 23). But he never told her about Mary Anne, and over the years never mentioned the ten bastard children he sired with her. Adelaide found out about Booth's double life in 1846, twenty-five years after he had deserted her. They were finally and officially divorced in 1851 (43). Booth's sexual misconduct can be traced to his minority: when Junius was still in his teens, he seduced one of his father's serving girls. She bore him a child and successfully sued him for debauching her. Typically, when officers came to collect the fine, Booth ran away, leaving his father, Richard, to pay (19).

22 Asia Booth Clarke, *Booth Memorials*, 78. Booth lists his home as "Harford, Maryland," but Joe Hall, who worked for the Booths, refers to it as "Belair."

23 Asia Booth Clarke, *Booth's Memorials*, 107.

24 Gordon Samples, *Lust for Fame*, 14.

25 Ibid., 17-18. Asia Booth Clarke noted that Joe Hall helped her brother John Wilkes Booth practice his Brutus, and that Joe was struck by how much John Wilkes Booth reminded him of Booth Sr. in the same role. Evidently, Joe Hall had been watching the Booths privately perform for decades.

Booth's battle with the master-actor, Edmund Kean? Might he have even, dare we ask, listened to or learned acting from Junius Brutus Booth, the man who was to sire a trio of actors, Junius Brutus Jr., Edwin, and John Wilkes?[26]

Mary Malone, in her biography of Aldridge, tosses away these stories. Aldridge, she writes, was born and raised in New York; his father was born in New York; they were not descendants of African royalty.[27] Even if we agree with Malone that anything other than the facts is the stuff bad mini-series are made on, Mr. Keene may have learned of Kean from yet another source. We know that by 1821 Aldridge was intermittently in New York, acting with James Hewlett, a mulatto native of the West Indies. Hewlett was known even in London—where he had appeared the year before—for his astonishing imitations of both Kemble and Kean. Returning to New York, Hewlett joined an all-black theater group, the African Company. The group played out of a theater on Mercer Street, which had a capacity of 300 or 400. While Aldridge was performing at Mercer Street with James Hewlett, Kean played the Anthony Street Theater in New York in March and April 1821.

Aldridge may well have attended one or many of these performances. While we might imagine that racism was rampant in America during this period, Ira Aldridge, like all African Americans living in the north, could legally attend any theatrical event. In fact, we have evidence that Negroes turned out in large numbers to see Kean. In 1825, while Kean was suffering under the weight of public scandal, a New York newspaper captured a performance of Kean in lively caricature—an audience united in pummeling poor Kean with fruit, eggs, and even a dead cat. The audience is, for the most part, black. The few whites in attendance sit in the more affluent boxes. While caricature is an art that tends toward exaggeration, it is an exaggeration of fact, not of pure fancy. If Negroes turned out in large number to see Kean in 1825, it is reasonable to suppose they did the same during the earlier 1820-21 tour.

If Aldridge saw Kean in New York, it was during Kean's first tour, as we know that, after the closing of the African Company in 1823, Aldridge moved to Scotland and was, by 1825, starring at the Coburg in London. One yarn has it that while in London, Aldridge worked as Kean's valet.[28] Again the story is not as ludicrous as it initially sounds. Aldridge came to England when the black theater in New York closed. He was already a gifted actor but stood little chance of starring in any of the predominantly white American companies or of finding another viable black company. In England, at least, there were two precedents for black Shakespeareans: Ignatius Sancho, an ex-slave, had starred as Othello in the 1760s, and more recently, the aforementioned James Hewlett had performed his principal Shakespearean

---

26 Certainly, the elder Booth taught his actor-sons his Keanian moves. Writes L. Terry Oggel: "The younger Booth [Edwin] had absorbed his father's style all unconsciously, just as he had learned most of his parts by hearing his father perform them over the years. Naturally, his attempts in the first years …[of his taking to the stage] were in imitation of his father" (*Edwin Booth: A Bio-Biography*, 12).

27 Mary Malone, *Actor in Exile*, 1-4.

28 The claim is made most recently in Fred Kelso's "Aldridge, Ira: Historically Important Marylanders."

roles in London.[29] As for working as Kean's valet, if Aldridge knew the Booths, it is possible that the name of Kean had been in his head since leaving Bel Air. Let us assume he never met the farmhand Joe Hall or the Booths, that he learned of Kean only after he met Hewlett in New York. Even in this scenario, it is likely that Aldridge was no less drawn to Kean's sympathetic portrayal of black men.

Plate 12: Kean performing in America, ca. 1825. Note the segregated audience. Was Ira Aldridge among the audiences that saw Kean perform? Reprinted from Personal Collection.

Aldridge might have sought Kean out, but would Kean hire him? It's not impossible. Meeting Kean would be easy enough. He was far from a recluse. He liked to drink in the worst sort of taverns, visit the lowest brothels. If Kean did hire Aldridge, it might have been a further declaration of his racial egalitarianism. No doubt, hiring Aldridge would also demonstrate Kean's flair. Perhaps keeping a Negro valet had *cachet*, or perhaps it just appealed to him that everyone would notice his newest servant? (We recall, for example, that Grattan was ushered in to see Kean by a black manservant.) Was employing Aldridge no different than buying a pet lion or walking around the house in his Huron chief outfit? Kean's biographers are remarkably silent on this point, but it is unlikely, though not impossible, that Aldridge worked for Kean. Accepting that Aldridge was in Scotland in 1824 and

29 William Torbert Leonard, *Masquerade in Black*, 43.

made his London debut in 1825, it's hard to see when he might have worked for Kean, who left for America in 1825.[30]

Adopting Kean's name was dangerous. As we have seen, Kean went out of his way to destroy all rivals. But Mr. Keene's timing was impeccable. In 1825, with the Charlotte Cox affair forcing him to consider moving to America, Kean had more pressing concerns than this envenomed snake. In time, Aldridge would have to fight for the right to use the stage name of "Mr. Keene," and all the legitimacy that the still-potent cognomen entailed. As for Kean, there was another enemy, far more dangerous and much closer to home—his own son.

Yet Another Mr. Kean

Charles Kean was born on 18 January 1811, at the low point of Edmund Kean's fortunes. His elder brother, Howard, who had died at age six, had been acclaimed as an acting genius of sorts, doing theatrical recitals and songs. This second son's path to the stage was not so direct. When Charles was of age, his father sent him to Eton, where he did well in Latin and excelled in "old-boy" sports. He was second captain of the rowing team and learned fencing from the master Angelo.[31] Kean, who had always claimed that he had been to Eton, must have been proud, but the result was that Charles grew up to be an expensive lay-about and a virtual stranger.

Their distant relationship was a non-issue when the money was pouring in, but, by 1827, Kean was broke. Despite earning an ungodly sum—think Tom Cruise's career wages—he was now living hand-to-mouth with a common prostitute named Ophelia Benjamin. To Kean, it was clear. He had worked hard for years to support his family, and the result was that he and his wife were estranged and his educated son was nothing more than a little ingrate who had sided with his mother.

All of Kean's biographers assume that Mary, disgusted with her husband's affair with Mrs. Cox, left him. It appeals to their Victorian values and, more importantly, describing Kean's sensuous excesses, his villainous behavior, allows for a dramatic fifth act of social rehabilitation and spiritual redemption.[32] What we might overlook is just how forced this narrative is. True, Mary, like every person, had her breaking point, but Kean's affairs had always been very public. There was nothing in the Cox affair that was new or more disturbing than any of Kean's other flings; Mrs. Cox was only one of a number of women he slept with every night. Whether Kean used sex as a theatrical tool or not, from the biographer's vantage, Kean's open affairs were also psychologically cruel acts. Each night at the theater offered further proof of his

---

30 That would still leave 1824, an acceptable window of opportunity, but, from early 1824 to early 1825, Aldridge was attending Glasgow University, where he received several medals for Latin composition. What is of interest is the reason why the story is repeated. Whether literally true or not, the story does suggest Aldridge's deference to Kean: Kean is the lord of the theatrical mansion, Aldridge, his obsequious butler.

31 John William Cole, *The Life and Theatrical Times of Charles Kean*, I:143-4.

32 Both aspects are discussed in the last chapter.

lack of commitment to his wife and their one remaining child, Charles. That Mary Kean stuck it out so long is, from any rational standpoint, a consecration to quietism, a proof that she too played her part, a Niobe, all tears.

All of Kean's biographers state that Mary left him. Yet, the truth of the matter was that he left her. In a hitherto unpublished letter, Mary writes, "Dearest Edmund do I deserve this treatment for god sake; if you have any feeling for me[;] you have made me miserable as your Heart can wish—let me see you—…. *I shall go to Bath* I cannot be *worse treated* than now[,] completely neglected & if I am to be miserable let me enjoy [illegible] with you … Why not come home…[?]"[33] Kean never replied and never returned. In another letter to Kean's solicitor, Mary writes, "You do not answer my inquiries as to Mr. Kean—*tell me at once* does he wish me to remain here?" Kean had sent Mary to his estate on the Island of Bute, probably in part to shield her from the scandal. Continuing, she wrote, "Will it give ease to his mind, my doing so? Does he wish to see me again…? I do not want a separation from my husband, not for worlds would I bring any such thing before the Public." The reply from his solicitor, Sivell, states that Kean wanted to separate from Mary but had settled on her £504 per annum: in addition Kean left further funds to pay for Charles' Eton education.[34]

Father and Son

Edmund Kean's biographer Hawkins deletes all mention of this provision for Charles. In his version, Mary leaves the actor, but Kean agrees to give her a generous allowance and then uses what is left of his influence to obtain a good job for Charles, a position in the East India Company, but Charles refuses. After learning of Charles' disinclination, Kean tries to explain the sad facts of life to his son:

> KEAN: My strength is on the wane; I cannot act Sir Giles as I used to. My money is gone; I have nothing to fall back upon should I be unable to play. At present it is not in my power to secure the *400l.* a year to your mother, or I would do so immediately. However, while I live, she shall never go in want of anything, and when I die it will be found that I have done something for her.
> CHARLES: Sir, your inability to secure the allowance to my mother compels me to decline the cadetship, and to announce to you my determination not to leave England during her lifetime.
> KEAN (*formally*): Listen to me, you either accept the cadetship, or give me up.
> CHARLES (*rises quickly and with anger*): I am sorry for it, but I do not think that you are so angry as you would make me believe. However, I won't leave my mother.[35]

---

33 Letter from Mary to Edmund Kean, in Kean E- Recip., HRC.

34 Gordon Craig, *The Life and Theatrical Career of Edmund Kean*, 52.

35 F.W. Hawkins, *Life of Edmund Kean*, II:295. I have adapted the dialogue into playlet, but the words themselves come from Hawkins' biography.

In John William Cole's biography of Charles Kean, Edmund Kean is more concerned with protecting his fame than with providing for his family. According to Cole, Kean walks out on Mary. Then the actor cuts off Charles' allowance and forces his withdrawal from Eton. Charles then comes back from Eton to find his mother living alone and in poverty.[36] Manfully, Charles stands up to his father and informs him of his decision to become an actor:

KEAN (*raging villainously*): What will you do when I discard you, and you are thrown entirely on your own resources?
CHARLES: In that case, I shall be compelled to seek my fortune on the stage. (*Kean smiling in derision. Charles, warming, continues*) and though I may never rise to eminence, or be a great actor, I shall at least obtain a livelihood for my mother and myself, and be obliged to no one.
KEAN: The name of Kean shall die with me.[37]

Who knows? Cole's narrative might be accurate. Kean had a mountainous ego and probably did resent his son. As for Kean cutting off Mary financially, it's either a nasty truth or a useful imposition, a handy reason for the reader to side with Charles. Maybe Kean did cut off Charles' college fund? But the known facts suggest that Charles could have stayed in school, had he so wished. Assuming Kean did not cancel the aforementioned funds, his rage was understandable. Charles could have stayed in school, could have become a gentleman. Instead, he became yet another competitor.

In any case, the aforementioned war of words between father and son is the climax of Cole's biography. There is no other section of the book that works upon us with such force. Yet, while we dislike the Edmund Kean of Cole's construction, we feel surprisingly little sympathy for his aloof Charles, who displays no guilt, no remorse for disobeying his father, and, perhaps more damagingly, little warmth or generousness of spirit to counterpoise Edmund Kean's cold villainies.[38] The biography is a wild narrative, a kind of *Tristram Shandy*, in which its hero (Charles) does not appear until he is full-grown. His first entry is in fact the aforementioned

---

36 John William Cole, *The Life and Theatrical Times of Charles Kean*, I:148.

37 Ibid., I:146-7. Again, I have turned the stated dialogue into a playlet. See also Henry Sedley, who writes, "Edmund Kean, and in truth, nearly all eminent players … disliked to have his children following in his footsteps" ("The Booths—Father and Son: Some Personal Reminiscences," 1082). Richard W. Schoch notes some difficulties in this father-son dynamic (*Shakespeare's Victorian Stages*, 22-3).

38 At times, he is downright unfilial. For example, John William Cole defends Charles for not buying more of his father's things in an estate sale:

The sale of Edmund Kean's valuables took place in the 17th of June, 1834. The world wondered, or affected to wonder; and it was said beyond a whisper, by more than one person, that Charles Kean *ought* to have bought in the personal effects of his father, and prevented a public auction. …. [but] the young man was still struggling for his own subsistence, that he had his mother to support, and that he had not yet had sufficient time to accumulate store. (*The Life and Theatrical Times of Charles Kean*, I:209)

confrontation with his villainous father. Concerning the first eighteen years of Charles' life, Cole simply informs us that he was shipped off to boarding school. Even here, Cole supplies no anecdotes from professors, gardeners, shop assistants or constables; Cole supplies no details of birthday parties, Christmas presents, or *impromptu* picnics.

Who knows, Charles may well have been one of those people who never stood out in a crowd, who left no strong or fond impressions on school chums and colleagues. But Cole goes still further to disassociate Charles from his famous father, even suggesting that the former was somehow a genetic leapfrog, that there was nothing of Edmund Kean's looks or personality in this, his only surviving son. Cole begins by reciting a variety of stories concerning Edmund Kean's parentage, that he was, alternatively, a bastard descendant of George Saville, Marquis of Halifax, a bastard descendant of Henry Carey, or the bastard son of the Duke of Norfolk. Cole then turns a nice rhetorical trick: "Birth and ancestry, and what we have not ourselves achieved, we can scarcely call our own. ... Nevertheless, everything must have a beginning; and there is more satisfaction in winning fame and fortune by personal merit than in being accidentally the 'tenth transmitter' of hereditary distinction."[39] In other words, Charles can take some satisfaction that he likely has royal blood in his veins, and more satisfaction that he rose to fame unaided by his bastard father. The next part is still trickier. Subtly associating Edmund Kean's "flashes of lighting" with a fickleness of personality, Cole goes on to suggest that Charles, though lacking in genius, compensates with two unKeanian virtues: steadiness and due diligence. Thus, Charles inherits nothing from Edmund, but "owes much to his own self-reliance, based upon upright principles, and innate integrity of heart and purpose. His genius has never burned with a flickering light; his perseverance has never faltered on the roughest track."[40]

Cole's Biography is a Fiction

Cole's narrative certainly works to Charles Kean's advantage, but this narrative of the self-created man is a pure myth, a way to misrepresent a career, which was, I will argue, based on nepotism and, as facts suggest in his coming encounter with "Mr. Keene," sustained by discrimination. After all, Kean might have hindered his son when the latter approached Stephen Price of Drury Lane. His father had been with Drury Lane since 1814 but had recently switched to Covent Garden. (Kean had been upset over a refusal for a salary advance. Drury Lane denied him the money, and the actor, outraged, signed with Covent Garden.) Price had lost a star with Kean;

---

39 Ibid., I:59-60. He further writes, "Of his [Edmund Kean's] own parentage and ancestry little is known, and that little is involved in much uncertainty" (I:58).

40 Ibid., II:378. Elsewhere, Cole writes, "Charles Kean, inheriting the genius and success of his father, but avoiding the fatal improvidence by which both were rendered unavailing, has, while yet within the meridian of life, placed himself at the head of a difficult profession, for which he was not trained or intended..." (I:58).

perhaps his son could take his place? On balance, "the name of Kean [was still] a powerful talisman."[41]

As we have seen, Edmund Kean had ingenious ways to control his supporting cast or to destroy rising talents. Keeping his son from the stage could have been managed easily. Even with Kean now at Covent Garden, he might have quietly spoken to Stephen Price, or he might have threatened actors appearing with Charles. It would have been just like Kean to whisper quietly to a starving actor, "Appear with my son, and you will never appear on stage with me." He might have taken legal action against the theater for billing Charles as "Mr. Kean"—a deliberate attempt to confuse Edmund Kean's fame and skills with those of his unknown and untested son. Instead, to the shock, no doubt, of many, Kean worked to aid Charles. In a hitherto unpublished letter, Ann (often called Nancy) Carey (Kean's birth mother) writes:

Thursday May 17 1827

Dear Edmund

I wrote to Mr. Reynolds this morning not knowing wether you was in London or not, have since leant that you are.

I bless God for your safe return to England and rejoice that you have put your enemies under your feet. May providence preserve your health and bestow on you grate favour because you have done a mercyfull act in placing Harry in Drury Lane.[42]

Kean's first child, Howard, died in 1813. The date of Ann Carey's letter, coming almost fifteen years later, but only months before Charles' première, suggests that Carey either confused the names of her grandchildren, or had been so infrequently part of the family environment—she didn't know whether Kean was in town or not—as to not recall which grandson was still living. But she understood one thing well enough: Kean had helped his son get a job at Drury Lane.

The Early Career of Charles Kean

On 1 October 1827, people flocked out of simple curiosity to see the son of the great actor make his first appearance in John Home's popular play, *Douglas*.[43] Charles played the lead role, Norval, a high-minded warrior. The play is obscure enough to warrant a brief summary. Raised in pastoral simplicity, Norval nonetheless yearns for the court and the battlefield. He soon saves Lord Randolph from assassination and finds himself oddly attached to Douglas' widow, who turns out to be his long-lost mother. Suffice it to say, by the close of the play, he will save the kingdom and reclaim, albeit briefly, his birthright.

For a debut, Charles' part was surprisingly large but straightforward enough. For the most part, all he had to do was swagger around the stage, look fierce, and deliver

---

41 Ibid., I:148.

42 Letter from Ann Carey to Edmund Kean, in Kean E- Recip., HRC.

43 John William Cole, *The Life and Theatrical Times of Charles Kean*, I:149-50.

his lines with bombast. Here's a typical scene in which Glenalvon, a scheming lord, baits Norval with a reminder of his humble upbringing:

> NOR. If I were chain'd, unarm'd, and bed-rid old,
> Perhaps I should revile; but as I am,
> I have no tongue to rail. The humble Norval
> Is of a race who strive not but with deeds.
> Did I not fear to freeze thy shallow valour
> And make thee sink too soon beneath my sword,
> I'd tell thee what thou art. I know thee well.
> GLEN. Dost thou not know Glenalvon, born to command
> Ten thousand slaves like thee.
> NOR. Villain, no more!
> Draw and defend thy life. I did design
> To have defy'd thee in another cause:
> But Heav'n accelerates its vengeance on thee.
> Now for my own and Lady Randolph's wrongs. (4.1.401-14)

Kean's name did half the trick. The theater was brimmed with the curious. But, once the curtain went up, Charles was on his own. It's likely that everyone, perhaps even his famous father, wanted the boy to do well. Sadly, Charles Kean failed, thoroughly and absolutely. All he had to do was act tough, but, as one theatergoer recorded: "He trembled exceedingly, supported himself on his sword, and appeared to have much ado to retain his self-possession." Even his enthusiastic biographer admits that the reviews were "unanimous in condemnation. Not simple disapproval, or qualified censure, but sentence of utter incapacity—stern, bitter, crushing, and conclusive."[44] Comparing father to son, George Henry Lewes concluded that Charles Kean was "wholly deficient."[45] An anonymous critic for *Oxberry's Dramatic Biography* thought Charles' performance was so unKeanian that he even suggested that the two actors could not possibly be related: "Unfortunately for our hero [Edmund Kean], these children of adoption evidently appear strangers to his heart—they seem not to come from him—and only give occasion for regret."[46]

When audience interest in Charles waned, he headed for America, where he billed himself as "Mr. Kean," no doubt upsetting at least some customers, who bought tickets with the expectation of seeing the father, not the son. Charles improved slowly, and he returned from America hopeful that he could garner legitimate support. But, before leaving for America, he had to defeat some "man of colour" promoting himself as "Mr. Keene."

---

44 Ibid., I:152.

45 George Henry Lewes, *On Actors and the Art of Acting*, 16.

46 *Oxberry's Dramatic Biography*, V:49-50. Anticipating Cole's strategy, *A Memoir of Edmund Kean* (1825) suggested that the stain was, paradoxically, a family trait: "Mr. K[ean]. has one child living, a son [Charles] about 12 years of age, who bears no resemblance to his father" (9).

Keene vs. Kean

There was no denying the stark visual, racial, and class distinctions between these two Kean actors. In many ways, it was more distinctive than any comparison of Othello and Iago. Charles was the product of the English Boarding School system, designed to educate the sons of England's wealthiest leaders and its political peers. Although his father was an actor with questionable pedigree, Kean's wealth and fame expunged the social stains of bastardy and class inferiority. Charles was, as long as his father was footing the bill, a part of men's clubs and tea parties.

Yes, Charles had social advantages, but, from his perspective, it was Mr. Keene who was in the wrong. Imagine his upper-class disgust when finding out that some son of a runaway slave, or some former valet of his father's, was now using his family's name for monetary profit. While Charles was being forced into the wilds of America to learn his craft, this Negro had lolled about London and, in a seeming instant, had achieved fame and fortune. Now there was talk of this upstart actually stealing his father's throne. Charles never discussed the matter with his father, but it was clear that there was only one course of action open to him. Edmund Kean had defeated all rivals. His son would have to prove that he could do the same.

The newspapers saw "Mr. Keene's" appropriation of Kean's name as a challenge and affront to Charles. *The Globe* framed the controversy in theatrical terms:

> Keene v. Kean. The African votary of Thespis, yclept Mr. Keene, goes on triumphantly at the Coburg. *Two sons*, they say, *cannot shine in the same hemisphere*, and the new and the old world have done well to exchange luminaries. (Emphasis my own.)

The italicized line is from Prince Henry's challenge to Henry Percy in Shakespeare's *1 Henry IV*. Although neither Charles Kean nor Mr. Keene had ever been associated with the play, the message was clear enough. The duel of the two Keans would leave only one actor as heir apparent to the theatrical kingdom of Drury Lane.

As we saw in his dealings with rival actors, delay had always been one of Edmund Kean's weapons, and Charles adopted it as his own. Their motives differed: Edmund Kean had used delay as a means of marginalizing rivals and solidifying in the public's mind his right to a certain part; Charles used delay as a prolonged tutorial, a training camp for his upcoming bout. That it would take two years of near-constant performance before Charles felt ready to duel with Mr. Keene indicates how much Charles feared defeat.

They finally met on 10 July 1829, at The Belfast Theatre, and Charles had every reason to expect that he would emerge triumphant.[47] Firstly, his father had always been a favorite with Irish audiences. Even at the height of the Charlotte Cox affair, Dublin audiences had cheered Kean, and it was likely they would extend their

---

47 Torbert Leonard dates the evening as 9 July 1829, but the playbill states "This present evening (Friday, July 10)."

approbation to his son.[48] In fact, the duel with Mr. Keene was scheduled on the last night of a very successful theatrical run for Charles. Secondly, Charles, following another of his father's tactics, picked his own part and, therefore, carefully choose the theatrical ground on which to duel with Mr. Keene. Thirdly, Charles made sure that Aldridge could not use his adopted cognomen. For this particular performance, he was billed as the "AFRICAN ROSCIUS."

Even with these safeguards, the risks were all on Charles' side. They had agreed to appear together in *Othello*—with Charles playing Iago and Mr. Keene playing the Moor—and in Thomas Southerne's *Oroonoko*—with Charles Kean as the black slave Oroonoko and Mr. Keene as Aboan, a fellow slave who goads Oroonoko to rebel. If Charles did in fact pick these roles to duel with "Mr. Keene," his strategy was surprisingly risky. Charles' stage skills had improved considerably, but why give Mr. Keene any chance at all?

It seems allowing Aldridge to play Othello and Aboan was suicidal for four reasons: firstly, Edmund Kean may have played a near-white Othello, but the audience would surely be aware that this was a radical innovation. For most, Othello was still very much black. Since Othello is a Negro, the audience might conclude that Mr. Keene made a great Othello because he, like Othello, was Negro.[49] Playing the Negro lead in *Oroonoko* was equally dangerous for Charles. With Mr. Keene, a Negro, playing the part of Aboan, Charles was inviting a direct comparison as to who could play a black man better. Secondly, Othello was one of Edmund Kean's best parts. Since Mr. Keene had been trained as a copy-Kean, a strong performance might reinforce in the audience's mind that, in comparison with Charles, Mr. Keene made the superior Kean. Thirdly, the audience might associate this duel with his father's famous duel with Booth. His father had played Othello against Booth's Iago. This Negro was playing his father's part, Charles, the part of the challenger. Fourthly, Edmund Kean had destroyed Booth. If Charles were not as equally devastating, the clear inference would be that Charles was not—as patrons and critics had already suggested—worthy of his father's name.

In the end, both received positive press, but these reviews give us little indication as to how each actor felt about the outcome. As for Mr. Keene, we have no letters, journals or anecdotes, but we can imagine that the actor was satisfied. Like Young's or Macready's encounter with Edmund Kean, anything outside of unmitigated defeat

---

48 *The National Advocate*, New York, 12 July 1825, reported: "Mr. Kean had made an engagement in Dublin and played Sir Giles Overreach. In the early part of the performance he met with considerable opposition. The tumult eventually subsided, he was loudly applauded, and called forward when the curtain had fallen.—He addresses the audience on the subject of '*Irish generosity.*' This was so agreeable to them, that they appeared sadly disappointed, when he stated the following night was intended to be his last—but *eight*"(Press Clippings, Personal Collection). The same source noted that Dublin audiences applauded Kean "to the skies," while English audiences treated him in contempt (Press Clippings, Personal Collection).

49 On the other hand, *The Douglas Jerrold Newspaper* 21 March 1848, called Aldridge's portrayal of the black character Zanga a "piece of vulgarity" (William Herbert Marshall and Mildred Stock, *Ira Aldridge, the Negro Tragedian*, 162).

was a triumph. Further, Mr. Keene could be proud of the way he had upheld the Kean name. Thanks to the groundwork laid by Kean, Mr. Keene could no longer be judged simply as a black man playing black parts. He was now an *actor* playing black parts.[50] As for Charles, legend has it that after the performance, he swore that his wife, Ellen Tree, would never act with Mr. Keene again, "Because he's a nigger."[51] Of course, the word "nigger" grates on our racially sensitive ears. It's likely that Victorians were less squeamish with the uses of the word. That being said, it's transparent that Charles doesn't use the word in a complimentary fashion. More than likely the story signals Charles' desire to overturn his father's politics by re-inscribing the strict limits of what was socially acceptable and theatrically allowable.

Edmund Kean Helps Mr. Keene

During all this, we shouldn't forget Edmund Kean himself. In 1829, Charles' father was still alive. How did he feel about this theatrical contest to replace him? By the time of the Keene vs. Kean duel, Charles had patched things up with his father.[52] But Edmund Kean would be good to this other theatrical son as well. In December 1831, Edmund Kean met Mr. Keene in Dublin. Kean began his Dublin run 19 December with his Richard III and followed on 20 December with his Shylock; on 22 December, Kean performed his Othello. He stayed in Dublin until 2 January 1832, performing in the interim his major parts, including: Overreach (23 December), Brutus (24 and 25 December), Lear (27 December), Mortimer (28 December), Reuben Glenroy (31 December), and, on his last night, a medley including Act IV of *Richard*; Act IV of *Merchant of Venice*; Act V of *A New Way to Pay Old Debts*; Act II of *Macbeth*; Act III of *Othello*.

Mr. Keene played the same theater on 21 December. His manager urged him not to play any of Edmund Kean's parts, but Mr. Keene refused and announced he'd perform as Othello.[53] The risks were clear to everyone. As a columnist for *The Standard* later wrote: "He [Mr. Keene] had chosen the part of Othello for his first appearance—an undertaking which at present was most hazardous" since Edmund

---

50 Herbert Marshall and Mildred Stock ignore Kean's color recoding and conclude their study of Aldridge by arguing that he, not Kean, was the first significant actor to break the color barrier. Aldridge was "a pioneer in laying the foundations of that still-to-come theatre of the human race, Ira Aldridge was the first to show that a black man … [could play white parts] with equal artistry" (*Ira Aldridge, the Negro Tragedian*, 335). They also downplay Aldridge's use of Kean's name.

51 Ibid., 105. *The Standard* for 14 April 1833 noted that some objected to "the Moor's familiarity with her face, and ridiculed his privilege." See Ira Aldridge, *Memoir and Theatrical Career of Ira Aldridge*, 17.

52 After Edmund Kean's return from a tour of France in 1828, he vacationed at his castle in Bute, Scotland. There, he received a letter from Charles, his son, asking for a meeting. Kean agreed and even offered to act on stage with his son in the famous performance of *Brutus*, detailed in the Introduction.

53 Herbert Marshall and Mildred Stock, *Ira Aldridge, the Negro Tragedian*, 99.

Kean considered "this character, and the genius by which he has made it, peculiarly his own."[54] It was an act of youth, but also of stupidity. Edmund Kean, all previous history indicated, was not one to ignore an insult or a challenge.

On 21 December, the great Edmund Kean went to the theater to see Mr. Keene act. As stated earlier, they might well have met years before. But even were this so, when Mr. Keene first came to Britain in 1824, he had been little more than an amateur. By 1831, Mr. Keene was at the apogee of his powers. What was Kean's reaction to Mr. Keene's Othello? How odd and fantastic it must have been for Kean to watch this dark reflection of himself, and what a missed opportunity as well. If only Edmund Kean had dueled with Mr. Keene! Might Kean have played Iago to Mr. Keene's Othello, or might both have donned makeup? Think of it: Kean as Othello, Mr. Keene as Iago. But it was not to be.

And as for duels, by 1831, Edmund Kean was in swift decline. His health was failing, and he now found himself acting at lesser playhouses, including the Coburg, where Mr. Keene had gotten his London start. He might not have wished to duel anyone.[55] Besides, what had Kean to prove? He had overthrown the best of the Kemble school, and he already met imitations of himself twice before: Kean had defeated Kean when he had acted with Booth, and Kean had reconciled with Kean when he had turned to Charles and asked his son to pity his poor father. Perhaps Kean sensed his own mortality and was trying to patch things up as best he could before he shuffled off this mortal coil; perhaps he had simply mellowed with age?

According to the *Dublin University Magazine*, after the performance, Kean sent for Mr. Keene and complimented him highly on his acting. But this account is dated October 1868. There is no contemporaneous record of their meeting face to face. That being said, Kean felt strongly enough about Mr. Keene's work to send the following note to a Mr. Bellamy, manager of Theatre Royal, Bath:

Dublin, January 3,1832.

Dear Bellamy,—I beg to introduce to your notice Mr. Aldridge, the African Roscius, whose performances I have witnessed with great pleasure. He possesses wondrous versatility, and I am sure, under your judicious generalship, will prove a card in Bath. I have not yet recovered from the fatigues of my journey, but hope to be myself in a day or two.

I remain, dear Bellamy, truly yours,

E. KEAN.[56]

---

54 *The Standard* (April 14, 1833), The Theatre Museum, Covent Garden, London, England.

55 On 27 June 1831, Kean played his *Richard III* at the Coburg. The theater stressed in its advertisement that audiences might expect a "ten-fold" increase by enjoying Kean in so intimate a venue (The Theatre Museum, Covent Garden, London, England).

56 Ira Aldridge, *Memoir and Theatrical Career of Ira Aldridge*, 15.

The Russian critic Sergei Durylin sees in Kean's letter nothing less than fear.[57] Kean wanted his rival out of town as soon as possible and, with him, all comparisons. It is unlikely that Kean was trying to push Mr. Keene out of Dublin. His dates were up anyway. More likely, as odd as it sounds, Kean may have simply been behaving generously. On the other hand, it is odd that Kean referred to Mr. Keene in his letter as "Mr. Aldridge", rather than "Mr. Keene". In any case, whether Kean was just getting rid of Aldridge or genuinely willing to help him, with letter in hand, doors were opened. Bellamy employed him immediately.

Crowning a New Kean

Was this letter of introduction a symbolic endorsement of Mr. Keene over Charles Kean? If it was, Kean was not alone in his preference. Less than three months before Kean died, the *Caledonian Mercury* of Glasgow (March 20, 1833) endorsed Mr. Keene, not Charles, as Kean's natural heir apparent: "He [Mr. Keene] reminds us of Kean in many of the best passages, and when time may have deprived us of that great master, the African Roscius will not be an unworthy successor."[58] On 10 April 1833, Mr. Keene appeared in *Othello* at Covent Garden. It was a coronation of sorts, with Edmund Kean's regular supporting cast in place.

But Covent Garden had moved too soon. Although Edmund Kean would be dead in 35 days, the audience was not ready to embrace fully Mr. Keene or any new Kean. On 11 April 1833 *The Theatrical Observer* stated its objections:

> We cannot, however, think him [Mr. Keene] calculated to fill the place of Mr. Kean, whose inimitable performance has spoiled us for seeing anyone else in the character [of Othello], while the remembrance of his excellence remains so vividly impressed on our minds.

Mr. Keene seems to have taken this review to heart. He retreated to the provinces and, for long stretches, toured Eastern Europe. Always retaining his Keanian style, Aldridge soon gave up the adopted cognomen. In the years to come, he would appear in London many times and would expand his repertoire to include many traditionally white roles, including King Lear, but never again would he challenge Charles' right to the name of Kean, or the right to think of himself as Edmund Kean's successor.

But audiences were none too hasty to embrace Charles either. Finally, on 16 May 1838, five years after Edmund Kean's death, *The Morning Post* gushed:

> Mr. Charles Kean appeared here last evening for the first time, as *Othello*. Under any circumstances, the character is an arduous one, but was rendered more so on the present occasion, from its having been considered the *chef-d'œuvre* of his lamented father. ... as the play progressed, and level speaking gave place to bursts of feeling, the genius of the actor shone forth in its brightest colours, and elicited from a crowded audience such

---

57 Sergei Durylin's argument cited in Herbert Marshall and Mildred Stock, *Ira Aldridge, the Negro Tragedian*, 104.

58 Ira Aldridge, *Memoir and Theatrical Career of Ira Aldridge*, 19.

manifestations of applause, as might fairly lead to an anticipation of the revival of the most flourishing days of the drama.[59]

If Charles' ascension to his father's throne heralded the possible return to Keanian brilliance, it was an option that Charles claimed but refused to exercise.

Revising Kean's Radical Acting

Charles found himself in a difficult position. To act Kean faithfully, he had to exhibit racial forbearance; a notion that was anathema to his Eton background. Yet to act Kean poorly would be the death of his career and a betrayal of his father. Charles decided on a midcourse. All extant commentary confirms that Charles acted like his father on stage.[60] However, offstage, he could not have differed from him more. His father was a whoremonger, a wild man, a drunk who snubbed class lines and racial distinctions; Charles was an Eton brat, happily married, politically conservative, sexually staid, and, if we accept anecdotal evidence, a bigot. He saw no problem in calling a black man a "nigger," an epitaph which strongly suggests that Charles' views were not as open-minded as those of his father.

Even on stage, Charles tried to contain his father's acting through the use of spectacular scenic productions. We have seen that Kean himself hated scenic spectacles because they took audience attention away from his movements. Yet once Charles had secured his hold on theatrical power, he set to work on projects designed to distract the audience from the actor, even if that actor was himself. In 1850, Charles Kean took the lease of the Princess's Theatre, in which he mounted the largest, most lavish Shakespeare spectacles the stage had ever seen: an ensemble of capable actors, hundreds of extras for the crowd scenes, three-dimensional backdrops, real horses on the stage; in short, everything his father had banned from his own productions. More importantly, Edmund Kean's acting, we recall, suggested that race was a fictional construction. Charles, on the other hand, used the constructedness of the stage to recreate the historical settings of Shakespeare's plays. Each character was carefully vested with appropriate and visually authentic garb, be it Roman, Illyrian, or Venetian. Such details obliged audiences to pass value judgments. Did Roman helmets really look like that? Were Illyrians really so gaudy? Could Desdemona, a daughter of a Venetian statesman, really marry a black man, who was also, by the

---

59 The article is quoted in John William Cole, *The Life and Theatrical Times of Charles Kean*, I:292.

60 A friend of Edmund Kean's informed him that Charles "copied your manner in attitude as much as possible" and received loudest applause when he "imitated your voice and style" (Ibid., I:155). His Hamlet was often eerily like his father's, especially the line "In my mind's eye, Horatio" which was, indeed, "most like Edmund Kean's manner of delivering that passage," and was highly applauded (Ibid., I:258). On 6 July 1840, Charles played Macbeth at the Haymarket; *The Morning Post* again compared his performance to his father's: he acted, "just as Edmund Kean did before him; and it would be impossible to accord higher praise"(Ibid., I:314).

way, a hired mercenary? Under this sort of withering scrutiny, Kean's own acting had to be rejected, because, asking a question such as "How sympathetic would the Venetians be to blacks?" required an answer that was incongruous with Kean's radical goals of color erasure. As such, Charles' claim to Keanian performance was not so much a succession as a rebellion. Kean's performances had called into question the nature of western racial superiority; now Charles was arguing that his father's ideas were all nonsense.

Charles Kean and John Wilkes Booth

Charles Kean was not the only Keanian who was out to stop Edmund Kean's message. John Wilkes Booth was taught the Keanian acting style by his father, Junius Brutus Booth, and, when donning make-up and costume for Othello, studiously avoided depicting the Moor as an African. His costume, for example, was entirely of Turkish origin.[61] But, off stage, he too rejected Kean's implicit idea of racial equality. One of the ironies of Booth's assassination of Lincoln is that the President had every reason to think Booth's views were in accordance with his own.[62] Indeed, Lincoln had seen Booth several times and could not help but notice the actor's interests in roles of color and ethnicity. Booth's standard stable included Othello, Charles De Moor in Schiller's *Robbers*, and Shylock from Shakespeare's *Merchant of Venice*; that's to say, Booth played black men and Jews.[63]

Lincoln was something of an amateur Shakespearean and enjoyed reciting lines from *Richard III*. He even took acting notes on the role from James Henry Hackett, an American actor who was a known Kean disciple.[64] Lincoln, then, was training in

---

61 Gordon Samples, *Lust for Fame*, 122.

62 Offstage, Booth himself did not hide his disgust at Lincoln's policies, particularly the emancipation of the slaves. In April and May of 1862, he was arrested for wishing "the whole government would go to hell"; he was released after paying a fine and swearing his allegiance to the Union (Gordon Samples, *Lust for Fame*, 138). On 13 April, a day before the assassination, Booth told a friend, "I feel like mounting my horse and tearing up and down the streets, waving a Rebel flag in each hand" (Ibid., 179). Booth's anger with Lincoln had stemmed from Lincoln's turnaround on the issue of slavery. Until 1860, Lincoln spoke of the need for a spirit of compromise and said he had no interest in the question of "slaves or slavery, in the states" (Letter to George T.M. Davis, 27 October 1860, *Abraham Lincoln, Slavery, and the Civil War*, 93). By 22 September 1862, Lincoln was offering slaves emancipation for any attempt to hinder or confront the rebel armies (Preliminary Emancipation Proclamation, 22 September 1862 (Ibid., 206-8; 207).

63 Hazlitt called Shiller's *Robbers* "barbarous, violent, and like Shakespear" (*Works*, XII: 329). On 7 March 1862, Baltimore had a "Boothian Festival" in which Wilkes Booth performed his best-known parts, Charles de Moor, Shylock, Richard III. On this occasion, Othello was not performed, although it had been featured in his previous engagement at the McVicker's Theater in Chicago.

64 Hackett went to London to record the master's moves in a promptbook, later published under the title, *Oxberry's 1822 edition of Richard III*. It should be noted that Hackett was a

the Keanian style of acting.[65] There is even a suggestion of "flashes of lightning" in Lincoln's dramatic expression. Joseph H. Choate recalled that when Lincoln gave a speech, "he was transformed before us. His eye kindled, his voice rang, his face shone and seemed to light up the whole assembly as by electric flash. For an hour and more he held his audience in the hollow of his hand."[66]

Legend has it that months before the assassination, Lincoln even requested a meeting with Booth. This request was highly unusual for Lincoln, who had a habit of sneaking into theaters unobserved and, normally, had no desire to go backstage. If the story is true, something about Booth must have caught the President's eye.[67] Might he have seen in Booth something that was very much in keeping with own Keanian oratory? In any case, Booth refused the request. He gave Lincoln no direct reason, but later told his friends that "I would rather have the applause of a Negro to that of the President!"[68]

The events of Lincoln's assassination are well rehearsed. But where did Charles Kean stand on the issue? As fate would have it, Charles Kean was in America at the time. His wife, Ellen, writing to their daughter, noted that Charles felt it necessary to meet with the British Consul and then with local actors to demonstrate his sympathies.[69] But such sympathetic outpourings were merely for show. Privately, Charles Kean's wife Ellen lamented, "All that sweet Plantation life is gone forever."[70] Killing Lincoln in the theater might have added dramatic flair, but it did not contain the very forces of equality, liberty, and fraternity which Edmund Kean's acting—and, because he was a copyist, even John Wilkes Booth's acting—helped to unleash.

---

wonderful Falstaff, a part Kean never played. It is possible that Hackett used Kean's style for the part.

65 Hackett's correspondences with the President are stored at the Library of Congress, Rare Books Division, The Alfred Whital Stern collection of Lincolniana, 1837-1912, Washington, D.C., 2 ft.

66 Harold Holzer, *Lincoln at Cooper Union*, 114. Holzer also argues that Lincoln studied rhetorical manuals, some of which stressed Shakespearean techniques. See *Lincoln Seen and Heard*, 173.

67 Lincoln stated his favorite play was *Macbeth*. See Albert Furtwangler's *Assassin on Stage: Brutus, Hamlet and the Death of Lincoln*, 70.

68 Gordon Samples, *Lust for Fame*, 126.

69 Ellen Kean, *Death and Funeral of Abraham Lincoln*. 18

70 Ellen Kean concludes, "England is the only land to live in." *Death and Funeral of Abraham Lincoln*, 27.

Chapter 6

Playing Kean Playing Kean

In 1821, after a performance of Kean's Hamlet in New York, the American painter and poet Washington Allston wrote:

> Who, then, dare wear the princely Denmark's form?
> Who starts before me? Ha!'tis he I've seen
> Oft in a day-dream, when my youth was green,—
> The Dane himself—the Dane!—who says 'tis Kean?
> Yet, sure, it moves, as if its blood were warm. ...
> Or *Kean* or Hamlet—what I see is real![1]

Allston's uncertainty turns on a simple question: what is real? After all, in his mind's eye Allston has dreamed of Kean before. Is the Kean he now sees the real Kean or merely a dream? Certainly, Allston believes that this Kean is real: "it moves, as if its blood were warm." What is this "it"? Kean or Hamlet? Even the poet is not sure. Is Hamlet a fictional "it," fleshed out by Kean, or is Kean a ghostly spirit who needs the "princely Denmark's form"? Seeing Kean as Hamlet, Hamlet as Kean, the clear steel of reality is turned into golden "Or."

Or is this golden ore merely fool's gold, a misspent reality not just for the actor but for the entranced audience as well? Allston's solution, that what he sees is real, is, even to Allston, inadequate. If illusion seems real, it does not make illusion reality. The "real" problem of Allston's poem is not the moment when Kean and Hamlet become confused, but how this confusion leaves Allston doubting his own ability to sift fact from fantasy. Allston becomes his own Hamlet doubting the reality and validity of what he sees. But Allston's hitch is much like Hamlet's theological adjudications. After seeing Kean, can Allston ever really know or trust anything again? There's the rub. If he denies the reality of Kean's Hamlet, if Kean is *not* Hamlet, then *nothing* appears as it seems; if he accepts the reality of Kean as Hamlet, then how does he account for his dream? The player-king has somehow caught Allston in a theatrical mousetrap, wherein the only solution is to accept that "What I see [, fantastical, perhaps even false, as it seems,] *is* real."

---

1   Excerpt from Washington Allston, "Kean As Hamlet," *New York Evening Post* 10 March 1821, written in celebration of Kean's New York performance of the same week also found in Gabriel Harrison, *The Life and Writing of John Howard Payne*, 387-8.

The Existential Actor

Of course, Allston's Kean is no more "real" than any other appropriation of the actor. (I suppose you might even argue that since Kean was always on stage, even he was never the "real" Kean.) It was this very aspect of Kean which intrigued Jean-Paul Sartre, who saw in the actor the archetypal existentialist, alienated from everyone, even himself: "He [Kean] was the Myth of the Actor incarnate. The actor who never ceases acting; he lives out his life itself, is no longer able to recognize himself, no longer knows who he is. And [sic] finally is no one."[2] To emphasize the problem of identity, Sartre went out of his way to state that the inspiration for his Kean was not the real Kean at all, but an actor who played Kean on stage: Frédérick Lemaître.

The Real Kean?

According to Sartre's narrative, when the actor Frédérick Lemaître played Kean in Dumas' play, he identified so fully with the character that his "real" self disappeared. The part "went to Lemaître's head, and he ended up completely merging his identity with Kean's."[3] There is some historical justification for this remarkable claim. "The actor," the *Revue et Gazette des Théâtres* commented, "took on the manner of his character to such an extent that the fiction seemed real."[4] More importantly, the resemblance between the two actors extended "beyond art to their private lives."[5] After the premiere of *Kean*, Lemaître began to drink heavily, to spend and to carouse as freely as had his hero; Lemaître became, like Kean, a spectacle of self-fashioning and self-obliteration.[6] Georges Duval, Lemaître's biographer, wrote:

> [Edmund] Kean and Frederick Lemaitre were one and the same character, and the latter was truly fitted, by his everyday violence and mood, to represent this existence of fencing-master and mountebank, drunkard and Lovelace, of the man spoiled by success and corrupted by every vice. Frederick was really all this![7]

When Ernesto Rossi played the lead role in Dumas' play in 1875 at the Ventadour, the press refused to accept another actor in the part. On the topic of Lemaître's Kean, The French newspaper *Le Sifflet* wrote, "Your name is carved in indestructible rock. Your glory is immortal. You shall not die. ... They have tried to compare him

---

2   Jean-Paul Sartre, "Kean," 243.

3   Jean-Paul Sartre, "Kean," 239. Victor Hugo thought that Lemaître combined the action of Kean with the emotion of Talma, but he does not note any manic need to imitate Kean. See George Henry Lewes *On Actors and the Art of Acting*, 78.

4   Quotation found in the undocumented Marie-Françoise Christout in "Kean ou désordre et génie," 63. Translation my own.

5   Robert Baldick, *The Life and Times of Frédérick Lemaître*, 158.

6   On Lemaître's lifestyle, see Edith Saunders, *The Prodigal Father*, 31, 52.

7   Manuscript translation of Georges Duval, *Frédérick-Lemaître et Son Temps: 1800-1876*, found in "Duval, Georges, Frederick Lemaitre," in Harry Ransom Collection (HRC).

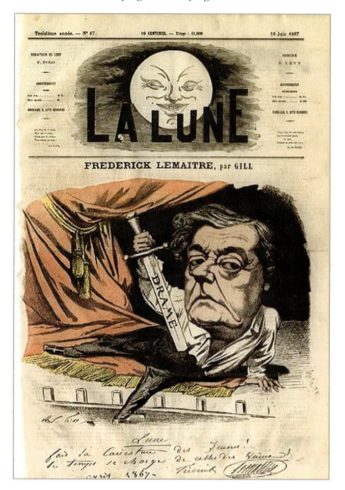

Plate 13: "The real Kean is me." Lemaître killing himself for his art. Reprinted by kind permission of the Harry Ransom Humanities Research Center; The University of Texas at Austin.

[Rossi] to you. They have attempted to efface your memory. ... They are fools or mercenaries!"[8] Now a seventy-five-year-old retired semi-invalid, Lemaître plastered notices around Paris in which he denounced Rossi's rival portrayal. The notices read, "The real Kean is me."[9]

---

8   Quote found in the undocumented Robert Baldick, *The Life and Times of Frédérick Lemaître*, 240.

9   Jean-Paul Sartre, "Kean," 239. The details of the story are probably fabricated. In bold strokes, however, there may be some truth. In his memoirs, Frédérick Lemaître writes that his version of Kean will never be forgotten, even if Rossi might on occasion play his part

It's clear that Lemaître's concept of being the "real Kean" consisted in breaking the traditional theatrical frame in favor of acting as a form of lifestyle and lifestyle as a form of acting. However, the "real Kean" had little to do with the "historical Kean." Instead, Dumas' pen and Lemaître's acting created a Kean directed against his own factual history, a countermemory—a makeover of the past, animated by the spirit of performance.[10]

The delicious quirk was that, as Lemaître's fiction was repeated, it became just as "real" as any historical record of the actor. Kean had moved the theatrical frame from the theater proper to the streets, his house, his bedroom. What may have surprised him were the many attempts to copy not just his acting technique, but his whole lifestyle. While Kean had power to crush attempts at the former, he was powerless to stop endeavors at the latter. Once Kean adroitly re-calibrated acting to social performance, he was incapable of stopping others from doing the same. If Kean played being Kean, anyone could play the part. From an existential point of view, the ability to remodel the self was (and is) not limited to the self. In a world where staged spectacle was (and is) often accepted as reality, Kean became (and remains) what people made (and make) of him.

Sartre's Existential Kean

In any play, characters are trapped in their roles, bound to say what has already been scripted. Freedom and free will in a play do not really exist. Actors repeat the same lines, move in the same patterns night after night, and then move on to a new work and do it all over again. But within Sartre's *Kean*, there is a hypersensitivity to each character's acting. Throughout the play, Kean metatheatrically observes that some characters are performing very well or making a great exit, etc. At one point, he says that he doesn't need money because someone will always give him what he wants. To prove the point, he demands that someone enter and give him flowers. There is a knock on the door. It is a delivery boy, who gives Kean, you guessed it, flowers!

Yet, much of the play explores whether this surreal dynamic is desirable or even escapable. Whereas the historical Kean went out of his way to stop others from acting like him, Sartre's Kean desires only to free himself from the parts others have been making him play. Unfortunately, this Kean has been playing roles for so long that he no longer has an identity of his own. At a christening party, for example, the

---

(*Souvenirs*, 12). Still later, referring to his performance of Kean and recent attempts to replace him in the role, he reminds his readers that Offenbach has not replaced Rossini and Harvé has not replaced Verdi (317).

10 Sartre also mentions in his notes to the play that he had seen the 1922 Mosjoukine film version of Dumas' *Kean*. Further, Sartre seems to have researched Kean's biography. What he found might have struck a personal chord. Sartre, like Kean, was a womanizer and a drunk. The day before his high school graduation, for example, Sartre got intoxicated and ended up at a local whorehouse.

lovesick actor demands that everyone call him Romeo.[11] He comes to realize that he is a kind of parasite living off the acceptance of others, unable to see or relate to moral and personal imperatives. Cheating on his friends, killing or being killed on stage—it's all unreal, all staged spectacle. Even alienation is seen as merely another form of acting: "Sometimes I wonder if real emotions are not merely false emotions acted badly."[12]

Sartre's Unreal Kean

Although Sartre's Kean is more a "man of theater" than any Kean before him, of all the Keans created since the original's demise, Sartre's is the least historically authentic. Sartre's Kean lacks all the fire, passion, and danger of the historical Kean. In Sartre's play, it is impossible to see the Kean who drank himself into a torpor, frittered fortunes carelessly, waved pistols from carriage tops, and seduced chambermaids, courtesans, actresses, and audiences. It is equally impossible that Sartre's Kean can move his audience to sighs or to tears.

This is a Kean devoid of delight, living in an endless routine that fills him with boredom and despair, even when on stage, even in the bedroom. Indeed, given the historical Kean's sexual appetites, Sartre's Kean has a curious lack of lust. When meeting Elena in his dressing room, he finds that she wants to make love, but he wants to talk, or more exactly, complain. When Anna, a rich heiress, offers herself, he plays Hamlet to her Ophelia, ordering her to "go to a nunnery in the first place."[13] It is a suggestion that the historical Kean, always ready for a quick debauch, would never espouse. But Sartre's Kean is hardly modeled on the historical character. Indeed, Sartre is anxious to overturn every aspect of the "real" Kean, hinting at one point that Kean is sexually impotent: "Kean is a pistol charged with blanks. He makes a noise [presumably of seduction], but he doesn't do any harm." Intimacy, we learn "bewilders" him.[14] Kean prefers a world in which he remains isolated, in which he might "dress in private to please [himself]."[15]

The words "private" and "please" are of interest, suggesting as they do a solitary pleasure, a moment, perhaps on its basest level, of masturbation or, in a grander sense, of personal peace. Blithely leaping from public flirtation to private impotence only stresses the actor's inability to realize and to desire a self that is not connected to his public performance. Thus, chased by adoring fans, Kean complains that his constant pleasing of others has come at a terrible cost: "What have you done? You took a child and turned him into an actor—an illusion, a fantasy"; "Kean the actor,

11 Jean-Paul Sartre, *Kean*, III.p.206.
12 Ibid., I.p.166-7.
13 Ibid., II.196.
14 Ibid., II.185.
15 Ibid., II.181.

died very young. Be quiet, murderers, it was you who killed him. It was you who took an infant and turned him into a monster."[16]

His devotees also speak of Kean as if he were a nothing, as if he existed merely to fulfill their fantasies:

> PRINCE: If they [the ladies] lose their hearts to Kean, they are chasing a shadow.
> ELENA: A shadow? Is Kean then not a man?
> PRINCE: Indeed no, madam. He is an actor.
> ELENA: And what is an actor?
> PRINCE: A mirage.[17]

Even his mistress says that she doesn't think Kean really exists: "Kean? Is there such a man?" She sees only the Shakespeare character: "I felt I was seeing Hamlet himself ... I saw the Prince of Denmark in person." Amy, another of Kean's willing paramours, agrees:

> Yes—as he was Romeo the night before, and the Thane of Glamis the night before that. How agreeable for his mistress .... Tonight she can sleep with the Prince of Denmark, and tomorrow in the arms of the Moor of Venice.[18]

We have already seen that Sartre has built an anti-Kean of sorts, someone uninspired by backstage sex or onstage intrigue. Sartre's Kean is a kind of Caliban, trapped in the timbers of his dressing room. This explains why his Kean is uninterested in stirring himself up through sex or theater. His prison, though dull, is the best that he (and, by extension, all men) can hope for.

Exit Boredom; Enter Kean

Is Sartre's Kean a representation of the alienated Everyman, or is he merely a convenient mouthpiece for Sartre himself? In Sartre's *Les Mots* (1964), we find a passage that is nearly identical to his sentiments concerning the actor:

> My retrospective illusions are all in pieces. Martyrdom, salvation, immortality: all are crumbling; the building is falling in ruins. I have caught the Holy Ghost in the cellars and flung him out. Atheism is a cruel, long-term affair: I believe I have gone through it to the end. I see clearly, I am free from illusions ... for about ten years, I have been a man who is waking up, cured of a long, bitter-sweet madness, who cannot recall his old ways without laughing, and who no longer has any idea what to do with his life .... I have renounced my profession, but I still write. What else can I do?[19]

---

16 Ibid., II.189; IV.251.

17 Ibid., I.165.

18 Ibid., I.155.

19 Jean-Paul Sartre, *Les Mots*, 210-11; translation my own. This image of a trapped and defeated Sartre/Kean is radically at odds with David Bradby's interpretation of both Sartre and Kean as twin monuments to freedom and the exercise of freewill. See his essay, "Sartre

Sartre's inability to think of anything to do other than what he has always done is premised on the notion that superior ability creates fame, and fame creates imposition. Likewise, Kean cannot do anything but act because that is what has brought him success: to do the opposite would be to evaporate the self, to do the same would be to imprison it further.

Kean and Sartre's Other Plays

In writing *Kean*, Sartre also restated many of the problems found in another play he wrote in the same year, *Lucifer and the Lord*. As the play opens, Goetz, a soldier, is about to march into a town and slaughter the inhabitants. Told that anyone can be evil, but no one can be good, Goetz takes up the challenge. Goetz sets up a commune for the poor, his City of the Sun, which is eventually destroyed in a peasants' revolt. Convinced that good acts come to no good, Goetz decides it is pointless to try to be a saint. Thereafter, he gets more satisfaction in being alone, and what better way to be alone than to go back to his original plan of killing everyone in the city?

Goetz's action-packed solution might be dramatically appealing but is only one of any number of options. He might just as reasonably argue that if all acts are meaningless, then the only solution is to do nothing, as non-action must, by logical inference, be meaningful. The fact that Goetz eventually chooses action over inaction is not a question of morality or even theatricality but of boredom. Goetz thinks he'll be more entertained by killing people than by ignoring them.

A similar philosophy is found in *Kean*. The actor allows that all acts are equally insignificant but does not slaughter his neighbors. Instead, he comes to a neater, though perhaps even gloomier, solution: social suicide. On stage, before his adoring public, Kean decides he has had enough of acting as if he were alive:

PRINCE: Mr. Kean! You are ruining yourself.
KEAN: And if I want to be ruined?[20]

Kean is delighted with the carnage he has caused to his career ("Last night, I pinched myself. A pretty suicide wasn't it?"[21]) and suggests that he is trading his illusionary image for personal freedom.

However, Kean finds that there is no reality outside of theatrical illusion. (If there were, it would mean there is a transcendent world, a point of view Sartre's own philosophy negates.) Longing for a world in which he can shout, "I shall be free! I shan't have to act!", Kean discovers that freedom is merely another way of acting. Even suicide, which many would consider the ultimate act of freedom, is taken away from him. It becomes a staged entertainment for others. Addressing Anna, Sartre's

---

as Dramatist," esp. 64. Given the repeated despairing comments of the actor in the play, I find his interpretation excessively upbeat.

20 Jean-Paul Sartre, *Kean*, IV.249.

21 Ibid., IV.249.

Kean cannot help but slip in and out of Shakespearean character and quotation: "To be or not to be. I am nothing my child. I play at being what I am. From time to time, Kean himself plays a scene for Kean"; "Act! Do I know myself when I am acting? Is there a moment when I cease to act?"[22]

There is no defeat in such role-playing. Indeed, the only solution to boredom that this Kean accepts is theatricality. Like Lemaître, who parades around Paris proclaiming he is the "real Kean," Sartre tells us that we too can all find some solace in becoming our own fictional heroes.

Sartre's Play?

Kean is in part a melodramatic comedy and in part a philosophical tract. This is both a fact and a design flaw or, rather, a *re*design flaw. Sartre stated that he did not construct *Kean* from scratch but adapted the play "attributed" to Dumas—"attributed" because Sartre begins his notes to the play by accusing Dumas of virtually stealing credit for *Kean*.[23] According to Sartre's research, Monsieur de Courcy, "the renowned hack," wrote the play first, Théaulon was called in second, and Dumas merely supervised the revision and then unfairly claimed sole authorship of the play.[24]

In what sometimes seems a petty vendetta, Sartre's version talks back to its authorial predecessors.[25] In the first act, Elena and Amy discuss Shakespeare, but they might as well have been discussing Dumas or any other revered author. Says Amy disparagingly, "The trouble with old authors is they never give us anything

---

22 Ibid., II.195; II.200.

23 Sartre's accusation that Dumas stole the play is especially unkind as Sartre was originally commissioned to update the play for the 150th anniversary of Dumas' birthday. I suggest that Sartre's rejection of Dumas' play ironically repeats that play's thematic rejection of tradition.

24 Jean-Paul Sartre, "Kean," 244-5. Sartre clearly has in mind the following letter, written by Théaulon de Lambert to Frédérick Lemaître. It concerning a new project he was developing:

> It is a five-act play and the title is *Kean, ou Désordre et Génie*. It is a mixture of all genres. I would willingly give all my successes, past, present, and to come, to produce something that satisfied you .... My desire [for it] to be played by the finest actor in Europe is so great, and I am so utterly convinced that the subject of *Kean* will please you, that I promise to deliver the complete play to you by Sunday next—I am going to work at it night and day.

Lemaître found the play to be unacceptable and called in John de Courcy for yet more revisions (Robert Baldick, *The Life and Times of Frédérick Lemaître*, 152-3). Even after these additional revisions, the play was said to have "no substance." He then took the play to Dumas (Claude Schopp, *Alexandre Dumas: Genius of Life*, 266).

25 In his notes to *Kean*, Sartre discusses Dumas' version, if only disparagingly: "Dumas the Existentialist! That's a joke" ("Kean," 241).

new."[26] Other quips are only apparent after a detailed study of the Dumas original and the Sartre rewrite. As such, they serve as little more than insider jokes, personal, if allusive, and scornful. Dumas' *Kean* is subtitled *Disorder and Genius*; in Sartre's version, Anna says that Kean is a "genius" who needs a woman in his life to organize things for him. Kean replies, "And genius—what would become of it if I had order?"[27] Another joke concerns the political nature of Dumas' play. Dumas, we recall, used the theater to challenge the *status quo*. Sartre scoffs at such notions. In Sartre's rewrite, Amy notes that plays are "not fatiguing. You can relax, close your eyes, even go to sleep, in the privacy of your box."[28] Dumas' Kean acts as Romeo and accuses himself of acting the part of Falstaff; Sartre's Kean warns Anna not to be "surprised if Romeo turns into Falstaff." Dumas' Kean states, "I play the comedy from eight o'clock in the evening till midnight, but never during the day." But Sartre's Kean, more aware of his existential state, is less certain: "I am playing. I am not playing. I don't know." Dumas' Kean lives in an Aristotelian comedy—five acts, ending in a marriage; Sartre's Kean self-consciously walks through five acts, in which he must observe the conventions of "comedy."[29] As for Dumas' penchant for sentimentality, Sartre's Kean asks Elena, "Why on earth did we both decide to be noble?"[30] Whereas Dumas' Kean learns the conventional wisdom necessary to achieve happiness (get married, go west young man), Sartre's play leads only to confusion and immobility ("Who is Kean? I don't know"). In short, Sartre's cynicism leads him to see and to ridicule the value of Dumas' Keanian revolutionary.

Playing Sartre's Kean

If Sartre's rewrite of Dumas demands that we choose a new kind of Kean, one differing from both the historical actor and Dumas' reconstruction, his Dumas-talking points suggest that it is difficult, if not impossible, to abandon utterly previous constructions of the actor. This is particularly true of the play's performance history. Sartre stated, "All the great actors who played the part successively enriched it with memories of them."[31]

Most reviews agree that the play works best when done as a straight comedy. In a review of a 1970 production, *The Observer* described Sartre's play as a "jolly period travesty"; *The Sunday Times* called it "a hilarious burlesque"; Michael Billington described the play as "a piece of extravagant, superior hokum." The last significant run of Sartre's *Kean* was Sam Mendes' 1990 production at the National Theatre.

26 Jean-Paul Sartre, *Kean*, I.155.
27 Ibid., III.213.
28 Ibid., I.154.
29 Ibid., V.279.
30 Ibid., V.267.
31 Jean-Paul Sartre, "Kean," 239.

Plate 14: Forrest's musical, *Kean* (1961), is based on Sartre's play, but instead of Kean being exiled to America, the Prince announces that he will have to make a public apology on the boards of Drury Lane. Kean agrees, but when the curtain rises he finds himself unable to speak in his own voice. Instead, Kean crafts his apology from bits and pieces of Shakespearean text. Whether sincere or not (the song is called "Apology?"), Kean fulfills his punishment even as he comes to realize that his stage personae are so well received that they ostensibly become, despite their multiplicity, his singular and "real" being. Reprinted from the Billy Rose Theater Collection, The New York Public Library for the Performing Arts, Astor, Lenox, and Tilden Foundations.

Benedict Nightingale wrote that, had he not known the piece to be Sartre's, he would have guessed that "Bertrand Russell had penned a sitcom for John Cleese."[32]

Penned for John Cleese, yes, but could it have been performed by Kean? Probably not. Kean himself is a less than ideal actor for Sartre's—or even Dumas'—play.

---

32 Benedict Nightingale, "Kean," *London Times*, August 7, 1990. In the same review, he calls the play a "Romantic comedy."

Even the genre (comedy) was one Kean disliked and studiously avoided.[33] Sartre went so far as to suggest that any association of the actor to the play was a detriment: "Kean ... is no longer a [*sic*] historical character; he has been elevated to the rank of myth, the patron saint of actors. ... an actor whose role is to play himself."[34]

Can we really say that the play *Kean* has nothing to do with the actor it celebrates? Two recent productions have explored this issue. Let's begin with the 1990 Sam Mendes production, starring Derek Jacobi, and then look at the older 1983 BBC TV version, starring Anthony Hopkins. The productions were selected not only because they both had famous players, but also because these players were so opposite in their respective approaches.

Derek Jacobi's Kean

Derek Jacobi is described variously as an "elocutionary master ...[possessing] wonderful operatic build"; the "man who speaks arias"; an actor whose style "consists of ... action, yet tempered by charm and grace."[35] Though of the aristocratic Kemble school, Jacobi was perfectly cast for Sartre's *Kean*, at least according to the needs of director Sam Mendes, who knew exactly what he wanted from Jacobi, and what he didn't want from the play. Mendes preferred a flamboyant histrionic bundle of comic and theatrical froth, not an evening of existential angst.

Judging by the reviews, Jacobi and Mendes succeeded. The *Times* critic Benedict Nightingale called it simply a "romantic farce." According to the *Independent*'s Paul Taylor, here was a man who did not take anyone or anything seriously and didn't expect things to change very much. Sartre's denial of an authentic self was handled "most unponderously"; Jacobi played Kean as a gentleman who had just wandered out of an Oscar Wilde play, full of quips and "lightness of touch"; the actor simply gave an "impersonation of the kind of thespian who, even if he were to set fire to his trousers, would still find it hard to be spontaneous." But Taylor also registered a concern. Was Jacobi being true to the spirit of that "kind of thespian"? Taylor didn't think so: "he [Jacobi] is naturally better suited to impersonating the flamboyant charmer rather than the lecher or the drunkard."

Agreed, Jacobi was (and is) a delight to the eye and a joy to the ear, but hardly a terror to the soul. His Kean was restrained, refined, and domesticated. In Jacobi's

---

33 Kean did infrequently appear in Burges' comic play *Riches*, but this was so odd that in 1815 the state used the novelty of a comic performance as a puff for the lottery: "For a Benefit at Drury Lane Theatre There is but One Kean in the Comedy of "Riches"; but at the Theatre-Royal, Bassinghall-Street, will be performed the Comedy of Riches in which Many who are Keen will be benefited...." See Jonathan Reynolds, *Dramatis Personæ*, 88 (2005):11. Kean's main roles were all tragic, and even within this genre, he had his limits. On Kean's dislike of sentimental or romantic roles such as Romeo, see Harold Newcomb Hillebrand, *Edmund Kean*, 141.

34 Jean-Paul Sartre, "Kean," 239.

35 Jacobi fanclub page.

lyrical style, Kean's declaration that he "doesn't exist at all" was said with the embarrassed good grace of a host who finds the last of the éclairs has been eaten, and what is one to do? There were no flashes of lighting, no roaring, and no real power in this Kean.

Anthony Hopkins' Kean

When Anthony Hopkins undertook the part, John Moffatt expected little difficulty: "It was probably easy for Tony to play Kean because he is an Edmund Kean type actor, a grand illusion, an outsized actor."[36] Moffatt couldn't have been more wrong. The play "produced more traumas and dramas" offstage than in any of Hopkins' other projects.

Hopkins took the role for scale wages, the theatrical equivalent of minimum wage. More telling than what he was paid for *Kean* is what he turned down to do it. At the time (pre-*Silence of the Lambs*), Hopkins was not yet an international star, though he was a useful and creditable actor.[37] Director Richard Attenborough had him in mind for his upcoming pet project. He told Hopkins, "This is our moment. Now we do *Ghandi*."[38]

After reading a "long and impassioned explanatory letter" by BBC director David Jones, Hopkins decided instead to star in *Kean*. While the contents of the letter and subsequent conversations remain private, Jones had stated that he "had wanted for ten years to do this bizarre and tricky play about Kean, the fabled, tragic nineteenth-century actor."[39] Hopkins shared that zeal:

> I feel just crazy about this part. It's such bloody hard work. It's the most emotionally demanding thing I've done ... Kean can't see the difference between reality and what is on stage. I suppose I am like him in parts. He is one of the greatest actors of his day, but a chronic drunk who died at forty-three a shattered man. I usually get to play this kind of crazy [*sic*] wild character. But it is immensely disturbing....[40]

The fact that Hopkins knew Kean's age at death is indicative of some sort of biographical knowledge of his subject, though just how much and from what source is impossible to tell.[41] In any case, one thing is clear: as rehearsals progressed, the part was clearly getting to Hopkins. Said cast member Cherie Lunghi, "It was hell. I

---

36 Zoe Heller, "Tony the Tiger," 231.

37 Hopkins, at this point, was just beginning to make a name for himself with his first box-office hit in *Magic*.

38 *Ghandi*, of course, was a huge hit and launched the career of Ben Kingsley, who also played Kean for many years in FitzSimons' play.

39 Michael Feeney Callan, *Anthony Hopkins*, 226.

40 Ibid., 229-30.

41 For details concerning Kean's age, see Introduction.

couldn't reach him. He went into a corner and gave this gabbling performance, with his eyes shut, to the floor."[42]

Why did Hopkins find the part so difficult? In part, for the same reasons Moffatt thought he would find it facile. Hopkins confused the historical Kean ("He is one of the greatest actors of his day, but a chronic drunk who died at forty-three a shattered man") with the histrionic construct ("I usually get to play this kind of crazy wild character"). This problem extended to the director as well. Jones confused the historical figure ("a nineteenth-century actor") with the fictional ("fabled, tragic").

It was easy enough for Hopkins to play the historical Kean; even before he became the top-tier movie star he is today, Hopkins' charm, skill, and cantankerous wit had brought him quizzical, perhaps even Keanian, distinction. He once walked away from a National Theatre production of *Macbeth* because he was asked to wear a false beard and what he described as "those fucking tights." A raging alcoholic, Hopkins once burst into Christopher Plummer's dressing room, steaming drunk, ready for a physical and verbal punch-up.[43] Further, Hopkins was (and one assumes, still is) a sexual rover, cheating, seemingly without compunction, on his wife of over 20 years. "She just says, 'Well, that's the way you are.'"[44]

Depending on the depth of Hopkins' knowledge of the subject, he may well have found other remarkable affinities with Kean's personality and even physique. Like Kean, Hopkins is short and stocky; like Kean, Hopkins has a difficult relationship with the British press: "What's the matter with you damn people?" he asked one British reporter, "I'm not going to sit here with your weak, whining negativity. I'm bored of you people. You want it dirty and raining, with dog shit on the pavement? Go back then! Go back to England. *Fuck off.*" Like Kean, Hopkins feels uncomfortable in high society: "You go to someone's house and you stand on the doorstep filled with dread and they come to the door and it's '*Hellllleeeh, daaaaarling!*' I stand there and I think, *Oh God, oh fucking hell.* I just cannot do it"; and like Kean, Hopkins is an avid boxing fan, "the only sport I care about."[45]

Hopkins did more than use Kean to vent his frustrations. He meticulously studied and recreated the actor's vocal technique and delivery. As we know from historical records, Kean used two basic techniques: slow to fast, and low to high. The actor George Vandenhoff broke down a memorable moment of Kean's from *The Merchant of Venice*:

He [Kean] hurried you on through the catalogue of Antonio's atrocities and unprovoked injuries to him, enforcing them with a strong accentuation, a rapid utterance, and a high pitch of voice; and when he had reached the *climax*, he came down by a sudden transition to a gentle, suffering tone of simple representation of his oppressor's manifest un-reason and injustice on the words—

---

42 Michael Feeney Callan, *Anthony Hopkins*, 228.

43 Hopkins joined AA in 1975. He was sober during *Kean*, but his years of alcoholism almost certainly informed his reading of the part.

44 Zoe Heller, "Tony the Tiger," 145.

45 Ibid., 144-5.

'I am a Jew!'

and the effect was instantaneous.[46]

It's clear that Hopkins followed Vandenhoff's notes, or a similar narrative that cataloged Kean's effects. In his first scene, a shabbily dressed Hopkins enters bleak-eyed and imperious. He barges in on the Prince of Wales, gabbling so quickly one must concentrate on him to understand his lines. He roves like a caged tiger, rambling, growling his words, turning fast, making guttural, unintelligible asides. But when he needs others to hear him, he is slow and clear. At another point, Hopkins uses Kean's low to high technique, combining it with slow to fast. For the line, "Every night I dress to please the English. Can't I have the right to undress myself?" Hopkins delivered the following score: [*soft and fast*] Ev'rynightIdress...[*rising voice, slow delivery*] to ... pla—lease [*loud and slow*] th'Eng—ggg—lish [*pause, followed by slow deliberate*] Can't—I—have—the—[*extremely loud*] right ... to [*soft and fast*] undresm'self?" Throughout, Hopkins also used grand gestures (waving his arms, wagging his fingers) and movement (roving the room, zigzagging around characters, who remain still or sitting).

Watching Hopkins in the BBC *Kean*, it's hard not to bear in mind Procter's description of Kean that night he acted with Booth:

> The fury and whirlwind of the passions seemed to have endowed him with supernatural strength. His eyes were glittering and blood-shot, his veins were swollen, and his whole figure restless and violent. It seemed dangerous to cross him and death to assault him.[47]

Booth, Procter later chronicled, walked around the stage half-stunned. The same might be said of Hopkins' cast members, who, for the most part, were confounded by him. Unlike the star, they spoke their parts in muted, though posh, BBC accents, and were, unless entrances and exits dictated otherwise, unmoving throughout.[48]

Given these differences, the production, for all of Hopkins' genius, was a failure. Even the director, Jones, called the project a "mess, a disaster, a bloodbath."[49] Hopkins blamed his director: "Jones didn't do his homework on Kean. He didn't prepare properly, and that was the problem."[50] Hopkins was being unfair. After all, Jones stated that he had been preparing for *Kean* for ten years. What was really at fault was Hopkins' inability to play the Kean of the play, a play written in the mid-twentieth century. Hopkins declaimed as the historical Kean had: grandly, loudly. He moved as Kean had done: restlessly, ominously. The problem was that his cast did

46 George Vandenhoff, *Leaves From an Actor's Note-Book*, 24.

47 Bryan Waller Procter, *The Life of Edmund Kean*, II:167.

48 I should point out that one other actor did vary from the BBC norm: Julian Fellowes played the Ambassador of Norway with an appallingly unrealistic delivery. "You're very welcome" was somehow transformed to "Veriare weary welccoomb." The effect was unintentionally comic.

49 Michael Feeney Callan, *Anthony Hopkins: In Darkness and Light*, 226.

50 Ibid., 228.

not see the use or purpose of twentieth-century players acting as if they were on a nineteenth-century stage.

Peter O'Toole's: Sartrean Kean or Keanian Satyr?

Here, we might make some preliminary comparisons between Jacobi's and Hopkins' approaches. For Derek Jacobi, there was no need for more than a polite comic turn. His Kean is a Saville Row tailor, professional and meticulous, inspired by the length of cuffs, rather than the breath of kings. Hopkins' Kean is a poetic madman, animated, arms flapping. But Sartre's play is charming and funny and calls for a clever and charming Kean, something that was beyond Hopkins' abilities. Hopkins is better suited to play the historical Kean, not the Kean of Sartre's play. However, even rating Hopkins by his ability to recreate the acting of the actual Kean, the actor falls well short of Peter O'Toole, who fancies himself the high priest of The Cult of Kean.

O'Toole begins his autobiography, *Loitering With Intent: The Apprentice* (1996) by slipping Edmund Kean's ring—a gift from Laurence Olivier[51]—onto his finger: "Come to me now and his ring in my hand while I tell you. ... the wonky old business of putting on plays for public performances on the stages of playhouses...."[52] Kean's ring is more than a relic.[53] The ring seems to talk to the actor, reminding him that Kean's spirit has always been with him. Looking back on O'Toole's childhood, the Kean spirit reminds him that, "Both our feet are to be warped into these bizarre and suffering right angles to the body"; "Ruined ... muscles, tendons, general bits of me ... pressed into such unexpected crude service."[54] At other points, O'Toole becomes the spirit, who, in turn, watches over Kean:

> The surgeons do it to anaesthetize you. When you are practically senseless, the surgeons will grip the young bones of your bent legs and will stretch and shove and pound and twist at those crooked limbs until they are straight. Thick iron rods with hinges and joints forming them into long splints and heavier than your body now is will then be clamped on your legs, from thigh to ankle. ... Night after day for five years you will wear leg irons, Ned, and at first your suffering will be much....[55]

---

51 Olivier was an avid collector of Kean memorabilia. His collection included Kean's stage sword, his lace collar and undergarments. See Roger Lewis, *The Real Life of Laurence Olivier*, 59. Olivier was buried with Kean's sword.

52 Peter O'Toole, *Loitering With Intent: The Apprentice*, 4.

53 Generically, a ring is commonly associated with marriage. It is also a sign of fraternity. For example, upon his death, Shakespeare bequeathed 26s.8d. apiece to Heminges, Burbage and Condell—fellow actors of the King's Men—for the specific provision of purchasing mourning rings.

54 Peter O'Toole, *Loitering With Intent: The Apprentice*, 125-6, 127.

55 Ibid., 59.

All right, let's fact check: O'Toole had bow legs, but did Kean? One of Kean's biographers, Hillebrand, does mention a legend that, as a child Kean, "might have had some trouble with his legs," probably no more than a broken leg.[56] Since Kean played Richard III as a child, it's possible that he played the invalid so well that it was assumed that he really was one. There is no verifiable document stating that he spent his childhood in leg irons. The fact that he was a child actor renders the idea rather improbable. But that is precisely beside the point. O'Toole has selected historical anecdotes to create his own Kean, if only as a means by which he can talk about himself.

O'Toole got his first big break in the play *The Long, the Short and the Tall* in 1959. This led to his feature film debut in *Kidnapped* (1960). Two years later, he achieved international star-status in the David Lean epic *Lawrence of Arabia*. Whether playing the fastidious English teacher in *The Last Emperor* or the private secretary hired to teach John Goodman royal manners in *King Ralph*, O'Toole has made a career out of his "classy" English accent and etiquette. However, it is O'Toole's well-known drunken behavior, his antic acting offstage, that solidifies his connection to Kean. As one recent article on the actor put it, "To this day, O'Toole specializes in men whose obsessions override—or deform—their wills."[57] Indeed, O'Toole's autobiography skips over his onstage or on camera performances. In their place, the actor tells us of his Keanian exploits behind the curtain:

> My majorette unwraps herself from the keyboard, sways her pompoms, tassels, silk and sexuality ... We could, perhaps, be of assistance to each other in this business of unbuckling, unbelting and unbuttoning rigid uniforms. Helpful and in no rush at all ... we ... mayhap could try each other on for size.[58]

Getting drunk and copulating in the Green Room with musicians and actresses is fun—at least O'Toole doesn't seemed pained by these staged, backstage encounters—but such behavior is also part of the official ritual, the Bacchanalian rites of Kean. O'Toole's actions are part of the carnal act of penis in vagina, bony finger in ring; King Dickie, crowned and holding sovereign sway with his bitch/whore/consort the theater.

O'Toole's Kean—Kean's tool—his name is happily well suited to this argument—is sexually protean. At some points in the book, he is a toddler: "You're all right, Kean, you're still here. You're on the floor .... Yes, I know, sweet Ned .... Leave it be. Brighten up. Look."[59] He is a young boy: "Back into my pocket goes your ring, little Ned, as we pick our way." At yet another point, O'Toole is Kean's brother, fondly remembering "poor Daddy."[60] He is O'Toole's co-actor, walking the stage, looking at the lights "Above our heads" and remembering "the night we

---

56 Harold Newcomb Hillebrand, *Edmund Kean*, 12.
57 Troy Patterson, "Peter O'Toole," 35.
58 Peter O'Toole, *Loitering With Intent: The Apprentice*, 23.
59 Ibid., 11.
60 Ibid., 58.

failed to kick the place to splinters."[61] He is O'Toole's drinking buddy: "Oh yes, Edmund Kean Esq. ... We are legless [drunk] at the Lyceum."[62] Kean is also his Ganymede, an effeminate boy, with "haunting" beauty and curly black hair, alluring and androgynous, able to satisfy any sexual hunger. At yet another point, Kean is dead, and O'Toole grieves for him, as if he were Kean's wife: "Here we go into what was once ours, mine and my widow's."[63]

These multiple Keans—the sweet boy, the drunken man, the failed father, the dutiful son, the thoughtful brother, the faithful husband, and these various O'Tooles— the father, the brother, the drinking confederate, the co-actor, the lonely widow— with their various limbs, heads above, legs splayed on the floor—"once ours, mine and my widow's"—simultaneously engage in copulative acts: "Come to me now and his ring in my hand while I tell you"; "down ... into Edmund Kean's Coal Hole." What is it that O'Toole tells us except how he and his multiple Keans "picked" and "sucked" whiskey from each other; how, in the bowel of Kean's favorite bar, The Coal Hole—a gay bar, one hopes!—he found himself drinking with Kean "sliding down my exploring throat."[64] All these adventures form yet another ring: a daisy chain, a ring of orgiastic excess.

For what its worth, O'Toole comes far closer than even Hopkins in recreating at least recognizable aspects of the historical Kean, but other facets of O'Toole's project remain anti-Keanian. For example, O'Toole is honored to preserve and to wear Kean's ring, but happier still that he got it on the cheap: "Yes, some deluded souls not fully understanding the property of a stage ring may believe you to be copper and paste, to be exquisitely fashioned costume jewelry but, my brother and sister actors and actresses, we know that you are a matchless adornment for the finger of a monarch."[65] O'Toole collects Kean memorabilia, a ring, and repeats stories with the gentle madness of a trainspotter—those weirdos who hang around British railway stations, recording, for fun, the serial numbers of trains.

To be fair, O'Toole does note that Kean's entire life has been about freeing himself from responsibility and restraint:

> in time, you will for good and all be rid of them and at that time you will be nine or so, you will for the first time know a miraculous sense of freedom such as few of us on earth can ever know.[66]

But O'Toole can't help but scold his god for his lack of parsimony; it offends his save-for-a-rainy-day sensibility:

---

61 Ibid., 11.
62 Ibid., 12 and 60.
63 Ibid., 9.
64 Ibid., 57.
65 Ibid., 3.
66 Ibid., 59.

Yes, King Bloody Dick, didn't the bed you died in have to be sold to pay for your burial? You, you hopeless little pillock, who had earned prodigious wages for nearly twenty years, snuffed it and left not a pot to piss in.[67]

O'Toole's deeply-rooted bourgeois attempts to collect Kean are inconsistent with Kean's own—let's not call them principles, let's call them—acts. O'Toole just isn't Keanian, except in his love of Kean. Even the logic of why and how to love Kean is at odds with what he loves about him. O'Toole's reverence is part of the world of accumulation, bourgeois proprietorship, and middle-class order—hardly Kean's strong suits.

Kean and O'Toole's Consumerism

Kean, we might recall, was quick to spend his fortune. Within days of his première at Drury Lane, Kean's salary was raised from £6 a week to £20 a week, later raised to £20 a day and then £30 a day. Further, Drury Lane shareholders presented him with a gift of £1000 and a share in the theater. Weeks after his London triumph, an anonymous diarist described Kean's new house and his newfound wealth: "bank notes were in heaps on the mantel-piece, table and sofa.... I think the receipts... amounted to £1150."[68] That's a lot of money to keep on your mantel, even today. But to understand these numbers by today's purchasing power, think extravagantly: Kean was keeping a sizeable down payment on a nice middle-class home on his mantelpiece as *spare change*.

We might say that Kean was flaunting his money. But money was the price of his art, which was then put on display as if it were an Oscar or an Emmy. However, the function of ornamentation is further revealed in relation to yet other *objects d'art* that Kean carefully placed next to the heaps of cash. In 1821, Kean was in New York and, according to his biographers, ordered that the body of George Frederick Cooke, a British actor who had died in 1812, be disinterred. While there are several solemn versions of the story, which will be revived in the concluding chapter, this one, light-hearted as it is, makes perhaps the most sober assessment of Kean's values. As Procter describes it, after examining the corpse, Kean took a toe-bone, which is described as "a little black relic, and might have passed for a tobacco-stopper."[69] As the story goes on, Kean returns to London and has the Drury Lane manager and some actors meet him for breakfast:

> On encountering the great actor, they were about to welcome him, each after his own fashion, when he stopped them, with a serious air. 'Before you say a word, my merry men,' said he—'Behold! Fall down, and kiss this relic! This is the toe-bone of the greatest creature that ever walked the earth—of George Frederic Cooke. ... Come, down with you all, and kiss the bone!' Elliston, between doubt and reverence, fell upon his knees and

---

67 Ibid., 11.
68 Raymund FitzSimons, *Edmund Kean: Fire From Heaven*, 76-7.
69 Bryan Waller Procter, *The Life of Edmund Kean*, II:196.

kissed the ridiculous relic. ... They then sat down to breakfast,—'with what appetite' we cannot pretend to say.[70]

This prized possession was also placed on his mantelpiece, where it moldered forgotten. Kean didn't even notice until some months later that his wife had thrown this "reverent" relic out the window.

In some ways, O'Toole's parsimony seems more in keeping with the habits of another Kean copyist, Junius Brutus Booth. Booth may have copied Kean's acting style and drinking habits, but unlike Kean, Booth kept scrupulous financial accounts. He was obsessed with how much he was worth, what he owned and the costs of maintaining his possessions. Kean, on the other hand, spent his entire fortune on wine, women, and song. O'Toole might like Kean's lifestyle, but his attempt to collect Kean becomes the organizing influence in his life. Kean's chaos becomes O'Toole's ritualized pattern. O'Toole stockpiles theatrical mementos; Kean misplaces human relics.

O'Toole, of course, doesn't have to be consistent; he can have his pint and drink it too. His book, though not in the strictest sense an autobiography, is not, even in the loosest sense, an academic essay. That being said, O'Toole's Kean—at least those aspects of what O'Toole prizes—is true to one important aspect of Kean's genius. It has become commonplace to say that we are all actors upon the stage of life. But this activity—and the acceptance of its condition as inevitable—can in large measure be traced to Kean's approach to acting. In one guise or another, Kean and early practitioners of Kean, anticipated Sartre's existential stance of making sense of the world in terms of stage dramatics. No actor before Kean experimented with wearing theatrical costumes, with living the character outside—and living his life inside—the theater.[71] For O'Toole the "real" work of playing Kean is never to forget that life itself is performance.

---

70 Ibid.,II:197.

71 A case in point: during the 1818-1819 season, Kean prepared for his much anticipated *King Lear*. "It was widely reported that he was studying the character with great care, even visiting lunatic asylums to observe the effects of madness.... He disturbed [his wife] Mary by wandering about the house with his eyes alternately vacant and filled with fierce light" (Raymund FitzSimons, *Edmund Kean: Fire From Heaven*, 138).

Chapter 7

The Final Curtain?

F.W. Hawkins's *Life of Edmund Kean* (1869), includes the following document:

REPORT OF POST-MORTEM EXAMINATION OF KEAN'S BODY
May 17, 1833.

The examination of the body of Edmund Kean, Esq., was commenced fifty-six hours after death by George Douchez, Esq., in the presence of J.C. Carpue, Esq., and James Smith, Esq., surgeons, Mr. Lee (Mr. Kean's secretary), and two of Mr. Kean's old and valued friends.

External appearance.—Face, neck, and the superior and the inferior extremities considerably emaciated. Decomposition rapidly taking place about the mouth, neck, and also about the face and extremities, but much more so about the former named parts of the body. Body well formed, and the external form of the thorax and the abdomen so beautifully developed as to serve as one of the finest models that could possibly be presented to the eye of the sculptor or painter. Body well proportioned, five feet six inches and three-quarters in length.

Head. On dissecting the scalp from the cranium we found the occipito frontalis muscles more developed than they are usually found; likewise the corrugatores supercilii uncommonly strong. The vessels of the dura mater very much distended. On examining the dura mater and exposing the hemispheres of the brain we found that there were adhesions of the tunica arachnoidea to the dura mater, more especially on the left side. The tunica arachnoidea was likewise found to adhere to the pia mater. There was also a considerable quantity of serum and coagulable lymph effused between many portions of those two membranes. The vessels covering both the cerebrum and cerebellum were in a highly vascular state.

The convolutions of the brain unusually strongly developed. Substance of the brain softer than natural. Lateral ventricules distended with fluid. The plexus choroides much more vascular than natural. There were likewise about two ounces of fluid found at the base of the skull, which appeared to extend down the theca vertebralis and the thorax.

Lungs.—Perfectly healthy, with the exception of two or three old standing adhesions of the pleura pulmonalis to the plura costalis of the anterior lobe of the left lung. Heart excessively loaded with fat, flabby, empty of blood, and its muscular structure much less developed than when in a healthy state. The trachea and bronchia were filled with frothy mucus.

Abdomen.—On cutting through the parietes of the abdomen we found the muscles covered by nearly two inches of fat. The omentum as well as the mesentery were also much loaded with that substance. The liver was of a green colour, but natural in size. The gall bladder contained numerous biliary calculi. On examining the stomach we found the mucous coat much thickened, and that had evidently suffered from chronic inflammation. The duodenum was of a deep orange tint, the internal coat presenting a somewhat similar appearance. The other small intestines were healthy in their structure but much contracted. The spleen, kidneys, and remaining viscera were perfectly healthy.

J. C. Carpue.
James Smith.
Geo. Douchez.

The use of the autopsy suggests that Hawkins' biography is purely interested in the facts of Kean; a scientific, objective exhumation performed by a nonjudgmental, cold and distant examiner. And yet we can see judgments at work even in this autopsy report, which places the management of the body in correlation to the logic, propriety, and regulation of the life. We are not talking about too much transfatty acid here. Studied lives, even medical reports, configure a biographical process of self-construction (you are what you eat). Kean's body is a physical record, evidence of the ways in which Kean lived, a full diary of capacity and fulfillment. The "unusually strongly developed" parts of the brain indicate his genius; the layers of fat, a diet of expensive meats; the gangrene of his liver, a record of his drinking binges; the lungs filled with frothy mucus signal tuberculosis in temporary abeyance; the deep orange tint of his small intestines, the result of his prescribed treatment for syphilis and gonorrhea.[1]

By definition and intent, biography, like autopsy, demands interpretation; even a medical narrative is a form of construal. By such standards, Kean's autopsy implicitly suggests its own judgments and pronouncements upon the subject.[2] If this were the corpse of an old man of moderate weight, we might say that his life was balanced and healthy; a man of enormous girth would be equally subject to the charge that he was out of control. Thus, although everyone must die, each body reveals how he or she functioned in relation to the norms of the society. Dying of AIDS in a homophobic society may be a fact of life for some, but it is far from a dispassionate fact. The way in which—and the way by which—a person dies suggests a variety of accountable codes by which we rank that person as good or bad, pitiable or contemptuous. Hawkins' inclusion of this autopsy record of Kean's death does not tell us *per se* how we should value Kean's life, but, given his protoVictorian sensibilities, we can assume that the lesion on Kean's legs, his bodily fat, his sexual diseases, all point to a wasteful life of immoderation and self-ruination.

If the autopsy is a nonlinear, textual witness of a life, a biography is a textual record that reorganizes these events in a linear taxonomy. The overall aim is to infuse the spirit of the life into the textual body of the narrative. Set in motion as a biological dynamic, the biography usually begins with the birth of the subject and traces in the course of a few hundred pages the events of a life. Richard Holmes calls this process the art of making "the dead walk again, to make the reader *see* a figure and *hear* a

---

1   In addition, the *New York Mirror, and Ladies Literary Gazette* reported that the actor had recently been diagnosed with palsy (20 June 1829, p.398, in Press Clippings, Personal Collection).

2   Hayden White questions whether any narrative is free of moralizing. See his *The Content of Form: Narrative Discourse and Historical Representation*, 25.

voice."[3] The mortal body's secrets, its mysteries and adventures, its triumphs and defeats, are preserved not in the lines of a face or folds of fat, but in the etchings of ink on paper and the folds of quartos and folios; the lessons of a life are not lost in the putrescence of the body but are preserved forever in a growing print culture, designed to corroborate or to extend existing wisdom.

Deathbed Confessions

We can see this narrative process at work in details concerning the actor's failing health and eventual death. In a letter dated 28 February [1827?], Kean apologizes for canceling an engagement. He explains that even the King of the English stage must sometimes be overruled: "My doctor has placed his veto against my quitting my room. I am sorry to lose the gratification but the Claims upon [the/my?] Constitution are imperative—& must be obeyed." Kean then asked Drury Lane for a £500 advance, but the theater, betting that he wouldn't live to repay the money, refused. Later that same year he switched to Covent Garden and performed well until 22 November, when he collapsed on stage.

Kean then planned a retirement tour, the first show of which was on 19 July 1830. Playing before the largest audience he had ever seen, Kean earned an astonishing amount: £1370. But debts had crippled Kean and, before the tour was over, his health gave out. Thus, Kean found himself having to give farewell performance after performance, which lasted years. As might be expected, the novelty soon wore off and audiences, suspecting that Kean was not in fact retiring, no longer saw a reason to pay exorbitantly to see an actor whose skills had so obviously eroded. He struggled through his physically demanding roles and had a chair set up in the wings so he could rest. To the audience "he seemed like a ghost, but a majestic ghost, leaving the audience to imagine how glorious it had been in life."[4]

His final collapse, as detailed in the Introduction, took place on 2 March 1833. According to a novelistic rendering by Otis Skinner, Kean sits in his dressing room, melancholy and alone. Charles enters to find his father haggard, wild-eyed, a shadow of his former self, mumbling incoherently and shivering over a fire. The great actor looks up, his eyes blood-shot, "You have come, my dear boy. It's very cold here. Charles, I am very ill. I fear there will be no performance tonight." Hot brandy and water fortifies him for the few scenes he stumbles through before he falls into his son's arms.[5] Biographers have filled the six-week interval between Kean's last stage performance and his death with a variety of bedside confessionals, the most famous being Hackett's tale that as Kean lay dying, he recited Lear's tender lines, "pray do not mock me."[6] Yet, Hackett, a second-rate actor, had no access to

---

3   Richard Holmes, *Sidetracks: Explorations of a Romantic Biographer*, 136.
4   "To My Dear Sir," Autograph note, HM 63344. Raymund FitzSimons, *Edmund Kean: Fire From Heaven*, 227-8.
5   Otis Skinner, "Three Madmen of the Theatre II," 633.
6   "Kean's Last Appearance on the Stage," *New York Mirror*, 22 February 1834, in Press

Kean's bedchamber, so how he came across this story is unknown. But good copy is good copy. Following Hackett, Molloy has Kean put to bed, where he passed into a lethargic state. But then:

> It was nine o'clock in the morning when he woke, and turned his eyes wistfully towards the light, then rested them on the faces of his secretary and the surgeon. Recognizing them, he strove to speak, but though they bent over him, no words fell upon their ears; then quickly and fearfully he flung out his arms, caught their hands, sighed, and was dead.[7]

Kean is now Cordelia, and we, his readers, are Lear, looking on as our beloved dies. Molloy would have us say with Lear-like elation, "Look on his lips. Look there! Look there!" But those lips remained silent, their secrets taken to the grave.

The nearly-always bathetic Philip Beufoy Barry has a wizened Kean reflecting on his lost fame and fortune:

> His life now was very lonely. It pains one to look upon Kean in those long days at Richmond, sitting in the little house, with windows that looked upon the Green, with no solace left to him but brandy and a memory. .... Kean, looking an old, old man, would sometimes sing and play for visitors. In the middle of a song, he would break off and flash out some reminiscence of an old triumph. Then he would cover his face with his hands, and say: 'All gone! All gone!'[8]

Giles Playfair does not have Kean explain himself; he does that for the actor. According to this psychic biographer, the actor clings to life because he "was still at war with his own conscience"; the actor "suffered agonies of mind for which there was no relief. He was then the prisoner of his remorse and was face to face with the awful realization that his tragedy was of his own making."[9] His Kean is a Buddha moonlighting as a Shakespearean. Even at age fifteen, Kean looks "back on his childhood as an old man does on crowded years that have gone before."[10]

The image of the all-wise, all-knowing Kean is at odds with both the chaos of his life and his characters. If Kean were so wise so young, a Buddha moonlighting as a Shakespearean, why had he repeatedly fallen into disastrous financial and personal decisions? The actor's own actions—not to mention his stage effects, which aimed at creating chaos, a shock to the system or "flashes of lighting"—are at odds with a life devoted to lining all one's ducks in a row. This grave Kean is not Kean at all, but a fantasy designed to win the hearts of his literary audience.[11]

Even though the facts of Kean's life are often shamefully sensual and hedonistic, it seems rather pointless to say that such biographies are false. True, Kean was a drunk

---

Clippings, Personal Collection.
7   J. Fitzgerald Molloy, *The Life and Adventures of Edmund Kean*, II:285.
8   Philip Beaufoy Barry, *Sinners Down the Centuries*, 257.
9   Giles Playfair, *Edmund Kean*, 313,315.
10   Ibid., 22.
11   Other aspects of Kean's deathbed confessions are dealt with in Gerald Weales, "Edmund Kean Onstage Onstage."

who spent his money recklessly, gambled, got into fistfights, slept with actresses, married women, and prostitutes. He was a bad husband, a worse father. Through it all, we have no evidence that Kean gave his life a second thought. There was always one more virgin to seduce, one more bottle to empty, one more stage to dominate. But, as we have seen, the logic behind the biography is more concerned with a constructed (and positive) message of Kean's life than a record of it. Negative assessments, of course, are possible, but they have their problems. Presenting Kean as a heartless villain begs the question why we should bother reading about him. To engage the reader, the biographer must make his subject knowable and likeable, even admirable.

Kean's Passion Play

In effort to rehabilitate Kean, many biographers prefer to dwell on episodes that would melt even the hardest of hearts. Thus, Molloy's Victorian biography evades Kean's sexual misdemeanors by stressing the near-biblical sufferings Kean, his wife, and children endured. The ultimate test comes on Easter Sunday, when Kean finds that he has no money to feed his wife and children:

> … bitter hardship and pitiless privation…. a Passion week he spent at Croydon. The theatre was closed until Easter Monday, when additional attractions were temptingly offered the public; but meanwhile the poor players were expected to live on air, and survive, that they might fulfil the promises which the bills set forth.[12]

But on Christmas Eve, with no food, no shelter and no friends, Kean and Mary watch on as their first born, Howard, dies from exposure and slow starvation. Kean goes wild. Half insane, he and Mary bury their first son, while a shivering Charles watched silently.

While the burial of Howard is seen as a private moment of grief, it is also narratively placed just before Kean's sudden rise to fame, as if the loss of Howard somehow gives the actor the last dram of genius needed to conquer London. Molloy even inserts a helpful explanation that the death of his son made him an unhappier man and an even finer actor: "He now played in tragedies with no need to simulate grief, and acted in comedies with a merry face and a sad heart…."[13]

Rehearsing *Hamlet*

Molloy also uses Howard's death as a rhetorical tool to link early and late periods of Kean's life with a neatness generally reserved for novelists or dramatists. Kean, too

---

12 J. Fitzgerald Molloy, The Life and Adventures of Edmund Kean, 1:43. Otis Skinner, speaking on behalf of Kean, tugs at our hearts: "It will be by the grace of God if poor Mary's baby [Charles or Howard—he doesn't specify] isn't born in a ditch. There is a haystack to sleep under and on again next day." (Otis Skinner, "Three Madmen of the Theatre II," 625).

13 J. Fitzgerald Molloy, *The Life and Adventures of Edmund Kean*, I:114-15.

busied by success to mourn for his son, puts off his tributary tears until much later in the biography, when he finds himself at the graveside of his spiritual father, the actor George Frederick Cooke, whose stage vigor partially anticipated Kean's own "flashing" style.

Kean asks the advice of his friend Dr. Francis and then Bishop Hobart, both of whom agree that Cooke deserves a monument. Rather than simply set a marker above his interred remains, they decide to move the body. In a scene reminiscent of *Hamlet*, Kean and his friend enter into a graveyard:

> One summer night, when all tumult was hushed and the world was calm, Kean and his friend set out for this city of the dead lying peaceful beneath the pale light of moon and stars. Workmen awaited them, lanterns were lighted, the heavy doors of the dark and humid vault forced open, and Kean, who exhibited a strong and morbid interest in the exhumation, descended to this charnel-house, where strangers in a strange land, homeless or nameless, found rest and peace in darkness and oblivion. The case in which the poor player had lain for over eight years was identified, and when, by Kean's request, the lid was raised, the yellow glare of lanterns fell upon a fleshless, eyeless skull, a few bones, and a handful of dust; this being all that was left of one whose soul had moved thousands to fear and pity, to hope and despair.

Kean's graveside visit becomes a kind of theater, the public outpouring of tears that have welled in him since Howard's death, which, in turn, becomes a final rehearsal of sorts for the actor's Drury Lane performances of the melancholy Dane. Holding Cooke's Yorrick-like skull in his hand, Kean, thinking of the deaths of both his first-born son and his spiritual father, cannot help but speculate "as to when his turn should come to perish in like manner."[14] The biographer is gratified by the display, which, he says, touches "the sympathies of the heart."[15]

---

14 Ibid., II:92. Kean's lament for Cooke may be less altruistic than has been hitherto suggested. The *New Monthly Magazine* warned Kean that Cooke was a fatal role that the actor must avoid playing:

> Too often we have had to lament that men, exalted by their genius, should suffer themselves to be precipitated from it by failings and vices which degrade them to the level of the lowest of their species. With the striking example of Cooke before his eyes, we trust that Kean will have prudence to avoid the fatal rock on which the former perished .... 'Remember Cooke!' (Don B. Wilmeth, *George Frederick Cooke, Machiavel of the Stage*, 7).

If Kean felt the same way, then his tears were not for Cooke, but for himself. Certainly, an argument might be made that Kean knew little of, and cared little for, Cooke. Kean told John Howard Payne that he never saw Cooke. See Gabriel Harrison, *The Life and Writing of John Howard Payne*, 45. Others felt Kean had hoodwinked London audiences: "G.F. Cooke was the great original of which Kean is the shadow.... Though only fifteen years have elapsed since the departure of Cooke, the present race of play-goers have forgotten him; and Kean's imitations remain undetected by the million, though they are obvious, though not as servile, as Young's attempts to copy Kemble" (*Oxberry's Dramatic Biography*, I:17).

15 J. Fitzgerald Molloy, *The Life and Adventures of Edmund Kean*, II:93.

Not all the versions of this story agree. According to the twentieth-century actor Donald Wolfit, upon Cooke's death, someone had decapitated his head and used it as Yorrick's skull in *Hamlet*. When Kean found out about the practice, he bought the skull and dug up Cooke's remains so that he could restore the head.[16] Even if this were the case, it's Kean's—and our own—emotional reaction that is of interest. Kean's actions demonstrate three ethical principles: (1) an understanding of right and wrong; (2) the need to avoid the bad and practice the good; (3) a concrete way of living life as either good or bad. These do-gooder narratives become a collective treatise on the qualities that make a profoundly sensitive human being a great actor; they operate as an incipient hagiography with a compelling and convenient association. Kean's personal tragedies made him a great actor; our ability to share in Kean's pain makes us better people. Kean's mourning for his son is natural, but his pity for Cooke suggests an important Christian virtue, an embracement of humanity well beyond the immediate family. Our pity for Kean teaches us the same.[17]

If this makes Kean's life useful, Hawkins observes that Kean's own life is also tragic in that the actor himself is cut off from the spiritual salvation his suffering art gave to others. Thus, on his deathbed, delirious with fear, Kean recalls his greatest moments at Drury Lane, but cannot help but reflect upon the pyrrhic costs:

> For several hours before his death Kean was quite insensible; but even in his unconsciousness his thoughts were with his acting .... 'Give me another horse!' he cried at another, half rising in his bed with delirious excitement; 'Howard,' he whispered tenderly at another.[18]

The same point is made in the recent Silvia Freedman musical, *The Meteoric Rise and Fall of Edmund Kean* (1997). In exchange for fame and fortune, the theatrical gods demand Howard's life. Immediately, after the funeral, Kean goes on stage and performs his hugely successful Shylock:

> Now he wins every game
> All the world knows his name
> He has learnt the price of fame....

The irony and significance of the family's loss and Edmund's personal gain is not lost on Mary. Kean is now at his peak, but, as Mary points out, it has come at a terrible price:

---

16 Donald Wolfit speech, "Edmund Kean," 2, in HRC. Arnold Hare states that Kean took an "abstract" of Cooke's head, along with a finger. See *George Frederick Cooke: The Actor and The Man*, 189.

17 Heinrich Heine notes that at a performance of Kean's Shylock, "a pale British beauty," sympathizing with the plight of the Jew, "wept passionately" and cried out many times: "The poor man is wronged!" See *Shakespeare's Maidens and Maids*, 377.

18 F.W. Hawkins, *The Life of Edmund Kean*, II:391.

MARY: You sacrificed your health, you sacrifice your sanity. You sacrificed our son. No matter how much they applauded you, cheer you, praise you, not all the applause in the world can waken him now. And what do you have in return for this sacrifice? What do you have in return for our sacrifice?

To Kean, it was worth the price; Mary disagrees:

KEAN: They [the audience] loved me.
MARY: They never loved you. (*Pulling Charles forward.*) We did.

The revelation comes too late. The ghosts of Shakespeare's characters step forward to doom him to an eternal drama of pain and sorrow.

Turning Cooke's body or Howard's death into sacrificial fodder for Kean's genius is morally repellant. By the same thinking, we should find the next Olivier in Kabul or in Croatia. If suffering and madness make a good actor, the possibilities are endless: Hitler as Hamlet; Manson as Mercutio. Nonetheless, there is no doubt that this equation is an easy way for the biographer to explain facets of Kean's acting and why Kean's onstage portrayals of grief seemed to be so real. Kean calls upon these dark memories when cradling Cordelia in his arms or when leaping into the grave to see his dear Ophelia one last time. However, concentration on these episodes, creating graveside scenarios as the defining moments of Kean's life, also creates an overtly religious narrative, one in which explaining why Kean succeeded on stage is no longer the issue. What is now paramount is the story of the actor on the stage of life, growing in spiritual awareness of his own physical limitations, preparing himself for the inevitable drawing of the theatrical curtain.

Given Kean's licentious life, it's easy to see why biographers rely upon these techniques. Further, as we have seen, Kean's own repertoire aids in these biographical narratives. The actor was known for his tragic roles. (He played very few romantic and even fewer comic parts, and those often incompetently.) However, Leigh Woods argues that biographers, in their need to "shape and tailor" Kean's life, create a "rivalry" with the actor.[19] Given the similarities of many Kean biographies, which present the actor in pseudo-hagiography, are other narratives even possible?

Julius Berstl, unhappy with the extant facts of Kean's debauched life, comes to a neat solution. The biographer "finds" (read: creates) Kean's private diary, in which the actor defends himself:

> With selfless burning devotion I have served the noble art of acting all my life as, when a half-fledged boy, I performed on the tight rope; as I sang my couplets in between the acts; as I played the clown in pantomime. Night after night I succeeded in establishing the mystic contact between the actor and the masses roused to fever heat by my performances. … An actor's work is divine service; the stage is the altar on which Audience and Actor together sacrifice to their unknown god! If ever by my acting I have brought home to

---

19 Leigh Woods, "Actors' Biography and Mythmaking: The Example of Edmund Kean," 240.

my audiences the fundamentals of drama and of my art, then by this act alone would my faults, weaknesses and vices be outweighed a hundredfold in the eyes of God![20]

Berstl's unapologetic addition hardly seems like something a man might say, much less pen, on his deathbed. It's another staged reading, another prepared speech, which Berstl both creates and quotes.

Kean and the Performative Self

Kean's most recent biographer, FitzSimons, simply has Kean passing away, *sans* quotation, *sans* moving lips, *sans* everything. FitzSimons is probably right to discard the abovementioned passages, but, as we have seen, Kean's life was deeply intertwined with dramatic fiction. Others may prefer to have Kean die with Lear on his lips. It's an interpretative move, to be sure. By quoting Lear, Kean concedes no hidden truth, but asks others to mask themselves as he had done, to speak in quotation, to see life as an actor, always on stage.

Seeing life as indistinguishable from performance is not a new way to look at Kean, nor it is a new approach to cultural studies concerning that early nineteenth century. *The Cult of Kean* might be numbered among a growing list of new historicist studies of nineteenth-century larger-than-life figures.[21] But it is Kean, Joseph Donohue suggests, that is perennially distinguished with the spirit of the nineteenth century, an era he calls "The Age of Kean."[22]

In many ways, we are still living in his epoch. This book is called *The Cult of Kean*. You could argue that, along with a handful of other Romantic figures, Kean grandfathered the whole cult concept.[23] His vocation didn't just produce "fans" but devotees of theatrical self-presentation.[24] Anticipating late twentieth-century pop icons such as David Bowie, Boy George, and Madonna, Kean was a character both

---

20 Julius Berstl, *The Sun's Bright Child*, 78-9.

21 Several recent studies have argued that Romantic heroes were often self-consciously marketed constructions: Peter J. Manning, *Byron and his Fictions* (1978), the collection, *Byron and the Limits of Fiction* (1988), James Soderholm, *Fantasy, Forgery, and the Byron Legend* (1996), Stephen Gill's *Wordsworth and the Victorians* (1998), Michael Dobson and Nicola J. Watson's *England's Elizabeth: An Afterlife in Fame and Fantasy* (2002), and Lucasta Miller's *The Brontë Myth* (2004). Other larger-than-life personalities have spawned similar studies: for example, Lois Potter's recent collection, *Playing Robin Hood: The Legend as Performance in Five Centuries* (1998). See also Peter Conrad, *Orson Welles: The Stories of His Life* (2003).

22 Joseph Donohue, *Theatre in the Age of Kean*, 176.

23 Julia Swindells notes that "Georgian theatre appears to have carried a much more fluid understanding of the actor than in the theatre of the nineteenth century. ... Audiences also acted, and stage actors were often witnesses to audience performance, as were other members of the audience" (*Glorious Causes*, 159).

24 On this point see William Hazlitt, who wrote, "If poetry is a dream, the business of life is much the same. If it is a fiction, made up of what we wish things to be, and fancy that they are, because we wish them so, there is no other nor better reality" (*Complete Works*, V:3).

on stage and off, a mannequin to be copied, his eccentricities to be emulated, his passions to be reproduced, his fame applauded, and his self-destructive capacities envied and aped.[25] Kean's offstage theatricality is now part of our everyday social conduct. We see such people all the time, indeed, with growing frequency: teenagers who copy the clothes and hair styles of their favorite pop stars, grown men who dress up as Elvis, even while assuming un-Elvis-like occupations: dock worker, barber, accountant, etc.

This brings us squarely to the heart of the matter: for good or bad, Kean's contributions are not the money and gifts he left to friends, but his innovations of dramatic representation. Kean took theater to the streets, turned life into art.[26] Acting like your hero, or simply living your life as a form of drama with yourself as the lead no longer seems like an illness or even odd. Jerry Springer and other talk-show hosts encourage people to expose shamelessly their darkest secrets on national television; more troubling are the "Reality TV" series such as *Survivor*, *The Bachelor*, *Who Wants to Marry My Dad?*, *Love or Money*, *Big Brother*, *Blind Date* and *Elim-i-date*, all of which encourage "ordinary" people to act outrageously in the name of ratings; internet sites offer us webcams where people urinate and defecate and fornicate for a fee; even true crime has become just another form of entertainment (*Judge Judy*, *America's Most Wanted*), and these "stars" have become famous, sometimes enduringly so, not because they are good, but because they are noticed.

I would go so far as to argue that in our era, Kean's escapades, memorable, if sometimes fictional, have become commonplace, perfectly in keeping with an age that is at once narcissistic and collectivist. As essayist Cintra Wilson observes:

> The good old way of getting famous was to be very good at something artistic, and have everybody fall in love with you for it. That doesn't really work now, because, as many critics have pointed out, nobody is very interested in art for its own sake anymore; now one only does 'art' as a necessary part of the equation, the means to the end of getting famous, so one can get plastic surgery and go to parties in order to lick and be licked upon by famous people like puppies in a basket.[27]

Media attention creates fame, and fame cancels all crimes, but, in so doing, our form of fame blurs our values. All this attention might make for good drama, but it's also a superficial excuse for a life.

---

25 On Kean and American culture: Leo Braudy dates the birth of the "fan" to circa. 1820s: "A large audience had begun to appear that sought to imitate the style of ostentation with little care for an actual accomplishment" (*The Frenzy of Renown: Fame and Its History*, 481). The date fits Kean's stage career nicely.

26 Leo Braudy argues that early American icons used theatrical tricks to get their message out to the masses (Ibid., 457).

27 Cintra Wilson, *A Massive* Swelling, XVI-XVII. For a reasonably similar—though less colorful—perspective, see Richard Schechner, *The End of Humanism*, 98-9.

A Moral to These Stories?

There is one last Kean to confront, my own. On Saturday, 25 May 1833, Kean was buried in a crypt in St. Mary Magdalene Church in Richmond. In his latter years, Kean had lived in Richmond and sometimes worked out of the local theater. Arrangements for the funeral extended beyond the standard casket and flowers, friends, and family. The event was accorded the status of a state funeral. Thousands thronged to see Kean one last time; twenty extra constables were hired to keep the peace; the shops on the main street were closed for business. Ophelia Benjamin, a prostitute with whom Kean had lived his last years, was not invited.[28]

In his last days, his fortune gone, the actor lived in filth and chaos. A sea captain the actor befriended has left us with a livid picture:

> The room we entered was almost unfurnished; a *deal* table, with divers intersecting circles, the marks of grog-glasses, and the ashes of cigars, showed that certain orgies had but recently broken up.

> … He [Kean] looked dreadfully dull and confessed that his o'er night potations had *not* been 'few and far between.' His eye was still brilliant, but the debauch had sadly impressed his other features … I was struck with his appearance; his face was livid, and of a Bardolph character; at the time. There was nothing classic in his features. A hard life had found him out, and he seemed a broken man….[29]

Another friend who visited him home in Scotland recalled:

> We then entered the library, a mere parlour, and nothing to recommend it, as what might have been anticipated from so great a reader as the late Mr. Kean. … Indeed, the books were by no means numerous, the principle part of which were secured by wires, and locked up in the bookcases, except a few scattered on some shelves of minor importance….[30]

Going through his private papers, his son, Charles, found his Will. In part, it read:

> My property in Bute, with the furniture of this House … goes to the possession of the Drury Lane Theatrical fund.
> My Dramatic Wardrobe, with all other clothing I leave to my worthy friend John Lee…[.][31]

---

28 In a letter to his secretary, John Lee, dated 20 January 1831, he writes: "Chance & circumstance have driven me to points I must get rid of this [wom]an. This is no association in feeling & the thread must be broken. I consent, but there are no positive commands to the contrary. God, they say—made man, The Devil the contrary." See Jonathan Reynolds, *Dramatis Personæ* 20 (1991):18. One presumes he is referring to Ophelia Benjamin.

29 See "'A Day With Mr. Kean'—by a Sea Captain who befriended him on the way to Edinburgh," in Kean, Edmund C. Newspaper Articles Messmore Kendall Collection, HRC.

30 Pierce Egan, *The Pilgrims of the Thames. In Search of the National*, 345.

31 A transcription of the will is found in Harold Newcomb Hillebrand, *Edmund Kean*,

Even Kean's last will is a theatrical spectacle of sorts. His personal effects—even his house—were listed as theatrical props, and his theatrical props—including his costumes—were listed as personal effects.

His remains were originally placed in the church's vaults but were moved by Peter O'Toole and friends, after they found, to their great surprise, no marker celebrating the life of England's greatest actor. Making his pilgrimage to St. Mary's, O'Toole noted:

> There was no tombstone. No gravemarker in the graveyard at the old grey parish church of St. Mary Magdalene on the Green. That was irritating, that was perplexing.... [We] had a tombstone carved up ... inside the church, in memory of Edmund Kean, together the pair of us laid it down. That ended our irritations, our perplexities, that was right. Tread softly.[32]

O'Toole's reverence is touching, but it is tinged with some trepidation. Why should we "Tread softly"? Is there some memory of Kean O'Toole would like to have buried? What do we remember about Edmund Kean, and what has that to do with the actor who lies buried at St. Mary Magdalene?

Setting out to answer these questions, I have returned to his grave. Finding the church was not easy. The officials at British Rail, where I disembarked, scratched their collective heads. I walked down to the Richmond Theatre. The girl at the box office had never heard of the church or the actor. A building agent knew of it. Down the High Street past the Starbucks to the Jigsaw and then left past the Tesco. (What have Thatcher, Major, and Blair done to this country?) And here I am. According to the yellowed brochure I bought for 20p, St. Mary's is the oldest church in Richmond, built at the end of the twelfth century.[33] O'Toole's monument is handsome enough, though neglected. Kean's body now rests under a children's play station, consisting of an elfish table and proportionally diminutive chairs. The table is covered in dried crayon and faded felt-tip markers. You've got to move the chairs and table aside for the tombstone to come to view:

Beneath this stone lies
EDMUND KEAN
Actor* DIED 1833
'The sun's bright child'

If we are to take the inscription at its word, Kean is a Promethean—"The sun's bright child"—both an actor and a myth. As we have seen, acting is what Kean did, even as a child, and interpretations of his acting and his genius varied even in his own lifetime. He was by turns seen as a thoroughly modern man who acted in old plays,

---

329.

32 Peter O'Toole, *Loitering With Intent: The Apprentice*, 299.

33 In 1827, another church, St. John the Divine, was added to the parish. It is closer to the Richmond Theatre and newer. I have been unable to ascertain why the family selected St. Mary's.

Plate 15: Kean memorialized as a Promethean god. Reprinted by kind permission of the Harry Ransom Humanities Research Center; The University of Texas at Austin.

a staunch—if iconoclastic—revolutionary who lived like an aristocrat, a bastard who protected his family name, a social activist and home wrecker, a sunshine-and-holiday Promethean playboy. The sheer number and variety of Keanian materials have helped his posthumous reputation, even if that reputation often depended (and depends) upon shouldering aside biographical facts in favor of bizarre, though compelling, fictions. He struts and frets with Napoleonic zeal in Grattan's memoirs, rages against the aristocracy in a play by Dumas, ridicules American culture in a comedic turn by Mark Twain, and confronts the existential riddle of mankind in Sartre.

This multivalence of perspective, itself a substantial crux for contemporary scholarship, exposes the serial nature of the Edmund-Kean character and calls attention to the tension between multiplicity and coherence in the production of popular culture. Different but equally valid, these various Keans do not always meet with our emotional/ideological/cultural approval. And it may well be our *dis*approval of Kean that unlocks the mystery of his continued reinvention. Kean's fictions work to rehabilitate Kean; by transferring our records of Kean from the actor to these fictions, Kean moves from the transitory to the archetypal. This transference does not necessarily change the facts of Kean's life, but it does monumentalize them. Kean's faults are redeemed in the serious world of literature and art, his personal actions, so often debased, are not expunged but are, nonetheless, redeemed in the literary record as political or philosophical expressions or as comical high jinx.

Ironically, had Kean been a giving, loving person, a man with integrity or a conscience, it's doubtful he would have made this leap into literature. Indeed, Theodore Norton was shocked that no poet had been inspired by Kean's passing to write an encomium to England's greatest actor:

> Not *one* lament? Not *one* 'melodious tear'
> To grace of mighty *Kean* the hollow bier?[34]

Given Kean's treatment of the poets and playwrights of the era, their reluctance to honor him is understandable. But we can go still further. After all, Kean's real behavior was rather disheartening. Here was a man who could summon thunder and lightning from the heavens, and what did he use it for? To turn Drury Lane into perhaps the biggest brothel London had ever known. In place of love, the original Kean gave us only arousal; commitment gave way to seduction; for creativity, Kean gave us flashes of lightning; for genius, Kean gave us ingenuousness. Given his talents, the results are disappointing.

What a waste, and for writers, what an opportunity. Kean may have held a position of power, but that power, so far from giving him license, merely imposed upon him higher duties, which, unfulfilled, manifested themselves, often with exaggeration, in the writings of others. Each of these writers projected their longings for mankind into Kean and measured their own accomplishments by how far their Keans diverged from the original, deficient model.[35]

In essence, this study suggests that Kean did and does serve a higher purpose, both as revolutionary practice and cautionary warning. Forging together the positives of these literary Keans, we might unveil a monument that states more than his name, more than his year of death, more than even the phrase, "The sun's bright child," a monument that would read:

> He was
> The first (unanswered) Metaphysician of the age.
> A despiser of the merely Rich and Great:
> A lover of the People, Poor or Oppressed:
> A hater of the Pride and Power of the Few,

---

34 Theodore Norton, *Kean, A Poem*, 9.

35 According to John Woolford, Kean's decrepit body constantly reminded his audience that he was not Richard III, but only a man. This "failure" of Kean's acting became the poetic fodder for one passage of Robert Browning's *Pauline*. See "The Influence of Edmund Kean," 26.

As opposed to the happiness of the Many;
A man of true moral courage,
Who sacrificed Profit and the present Fame
To Principle,
And a yearning for the good of Human Nature.
Who was a burning wound to an Aristocracy,
That could not answer him before men,
And who may confront him before their Maker.

He lived and died
The unconquered Champion
Of Truth, Liberty, and Humanity,
'Dubitantes opera legit.'

This stone
Is raised by one whose heart is
With him, in his grave.

The epitaph is real enough, though not written for Kean, but for Kean's readiest champion, William Hazlitt. Kean gave us an example of a man who inscribed, re-inscribed, erased, and rewrote his identity as he (and others) saw fit, and for that we remember him, but the message of The Cult of Kean is the one lesson the actor never understood: *noblesse oblige.*

Bibliography

Abel, C. Douglas. " 'Alexander the Little': The Question of Stature in Edmund Kean's Othello." *Theatre History Studies* 9 (1989): 92-105.

———. "Edmund Kean's Masonic Career." *Theatre Notebook* (1989): 69-70.

———. "Venom in His Blood: Edmund Kean's Othello Contests." *New England Theatre Journal* 6 (1995):69-89.

Abraham Lincoln, Slavery, and the Civil War: Selected Writings and Speeches, ed. Michael P. Johnson. Boston and New York: Bedford/St. Martin's, 2001.

Ackerman, Alan L., Jr. *The Portable Theater: American Literature & the Nineteenth-Century Stage*. Baltimore and London: The Johns Hopkins University Press, 1999.

The Actor; Or, A Peep Behind the Curtain. New York: Wm. H. Graham, 1846.

Actors and Actresses of Great Britain and the United States, eds Brander Mathews and Laurence Hutton. 2nd edn. 5 vols. Boston: L. C. Page, 1900.

Actors and Editors, A Poem By An Undergraduate. London: W. Smith and Co., 1817.

Adams, John Quincy. "The Character of Desdemona." www.classicaltheatre. com/id14.htm

Airksinen, Timo. *The Philosophy of the Marquis de Sade*. London and New York: Routledge, 1991.

Aldridge, Ira. *Memoir and Theatrical Career of Ira Aldridge*. London: Onwhyn, [1849?].

Allston, Washington. "Kean As Hamlet." *New York Evening* Post 10 March 1821.

Apostolidès, Jean-Marie. "Molière and the Sociology of Exchange." *Critical Inquiry* 14 (1988):477-92.

Archer, Stephen M. *Junius Brutus Booth Theatrical Prometheus*. Carbondale and Edwardsville: Southern Illinois University Press, 1992.

Archer, William. *Eminent Actors: Macready, Betterton, Macklin*. London: Kegan Paul, Trench, Trüber and Co., 1890-91.

———. *William Charles Macready*. London: Kegan Paul, Trench, Trübner & Co., 1890.

Ashe, Geoffrey. *The Hell-Fire Clubs: A History of Anti-Morality*. Phoenix Mill, Thrupp, Stroud, Gloucester: Sutton Publishing Limited, 2000.

The Assailant Assailed. Being A Vindication of Mr. Kean. London: Fearman's Public Library 1819.

Austen, Jane. *Jane Austen's Letters to Her Sister Cassandra and Others*, ed. R.W. Chapman. 2nd edn. Oxford and New York: Clarendon Press, 1932.

Austin, Wiltshire Stanton and John Ralph. *The Lives of the Poets-Laureate*. London: Richard Bentley, 1853.

Baer, Marc. *Theatre and Disorder in Late Georgian London*. Oxford: Clarendon Press, 1992.

Baillie, Joanna. *The Collected Letters of Joanna Baillie*, ed. Judith Bailey Slagle. 2 vols. Madison: Fairleigh Dickenson University Press; London: Associated University Presses, 1999.

————. *Dramatic and Poetical Works*. 2nd edn. London: Longman, Brown, Green, & Longmans, 1851.

Baker, Henry Barton. *Our Old Actors*. 2 vols. London: R. Bentley and Son, 1878.

Baker, Herschel. *John Philip Kemble: The Actor in His Theatre*. New York: Greenwood Press, 1942.

Baldick, Robert. *The Life and Times of Frédérick Lemaître*. London: Hamish Hamilton, 1959.

Ballad: Little Breechs in Kean, Edmund C. Newspaper Articles Messmore Kendall Collection. Harry Ransom Collection (HRC), University of Texas, at Austin.

Barish, Jonas. *The Antitheatrical Prejudice*. Berkeley: University of California Press, 1981.

Barry, Philip Beaufoy. *Sinners Down the Centuries*. Philadelphia: Macrae Smith Company, 1929.

Bate, Jonathan. "The Romantic Stage," in *The Oxford Illustrated History of Shakespeare on Stage*, eds. Jonathan Bate and Russell Jackson. Oxford: Oxford University Press, 2001.

————. *Shakespeare and the English Romantic Imagination*. Oxford: Clarendon Press, 1986.

————. *Shakespearean Constitutions: Politics, Theatre, Criticism 1730-1830*. Oxford: Clarendon Press, 1989.

Bauer, Susan Wise. "Y2Krazy: You'd better stock up. Only those who purchase will survive." *Books & Culture*, Sep/Oct 1999. http://www.christianitytoday.com/bc/9b5

Beatty, Bernard and Vincent Newey (eds). *Byron and the Limits of Fiction*. Liverpool: Liverpool University Press, 1988.

Berret, Anthony J. *Mark Twain and Shakespeare: A Cultural Legacy*. Lanham, New York and London: University Press of America, 1993.

Berstl, Julius. *The Sun's Bright Child: The Imaginary Memoirs of Edmund Kean*. London: Hammond, Hammond & Co., 1946.

Billington, Michael. "Kean." *The Times* 22 September 1970.

Birkin, Lawrence. *Consuming Desire: Sexual Science and the Emergence of a Culture of Abundance 1871-1914*. Ithaca, NY: Cornell University Press, 1988.

"The Bishop!! Particulars of the Charge against the Hon. Percy Jocelyn, Bishop of Clogher." reprinted in Ian McCormick (ed.), *Sexual Outcasts 1750-1850*. Vol. III. London and New York: Routledge, 2000.

Blainey, Ann. *Immortal Boy*. New York: St. Martin's Press, 1985.

Boaden, James. *Memoirs of the Life of John Philip Kemble, Esq., Including a History of the Stage, From the Time of Garrick to the Present Period*. 2 vols. London: Longman, Hurst, Rees, Orme, Brown, and Green, 1825.

Bowdler, Thomas. *The Family Shakspeare.* 4 vols. London: Richard Cruttwell and J. Hatchard, 1807.

———. *A Letter to the Editor of the British Critic.* London: Longman, Hurst, Rees, Orme, and Brown, 1823

Bradby, David. "Sartre as Dramatist." *The Philosophical Journal* 7.1 (1970): 63-77.

Braudy, Leo. *The Frenzy of Renown: Fame and Its History.* New York and Oxford: Oxford University Press, 1986.

Brawne, Fanny. *Letters of Fanny Brawne to Fanny Keats (1820-1824),* ed. Fred Edgcumbe. London: Oxford University Press, 1936.

Bristol, Michael D. *Big-Time Shakespeare.* London and New York: Routledge, 1996.

———. *Carnival and Theatre.* London: Methuen, 1985.

Bucke, Charles. *The Italians: Or, The Fatal Accusation: A Tragedy.* London: G. and W.B. Whittaker, 1819.

Burke, Edmund. *Reflections on the Revolution in France,* ed. Conor Cruise O'Brien. London: Pelican, 1968, rpt. Penguin Classics, 1986.

Burnim, Kalman A. *David Garrick, Director.* Pittsburgh: University of Pittsburgh, 1961.

Burroughs, Catherine. "Acting in the Closet: A Feminist Performance of Hazlitt's *Liber Amoris* and Keats's *Otho the Great.*" *European Romantic Review* 2.2 (1992): 125-44.

Byron, Lord George Gordon. *The Selected Letters of Lord Byron,* ed. Jacques Barzun. New York: Farrar, Straus and Young, Inc., 1953.

Callan, Michael Feeney. *Anthony Hopkins: In Darkness and Light.* London and New York: MacMillan, 1995.

Carhart, Margaret S. *The Life and Work of Joanna Baillie.* Yale Studies in English (LXIV). New Haven: Yale University Press; Oxford: Oxford University Press, 1923.

Carpenter, Scott. *Acts of Fiction: Resistance and Resolution from Sade to Baudelaire.* Pennsylvania: Pennsylvania State University Press, 1996.

Carson, William G.B. *Managers in Distress: The St. Louis Stage 1840-1844.* St. Louis: St. Louis Historical Documents Foundation, 1949.

———. *The Theatre on the Frontier: The Early Years of the St. Louis Stage.* 2nd edn. New York: Benjamin Blom, 1935, rpt. 1965.

Cartelli, Thomas. *Repositioning Shakespeare: National Formations, Postcolonial Appropriations.* London, New York: Routledge, 1999.

Casanova, Giacomo. *The Memoirs of Jacques Casanova de Seingalt.* New York: Putnam [1959-61].

Clarke, Asia Booth. *Booth's Memorials: Passages, Incidents and Anecdotes in the Life of Junius Brutus Booth, (The Elder) By His Daughter.* New York: Carleton, 1866.

Clubbe, John. "Napoleon's Last Campaign and the Origins of Don Juan." *The Byron Journal* 25(1997):12-22.

Cole, John William. *The Life and Theatrical Times of Charles Kean, F.S.A.* 2 vols. New York and London: Richard Bentley, 1859.

Coleridge, Samuel Taylor. *The Collected Works of Samuel Taylor Coleridge*, eds James Engell and W. Jackson Bate. 16 vols. London: Routledge & Kegan Paul; Princeton: Princeton University Press, 1971-2001.

Colman, George (the Younger). *The Iron Chest*, Inchbald's British Theatre. vol. 21. London: Longman, Hurst, Rees, and Orme, 1808.

Conrad, Peter. *Orson Welles: The Stories of His Life.* New York: Faber & Faber, 2003.

Cox V. Kean: For Criminal Conversation With Plaintiff's Wife, Damages £800. Full Particulars of This Interesting Trial, With the Letters. London: John Fairburn, [1825].

Craig, Gordon. *The Life and Theatrical Career of Edmund Kean,* 1787-1833. London: Private Printing, 1938.

Critical Remarks on the Astonishing Performance of Mr. Kean, at Drury Lane Theatre. London: John Fairbun: 1814.

Crochunis, Thomas C. "Byronic Heroes and Acting: The Embodiment of Mental Theater." *Contemporary Studies on Lord Byron,* ed. William D. Brewer. New York: Edwin Mellon, 1991. 73-94.

Daniel, George. *Ophelia Keen!!! A Dramatic Legendary Tale.* London: John Cumberland, 1829.

Danto, Arthur C. *The Transfiguration of the Commonplace: A Philosophy of Art.* Cambridge, Mass.: Harvard University Press, 1981.

David, Saul. *Prince of Pleasure: The Prince of Wales and the Making of the Regency.* New York: Grove Press, 1998.

Davis, Jim and Victor Emeljanow. *Reflecting the Audience: London Theatregoing, 1840-1880.* Iowa City: University of Iowa Press, 2001.

" 'A Day With Mr. Kean'—by a Sea Captain who befriended him on the way to Edinburgh," in Kean, Edmund C. Newspaper Articles Messmore Kendall Collection, Harry Ransom Collection (HRC), University of Texas, at Austin.

A Defence of Edmund Kean, Esq. London: John Lowndes, 1819.

Delécluze, Etienne-Jean. *Journal de Delécluze, 1824-1828.* Paris: Editions Bernard Grasset, 1948.

Dibdin, Charles. *Professional & Literary Memoirs of Charles Dibdin the Younger,* ed. George Speaight. London: The Society for Theatre Research, 1956.

Diddler, Jeremy. *Theatrical Poems: Comic, Satirical, and Descriptive; Containing The Strolling Manager, The Scene Painter's Blunder, Studies from Nature, Kean, and his Imitators, &c.&c.&c.* [London]: H. Price, 1822.

Dimond, William. *The Bride of Abydos, A Tragick Play in Three Acts As Performed at the Theatre Royal, Drury-Lane.* London: Richard White, 1818.

Dircks, Phyllis T. *David Garrick. Twayne's English Authors,* Gen. Ed. Herbert Sussman. Boston: Twayne Publishers, 1985.

Disher, Maurice Willson. *Mad Genius: A Biography of Edmund Kean With Particular Reference to the Women Who Made and Unmade Him.* London and New York: Hutchinson and Co., 1950.

Dobson, Michael and Nicola J. Watson. *England's Elizabeth: An Afterlife in Fame and Fantasy.* Oxford: Oxford University Press, 2002.

Donaldson, Ian. *Jonson's Magic Houses: Essays in Interpretation.* Oxford and New York: Clarendon Press, 1997.

Donohue, Joseph. *Theatre in the Age of Kean.* Totowa, New Jersey: Rowman and Littlefield, 1975.

Doran, John. *"Their Majesties' Servants." Annals of the English Stage From Thomas Betterton to Edmund Kean.* 2 vols. New York: W.J. Widdleton, 1865.

Dumas, Alexandre. *Edmund Kean: Or, The Genius and the Libertine.* London: G. Vickers, E. Appleyard, William Strange, 1847.

————. *Edmund Kean* in *The Great Lover and Other Plays*, trans. Barnett Shaw. New York: Frederick Ungar Publishing Co., 1969.

Dunn, Esther Cloudman. *Shakespeare in America.* New York: Macmillan Company, 1939.

Duval, Georges. *Frédérick-Lemaitre et Son Temps: 1800-1876.* Paris: Tresse Éditions, 1896.

Edelman, Charles. *Brawl Ridiculous: Swordfighting in Shakespeare's Plays.* The Revels Companion Library. Manchester: Manchester University Press, 1992.

Egan, Pierce. *Boxiana, or Sketches of Ancient and Modern Pugilism.* 5 vols. London: For the Booksellers, 1818.

————. *The Life of An Actor.* 2nd edn. London: C.S. Arnold, 1825; rpt. London: Methuen, 1904.

————. *The Pilgrims of the Thames. In Search of the National..* London: Thomas Tegg, 1839.

Erdman, David V. "Byron's Stage Fright: The History of His Ambition and Fear of Writing for the Stage." *ELH* VI (1939): 219-43.

Evans, Nicholas M. "Ira Aldridge: Shakespeare and Minstrelsy." *ATQ* 16 (2003): 165-87.

"An Exhibition About the Fisher Family." The Theatre Museum in Covent Garden. Exhibition, Spring 2002.

Falk, Robert. "Shakespeare in America: A Survey to 1900." *Shakespeare Survey* 18 (1965): 102-18.

The Fancy. London: J. M. Gowan: 1821.

Farington, Joseph. *The Diaries of Joseph Farington.* 8 vols. London: Hutchinson & Co., 1922-29.

Finney, Claude Lee. *The Evolution of Keats's Poetry.* 2 vols. Cambridge, Mass.: Harvard University Press, 1936.

FitzSimons, Raymund. *Edmund Kean: Fire From Heaven.* London: Hamish Hamilton, 1976.

Forster, John and George Henry Lewes. *Dramatic Essays*, eds William Archer and Robert W. Lowe. London: Walter Scott, Ltd., 1896.

Frank, Frederick S. *The First Gothics*. New York: Garland, 1987.

Frappier-Mazur, Lucuienne. *Writing the Orgy: Power and Parody in Sade*, trans. Gillian C. Gill. Philadelphia: University of Pennsylvania Press, 1996.

Freedman, Sylvia (with music by Michael Jeffrey). *The Meteoric Rise and Dramatic Demise of Edmund Kean, A Musical In Two Acts*. Watford Palace Theatre, August, 1997.

Freeman, Lisa A. *Character's Theater: Genre and Identity on the Eighteenth-Century English Stage*. Philadelphia: University of Pennsylvania Press, 2002.

Friedland, Paul. "Parallel Stages: Theatrical and Political Representation in Early Modern and Revolutionary France." *The Age of Cultural Revolutions: Britain and France, 1750-1820*, eds Colin Jones and Dror Wahrman. Berkeley: University of California Press, 2002. 218-50.

Frow, Gerald. *"Oh Yes It Is": A History of Pantomime*. London: British Broadcasting Corporation, 1985.

Fruman, Norman. *Coleridge, the Damaged Archangel*. New York: George Braziller 1971.

Fuller, Thomas. "Excerpt from *Worthies, Warwickshire* (1662)," in *Four Centuries of Shakespearian Criticism*, ed. by J. Frank Kermode. New York: Avon Books, 1965.

Furtwangler, Albert. *Assassin On Stage: Brutus, Hamlet, and the Death of Lincoln*. Urbana: University of Illinois Press, 1991.

Gaer, Joseph. Introduction. *The Theatre of the Gold Rush Decade in San Francisco*. New York: Burt Franklin, 1935. 1-8.

Gates, David. "The Last Titan of The Theater: Sir John Gielgud, 1904-2000." *Newsweek* 5 June (2000): 75.

Genest, John. *Some Account of the English Stage From the Restoration in 1660 to 1830*. 10 vols. Bath: H.E. Carrington, 1832.

George, David. "Restoring Shakespeare's *Coriolanus*: Kean Versus Macready." *Theatre Notebook* 44.3 (1989): 101-18.

Gill, Stephen. *Wordsworth and the Victorians*. Oxford: Clarendon Press, 1998.

Gipson, Alice Edna. *John Home: A Study of His Life and Works*. Cadwell, Ida.: The Caxton Printers, [1916?].

Goulemot, Jean Marie. *Forbidden Texts: Erotic Literature and its Readers in Eighteenth-Century France*, trans. James Simpson. Philadelphia: University of Pennsylvania Press, 1994.

Grattan, Thomas Colley. *Beaten Paths; and Those Who Trod Them*. 2 Vols. London: Chapman and Hall, 1862.

———. *Ben Nazir The Saracen. A Tragedy In Five Acts*. London: Colburn, 1827.

Grayling, A.C. *The Quarrel of the Age: The Life and Times of William Hazlitt*. London: Phoenix Press, 2000.

Gross, Jonathan David. *Byron: The Erotic Liberal*. Lanham, Md.: Rowman & Littlefield, 2001.

Hackett, James Henry. Correspondence. Library of Congress, Rare Books Division, The Alfred Whital Stern collection of Lincolniana, 1837-1912, Washington, DC.

————. "Kean's Last Appearance on the Stage." *New York Mirror*, 22 February 1834. 270.

————. *Notes and Comments Upon Certain Plays and Actors of Shakespeare*. New York: Carleton, 1863.

————. *Oxberry's 1822 Edition of Richard III, With Descriptive Notes Recording Edmund Kean's Performance Made By James H. Hackett*, notes by Alan S. Downer. London: The Society for Theatrical Research, 1959.

Hadley, Elaine. *Melodramatic Tactics: Theatricalized Dissent in the English Marketplace, 1800-1885*. Stanford: Stanford University Press, 1995.

Hale, William. "Considerations on the Causes and the Prevalence of Female Prostitution." reprinted in Ian McCormick (ed.), *Sexual Outcasts 1750-1850*. Vol. III. London and New York: Routledge, 2000.

Harbage, Alfred. *As They Liked It: An Essay On Shakespeare and Morality*. New York: Macmillan Company, 1947.

Hare, Arnold. *George Frederick Cooke: The Actor and The Man*. Bath: The Pitman Press for The Society of Theatre Research, 1980.

Harrison, Gabriel. *The Life and Writing of John Howard Payne*. Albany, New York: Joel Munsell, 1875.

Hawkins, Frederick William. *The Life of Edmund Kean*. 2 Vols. London: Tinsley Brothers, 1869.

Hazlitt, William. *The Complete Works of William Hazlitt in Twenty-One Volumes*, ed. P.P. Howe. London and Toronto: J.M. Dent and Sons, Ltd., 1930-34.

Hearn, Michael Patrick (ed.). *The Annotated Huckleberry Finn*. New York and London: W.W. Norton and Co., 1981.

Heine, Heinrich. *Shakespeare's Maidens and Maids*. New York: John W. Lovell Company, 1891.

Heller, Zoe. "Tony the Tiger." *Harper's Bazaar* (June 1999): 143-5.

Henderson, Tony. *Disorderly Women in Eighteenth-Century London: Prostitution and Control in the Metropolis, 1730-1830*. London and New York: Longman, 1999.

Hillebrand, Harold Newcomb. *Edmund Kean*. New York: Columbia University Press, 1933; rpt. New York: AMS Press, 1966.

Hirsh, James. "Samuel Clemens and the Ghost of Shakespeare." *Studies in the Novel* 24.3 (2002): 251-72.

Holmes, Richard. *Darker Reflections: 1804-1834*. London: HarperCollins, 1998.

————. *Sidetracks: Explorations of a Romantic Biographer*. New York: Pantheon Books, 2000.

Holzer, Harold. *Lincoln at Cooper Union*. New York and London: Simon & Schuster, 2004.

————. *Lincoln Seen and Heard*. Lawrence, Kansas: University of Kansas, 2000.

Honan, Park. *Authors' Lives: On Literary Biography and the Arts of Language*. New York: St. Martin's Press, 1990.

Honigmann, E.A.J. (ed.) Introduction. *Othello*. The Arden Shakespeare. Walton-on-Thames, Surrey: Nelson Thomas & Sons, 1997. 1-111.

Horne, Charles. "Serious Thoughts on the Miseries of Sedition and Prostitution." reprinted in Ian McCormick (ed.), *Sexual Outcasts 1750-1850*. Vol. III. London and New York: Routledge, 2000.

Howell, Margaret J. *Byron Tonight: A Poet's Plays on the Nineteenth Century Stage.* Windlesham, Surrey: Springwood Books, 1982.

Huizinga, J.H. *Rousseau: The Self-Made Saint*. New York: Viking, 1976.

Hunt, Leigh. *Dramatic Criticism, 1808-1831*, ed. Lawrence Houston Houtchens and Carolyn Washburn Houtchens. New York: Octagon Books, 1977.

———. *Leigh Hunt: A Life in Letters*, ed. Eleanor M. Gates. Essex, Connecticut: Fall Rivers Publications, 1998.

Hunt, Lynn. "Pornography and the French Revolution." *The Invention of Pornography: Obscenity and the Origins of Modernity, 1500-1800,* ed. Lynn Hunt. New York: Zone Books, 1993. 301-39.

Ireland, William Henry. *The Confessions of William-Henry Ireland. Containing the Particulars of His Fabrication of the Shakspeare Manuscripts; Together With Anecdotes and Opinions (Hitherto Unpublished) of Many Distinguished Persons in the Literary, Political, and Theatrical World.* London: Ellerton and Byworth, for T. Goddard, 1805.

———. *Confidential Friend of the Departed, A Public and Private Life of That Celebrated Actress, Miss Bland.* London: J. Duncombe, 1830.

Jacobi fanclub page. http://www.linsdomain.com/jacobi.htm.

"Jeff DeMarco's Twain *1601* Page." www.mbay,net/~jmd/1601w.html.

Kahan, Jeffrey. *Reforging Shakespeare*. Bethlehem: Lehigh University Press, 1998.

"Kean." *The Observer*. 27 September 1970. 1-37.

"Kean." *The Sunday Times* 27 September 1970, on file at The Theatre Museum, Covent Garden.

The Kean Banquet, Wednesday, July 20, 1859: His Grace the Duke of Newcastle in the Chair. T.H. Taunton, Esq., Hon. Sec. London: Walter Brettell, [1859].

Kean, Edmund. "To My Dear Sir." Autograph note, dated 28 February 1825, in Huntington Manuscripts 63344.

Kean, Edmund C. Newspaper Articles. Messmore Kendall Collection. Harry Ransom Collection (HRC), University of Texas, at Austin.

Kean, Edmund E. –1m.-1. Programs, 1796. Harry Ransom Collection (HRC), University of Texas, at Austin.

Kean E- Recip. Harry Ransom Collection (HRC), University of Texas, at Austin.

Kean, Ellen. *Death and Funeral of Abraham Lincoln, With Some Remarks on the State of America at the Close of the Civil War. A Contemporary Account Contained in Two Long Descriptive Letters From Mrs. Ellen Kean, the Actress, Whilst Touring the United States in 1865. With Prefatory Note By John Drinkwater.* London: Priv. Print, January, 1921.

Kean, Mary. Letters from Mary Kean to Jane Porter. Harry Ransom Collection (HRC), University of Texas, at Austin.

Keats, John. *The Letters of John Keats,* Maurice Buxton Forman. 4th edn. London: Oxford University Press, 1952.

————. *Otho: A Tragedy in Five Acts*. Manuscript of Acts I-IV, at Harry Ransom Collection (HRC), University of Texas, at Austin.

————. *The Poetical Works and Other Writings of John Keats*, revised with additions Maurice Buxton Forman. Vol. 5. New York: Charles Scribner's Sons, 1939.

Kelly, Linda. *The Kemble Era: John Philip Kemble, Sarah Siddons and the London Stage*. New York: Random House, 1980.

Kelso, Fred. "Aldridge, Ira: Historically Important Marylanders." www.msstate.edu/listarchives/afrigeneas/199710/msg00340.html.1-3.

Kemble & Cooke: Or, A Critical Review. 2nd edn. London: J. Bonsor, n.d.

Lamb, Charles. *Plays and Dramatic Essays*, ed. Rudolf Dircks. London: Walter Scott, Ltd., [1893].

Lemaître, Frédérick. *Souvenirs de Frédérick Lemaître Publiés Par Son Fils*. Paris: Paul Ollendorff, 1880.

Lennox, William Pitt. *Plays, Players, and Playhouses*. 2 vols. London: Hurst and Blackett, 1881.

Lenz, Joseph. "Base Trade: Theater as Prostitution." *ELH* 60.4 (1993): 833-55.

Leonard, William Torbert. *Masquerade in Black*. Metchen, N.J. and London, England: The Scarecrow Press, Inc., 1986.

Levine, Lawrence W. *Highbrow/Lowbrow: The Emergence of Cultural Hierarchy*. Cambridge, Mass.; London: Harvard University Press, 1988.

Lewes, George Henry. *On Actors and the Art of Acting*. London: Smith, Elder & Co., 1875.

Lewis, Roger. *The Real Life of Laurence Olivier*. New York and London: Applause, 1996.

The London Stage, 1660-1800: A Calendar of Plays, Entertainments and Afterpieces, Together With Casts, Box-Receipts and Contemporary Comment. Compiled From the Playbills, Newspapers and Theatrical Diaries of the Period. Carbondale: Southern Illinois University Press, 1965-1968.

Lowell, Amy. *John Keats*. 2 vols. Boston and New York: Houghton Mifflin Company, 1925.

Lower, Charles B. "Othello as Black on Southern Stages, Then and Now." *Shakespeare in the South: Essays on Performance*, ed. Philip C. Kolin. Jackson: University Press of Mississippi, 1983. 199-228.

Macauley, Elizabeth. *Theatrical Revolution, or Plain Truth Addressed to Common Sense*. London: Printed for the Author, 1819.

MacQueen-Pope, W.J. *Edmund Kean*. Edinburgh: Thomas Nelson and Sons, 1960.

————. *Pillars of Drury Lane*. London: Hutchinson, 1955.

————. *Theatre Royal Drury Lane*. London: W.H. Allen, 1945.

Macready, William C. *Diaries of William Charles Macready*, ed. William Toynbee. 2 vols. New York: G.P. Putnum's Sons, 1912.

————. *Macready's Reminiscences, and Selections From His Diaries and Letters*, ed. Sir Frederick Pollack. New York: Macmillan and Co., 1875.

Makdisi, Saree. *William Blake and the Impossible History of the 1790s*. Chicago: University of Chicago Press, 2003.

Malone, Mary. *Actor in Exile: The Life of Ira Aldridge*. London: Crowell-Collier Press, 1969.

Manning, Peter J. *Byron and His Fictions*. Detroit: Wayne State University Press, 1978.

———. "Edmund Kean and Byron's Plays." *Keats-Shelley Journal*. Double Issue. (XXI-XXII (1972-1973):188-206.

Marder, Louis. *His Exits and His Entrances: The Story of Shakespeare's Reputation*. Philadelphia: Lippincott, [1963].

Marshall, Herbert and Mildred Stock. *Ira Aldridge, the Negro Tragedian*. Carbondale and Edwardsville: Southern Illinois University Press 1958; rpt. London and Amsterdam: Feffer and Simons, Inc., 1968.

Matthews, G.M. (ed.). *Keats: The Critical Heritage*. The Critical Heritage Series. Gen. ed. B.C. Southam. London: Routledge, & Kegan Paul, 1971.

Maturin, R.C. [actual given names: Charles Robert]. *Bertram: Or The Castle of St. Aldobrand*. London: John Murray, 1816.

———. *Manuel; A Tragedy in Five Acts*. London: John Murray, 1817.

McCracken, Peggy. *The Romance of Adultery: Queenship and Sexual Transgression in Old French Literature*. Philadelphia: University of Pennsylvania Press, 1998.

Mee, Bob. *Bare Fists: The History of Bare-Knuckle Prize-Fighting*. Woodstock: The Overlook Press, 2001.

A Memoir of Edmund Kean. Oxberry's Dramatic Biography. Vol.1. No.1, 1 January 1825.

Memoirs of Junius Brutus Booth, From His Birth to the Present Time. London: E. Thomas, 1817.

Mendoza, Daniel. *The Memoirs of the Life of Daniel Mendoza*, ed. Paul Magriel. London, New York: B.T. Batsford Ltd., 1951.

Miller, Lucasta. *The Brontë Myth*. New York: Alfred A. Knopf. 2004.

Moe, Doug. "Mixing mysteries and fine cuisine." *The Capital Times: Web Edition*, 24 August 2004. http://www.madison.com/tct/ opinion/ column/ moe/ index. php?ntid=8867&ntpid=2.

Molloy, J. Fitzgerald. *The Life and Adventures of Edmund Kean*, 2 vols. London: Ward and Downey, 1888.

Moody, Jane. *Illegitimate Theatre in London, 1770-1840*. Cambridge: Cambridge University Press, 2000.

Mullenix, Elizabeth Reitz. "The Sublime or the Ridiculous?: *Hamlet's* enigmatic positioning within the American cultural hierarchy." http://orathost.cfa.ilstu.edu. shakespeare/research/hamlet.html. 1-4.

Mulrooney, Jonathan. "Keats in the Company of Kean." *Studies in Romanticism* 42.2 (Summer 2003): 227-50.

Murray, Venetia. *An Elegant Madness: High Society in Regency England*. London: Penguin Books, 1998.

Nelson, Robert J. *Play Within A Play: Shakespeare To Anouilh*. New Haven: Yale University Press, 1958.

New Monthly Magazine. Philadelphia: E. Littell; New York, 1821-1823.

The New Way to Act Old Plays: A Familiar Epistle to the Management of Drury Lane Theatre on the Present State of the Stage. London: Robert Stodart, 1818.

Nicoll, Allardyce. *A History of English Drama: 1660-1900*, 3rd edn. 6 Vols. Cambridge: Cambridge University Press, 1955-59.

Nightingale, Benedict. "Kean." *London Times*, 7 August 1990. www.sparrowsprovidence.org/ articles/sartre_homage_to_dumas.htm.

Norton, Theodore. *Kean, A Poem.* London: W. Kenneth, 1835.

Odell, George C.D. *Shakespeare From Betterton to Irving.* 2 vols. New York: Scribner's Sons, 1920.

Oggel, L. Terry. *Edwin Booth: A Bio-Biography.* New York and West Port, Connecticut: Greenwood Press, 1992.

O'Toole, Peter. *Loitering With Intent: The Apprentice.* New York: Hyperion, 1996.

Oxberry's Dramatic Biography, and Histrionic Anecdotes. 5 vols. London: George Virtue, 1825-26.

Oxberry's Dramatic Mirror: Containing the Biography, and an Excellent Likeness on Steel, of the Following Eminent Performers: Bland, Booth, Carew, Elliston, Emery, Fawcett, Foote, Etc. London: C. Baynes for G. Virtue, 1827.

Parsons, Clement [Florence Mary Wilson Parsons]. *Garrick and His Circle.* New York and London: Benjamin Blom, 1906.

Patterson, Troy. "Peter O'Toole." *Entertainment Weekly* 591(13 April 2001): 33-9.

Payne, John Howard. *Brutus; Or The Fall of Tarquin. A Comedy in Five Acts.* New York: Wm. Taylor & Co., 1848.

Phillips, John. *Sade: The Libertine Novels.* London and Sterling, Va.: Pluto, 2001.

Playbills. Huntington Manuscript Collection, Huntington Library, 182799.

Playfair, Giles. *The Flash of Lightning: A Portrait of Edmund Kean.* London: William Kimber, 1983.

————. *Edmund Kean: Paradoxical Genius.* Westport, Connecticut: Greenwood Press, 1939.

Playing Robin Hood: The Legend as Performance in Five Centuries, ed. Lois Potter. Newark: University of Delaware Press, 1998.

The Poetic Epistles of Edmund. London: Effingham Wilson, 1825.

Press Clippings, Huntington Manuscript Collection, Huntington Library, 182799.

Press Clippings, in Kean, Edmund C. Newspaper Articles Messmore Kendall Collection, HRC.

Press Clippings, Personal Collection.

Procter, Bryan Waller [Barry Cornwall]. *The Life of Edmund Kean.* 2 vols. London: Edward Moxon, 1835.

Raymond, George. *The Life and Enterprises of Robert William Elliston, Comedian.* London: G. Routledge and Company, 1857.

"Reckless, courageous and a little bit crazy." *The Guardian* 19 March 2003. http://www.realitymouse.com/otoole/articles/guardianUKmar1903.html.

Reynolds, Bryan. *Performing Transversally: Reimagining Shakespeare and the Critical Future.* New York: Palgrave Macmillan, 2003.

Reynolds, Jonathan. *Dramatis Personæ Booksellers Catalogue* 20 (1991) and *Dramatis Personæ Booksellers Catalogue* 88 (2005).

Richardson, John. "Story of Mr. Kean." Manuscript, Harry Ransom Collection, Theatrical Arts Harry Ransom Collection (HRC-TA), University of Texas, at Austin.

Ripley, John. *Coriolanus on Stage in England and America, 1609-1994*. Madison, Teaneck: Fairleigh Dickenson University Press; London: Associated University Presses, 1998.

Roach, John. *Authentic Memoirs of the Green-Room; Including Sketches, Biographical, Critical & Characteristic, of the Performers of the Theatres Royal Drury Lane, Covent-Garden, and The Haymarket*. London: J. Roach, 1814.

Robinson, Henry Crabb. *The London Theatre 1811-1866. Selections From the Diary of Henry Crabb Robinson*, ed. Eluned Brown. London: The Society for Theatre Research, 1966.

Robson, William. *The Old Playgoer.* London: Joseph Masters, 1846.

Rousseau, Jean-Jacques. *Les Confessions de J.J. Rousseau.* 2 vols. Geneve: [No publisher listed], 1782.

———. *On the Social Contract and Discourses*, trans. Donald A. Cress; Introduction Peter Gay. Indianapolis: Hackett, 1983.

Ruggles, Eleanor. *Prince of Players: Edwin Booth*. New York: W.W. Norton and Company, Inc., 1953.

Rule, John. *The Labouring Classes in Early Industrial England 1750-1850*. London and New York: Longman, 1986.

Rzepka, Charles J. "*Theatrum Mundi* and Keats's *Otho The Great:* The Self in Society." *Romanticism Past and Present* 8.1 (Winter 1984): 35-50.

Sade, Donatien-Alphonse-François de. *Oeuvres Completes du Marquis de Sade*, ed. Annie Le Brun. Paris: Société Nouvelle des Editions Pauvert, 1987.

Sartre, Jean-Paul. *Les Mots*. Paris: Gallimard, 1964.

———. "Kean." *Sartre on Theater*, eds Michel Contat and Michel Rybalka, trans. Frank Jellinek. New York: Pantheon Books/Random House Inc., 1976. 238-46.

———. *Kean*, ed. David Bradby. London: Oxford University Press, 1973.

Samples, Gordon. *Lust for Fame: The Stage Career of John Wilkes Booth*. Jefferson, North Carolina and London: McFarland and Company Inc., 1982.

Saunders, Edith. *The Prodigal Father*. London, New York, Toronto: Longmans, Green and Co., 1951.

Schechner, Richard. *The End of Humanism: Writing on Performance*. New York: Performing Arts Journal Publication, 1982.

Schoch, Richard W. *Shakespeare's Victorian Stages: Performing History in the Theatre of Charles Kean*. Cambridge: Cambridge University Press, 1998.

Schopp, Claude. *Alexandre Dumas: Genius of Life*. New York: Franklin Watts, 1988.

The Secret History of the Green-Room. 2 vols. London: J. Owen, 1795.

Sedley, Henry. "The Booths—Father and Son: Some Personal Reminiscences." *Harpers* (no date), p. 1082 in "Magazine Articles D-1," Harry Ransom Collection (HRC), University of Texas, at Austin.

Shakespeare Imitations, Parodies and Forgeries 1710-1820, ed. Jeffrey Kahan. 3 vols. London and New York: Routledge, 2004.

Shakespeare, William. *Coriolanus, or, The Roman Matron: A Historical Play Adapted to the Stage, With Additions From Thomson, by J. P. Kemble*. London: Longman, Hurst, Rees, and Orme, 1806

————. *The Riverside Shakespeare*, ed. G. Blakemore Evans. 2nd edn. Boston: Houghton Mifflin Company, 1997.

Sharma, Kavita A. *Byron's Plays: A Reassessment. Poetic Drama and Poetic Theory*, ed. Dr. James Hogg. Salzburg: Institut für Anglistik und Amerikanistik, 1982.

Shattuck, Charles H. *Shakespeare on the American Stage: From the Hallams to Edwin Booth*. Washington: The Folger Shakespeare Library, 1976.

Shelley, Percy Bysshe. *A Defence of Poetry*. Portland, Maine: Thomas B. Mosher, 1910.

Siebenschuh, William R. *Fictional Techniques and Factual Works*. Athens, Ga.: The University of Athens, 1983.

Skinner, Otis. "Three Madmen of the Theatre II." *Scribner's Magazine*, LXXX. (6 December 1926): 622-633.

Slote, Bernice. *Keats and the Dramatic Principle*. Nebraska: University of Nebraska, 1958.

Smith, Gene. *American Gothic: The Story of America's Legendary Family—Junius, Edwin, and John Wilkes Booth*. New York and London: A Touchstone Book/ Simon & Schuster, 1992.

Smith, Tomaso (screenwriter), Guido Brignone (director). *Kean, gli amori di un artista*. Scalera Films, 1940.

Soane, George. *Dwarf of Naples. A Tragi-Comedy in Five Acts: First Performed at the Theatre Royal, Drury-Lane, on Saturday, March 13, 1819*. London: T. Rodwell, 1819.

Soderholm, James. *Fantasy, Forgery, and the Byron Legend*. Kentucky: University Press of Kentucky, 1996.

Stam, Robert. *Subversive Pleasures: Bakhtin, Cultural Criticism, and Film*. Baltimore and London: Johns Hopkins University Press. 1989.

Steiner, George. *The Death of Tragedy*. New York: Knopf, 1961.

Stirling, Edward. *Old Drury Lane: Fifty Years' Recollections of Author, Actor, and Manager*. 2 vols. London: Chatto and Windus, 1881.

Stowe, Richard S. *Alexandre Dumas père*. Boston: Twayne Publishers/G.K. Hall and Co., 1976.

Sturgess, Kim C. *Shakespeare and the American Nation*. Cambridge: Cambridge University Press, 2004.

Swindells, Julia. *Glorious Causes: The Grand Theatre of Political Change, 1789 to 1833*. Oxford: Oxford University Press, 2001.

Taylor, George. *The French Revolution and the London Stage, 1789-1805.* Cambridge: Cambridge University Press, 2000.

Taylor, John Russell. *The Rise and Fall of the Well-Made Play.* New York: Hill and Wang, 1967.

Taylor, Paul. "Cracked Actor." *Independent.* 8 August 1990.

Theatrical Inquisitor, and Monthly Mirror. London: C. Chapple, 1812-1820.

The Thespian Dictionary, or, Dramatic Biography of the Present Age. 2 vols. 2nd edn. London: James Cundee, 1805.

Thompson, E.P. *Customs in Common: Studies in Traditional Popular Culture.* New York: The New Press, 1993.

Thorpe, Clarence DeWitt (ed.). *John Keats: Complete Poems and Selected Letters.* New York: Odyssey Press, 1935.

Tobin, John. *The Curfew; A Drama in Five Acts.* New York: David Longworth, 1807.

Turner, James Grantham. *Libertines and Radicals in Early Modern London: Sexuality, Politics, and Literary Culture, 1630-1685.* Cambridge and New York: Cambridge University Press, 2002.

Twain, Mark [Samuel Clemens]. "About Play-Acting." in *The Complete Essays of Mark Twain*, ed. Charles Neider. Garden City, N.Y.: Doubleday, 1963; rpt. 1985.

————. *Adventures of Huckleberry Finn*, eds Walter Blair and Victor Fischer. Berkeley, Los Angeles, London: University of California Press, 1985.

————. "The Killing of Julius Caesar 'Localized.'" *Early Tales and Sketches*, in *The Works of Mark Twain*, eds Edgar Marquess Branch and Robert H. Hirst, with the assistance of Harriet Elinor Smith. 15 vols. Berkeley: Published for the Iowa Center for Textual Studies by the University of California Press, 1979-1981.

Vandenhoff, George. *Leaves From an Actor's Note-Book.* New York: D. Appleton and Company, 1860.

Wang, Shou-ren. *Theatre of the Mind: A Study of Unacted Drama in Nineteenth-Century England.* London: MacMillan, 1990.

Wardlaw, Ralph. *Lectures on Female Prostitution.* Glasgow: James Maclehose, 1843.

Weales, Gerald. "Edmund Kean Onstage Onstage." *Shakespeare and the Dramatic Tradition*, eds. W.R. Elton and William B. Long. Newark: University of Delaware Press; London and Toronto: Associated University Presses, 1989. 151-67.

Webb, Nancy and Jean Francis Webb. *Will Shakespeare and His America.* New York: The Viking Press, 1964.

White, Hayden. *The Content of the Form: Narrative Discourse and Historical Representation.* London and Baltimore: John Hopkins University Press, 1987.

White, R.S. *Keats As a Reader of Shakespeare.* London: Athlone Press, 1987.

Wilmeth, Don. B. *George Frederick Cooke, Machiavel of the Stage.* Westport, Connecticut: Greenwood Press, 1980.

Williams, Raymond. *Modern Tragedy.* Stanford, Calif.: Stanford University Press, 1966.

Williams, Simon. "Actorial Representations of the Self in the Romantic Age: Edmund Kean and Ludwig Devrient." *New Comparison* 9 (1990): 103-16.

Wilson, Cintra. *A Massive Swelling: Celebrity Re-Examined As a Grotesque, Crippling Disease and Other Cultural Revelations.* New York: Penguin, 2000.

Wingate, Charles E.L. *Shakespeare's Heroes On The Stage.* 2 vols. New York and Boston: Thomas Y. Crowell & Company, 1896.

Winston, James. *Drury Lane Journal: Selections from James Winston's Diaries 1819-1827,* eds Alfred L. Nelson and Gilbert B. Cross. London: Society for Theatre Research, 1974.

Wolfit, Donald. Speech. 2 pages. No date in "Edmund Kean." Harry Ransom Collection (HRC), University of Texas, at Austin.

Woods, Leigh. "Actors' Biography and Mythmaking: The Example of Edmund Kean." *Interpreting the Theatrical Past: Essays in the Historiography of Performance,* eds Thomas Postlewait and Bruce A. McConachie. Iowa City: University of Iowa Press, 1989. 230-47.

Woolford, John. "The Influence of Edmund Kean On Browning's *Pauline.*" *Studies in Browning and His Circle* 17 (1989): 23-31.

Wright, Frances. *Altorf: A Tragedy.* London: Longman, Hurst, Rees, Orme, and Brown, 1822.

Wright, Robert and George Forrest. *Kean: Selections.* New York: Columbia Records, 1961.

Young, Julian Charles. *A Memoir of Charles Mayne Young, Tragedian.* London, New York: Macmillan and Co., 1871.

Ziter, Edward. "Kean, Byron, and Fantasies of Miscegenation." *Theatre Journal* 54 (2002). 607-26.

Index